From

MARX

To

KANT

SUNY SERIES IN PHILOSOPHY
Robert C. Neville, Editor

From

MARX

To

KANT

Dick Howard

State University of New York Press

PUBLISHED BY
STATE UNIVERSITY OF NEW YORK PRESS, ALBANY

PRINTED IN THE UNITED STATES OF AMERICA

FOR INFORMATION, ADDRESS STATE UNIVERSITY OF NEW YORK
PRESS, STATE UNIVERSITY PLAZA, ALBANY, N.Y., 12246

LIBRARY OF CONGRESS CATALOGING IN PUBLICATION DATA

Howard, Dick, 1943-
Systematic political theory from Marx to Kant.
(SUNY series in political thought)
1. Political science—History. I. Title. II. Series.
JA83.H69 1985 320′.01 84-24427
ISBN 0-88706-042-0
ISBN 0-88706-043-9 (pbk.)

10 9 8 7 6 5 4 3 2 1

Contents

Acknowledgements

This book is the product of twenty years of reading, thinking, talking, and doing. My debts are enormous and multiple. The most important is to my wife, for all the reasons she knows.

I have been much influenced by my experiences living and working in France and in Germany. Cornelius Castoriadis, Claude Lefort, and Paul Thibaud have been friends and teachers from one side of the Rhine; Jürgen Habermas and, for a time, Klaus Hartmann, from the other. The group around the journal *Esprit* has been a constant encouragement and stimulus over the years, teaching me above all respect for the new and constant curiosity, which are the qualities shared by what I call originary—not original!—philosophy and politics alike. André Gorz helped enormously at a crucial stage at which self-doubt was becoming painful.

There has been support in the United States as well, of course. The years of work with *Telos* were, and have become again, important. Andrew Arato, and Jean Cohen have been intellectual companions during much of the time that this project was going through its various revisions. Karl Klare has been a constant questioner whose own important work in critical legal theory has given me much to chew upon. The Europe-in-Formation radio group with whom I have worked for four years, especially John Mason and Tom Whelan, has helped give perspective time and again. Two professional colleagues have been particularly supportive in criticizing this manuscript, Richard Bernstein and Charles Sherover. Robert Neville deserves thanks as an editor and as a colleague. Niall Caldwell was a critical, and thus useful, proofreader.

Institutional support has been forthcoming as well. The philosophy department at the State University of New York at Stony Brook is a nice place to work. Participation in the weekly luncheons at the Research Institute on International Change at Columbia University has been invaluable in providing a continual help intellectualy and personally. Its administrative assistant, MarJean Knokey, has arranged for the typing and retyping of variants of variants of this manuscript.

Drafts that were written to satisfy institutional exigencies require acknowledgment and thanks. A first draft was written for Duquesne University, at the invitation of John Scanlon. The penultimate version was presented as a graduate course in the political science department at Columbia University at the invitation of its chairman, Douglas Chalmers.

Fellowship support is also gratefully acknowledged. Summer grants from the Research Foundation of the State University of New York helped me continue the work during some summers. A semester's leave permitted another draft. An American Council of Learned Societies (ACLS) grant provided for a six-months leave. Finally, a fifteen-month fellowship from the German Alexander von Humboldt Stiftung permitted me to work first at the Max Planck Institut in Munich and then at the philosophy department in Frankfurt under the sponsorship of Jürgen Habermas.

Note on Text and Translations

This is a work of philosophy, not philology. I have not loaded the text with references either to primary or to secondary sources, save where I have explicitly borrowed from, felt a debt to, or needed to clarify my own position. I have not footnoted the primary sources from which I take short quotations, save in the event that the context is not clear. I have used texts that are widely known and available and have tried to clarify always the source of any citations.

All translations are my own, unless otherwise indicated.

The systematic character of the work made the drafting of an index redundant. The systematic character of each chapter is explained in the introduction.

Preface

The introduction to this volume explains briefly the systematic philosophical claim implied by the anachronistic movement "from Marx to Kant." Although the system stands on its own, these prefatory remarks indicate politically why I came to see the need for a systematic account of the relation of philosophy and politics. Two decades of political involvement in the United States and Europe have left their traces in my books, articles, translations, and editorial activities. Sometimes the theoretical work moved ahead of the political implications; sometimes politics suggested new theoretical directions.[1] The present work brings the two moments together in a philosophical unity. Although they do not explain the at-first enigmatic conceptual use that I will make of the substantive *the political,* its political implications should briefly be mentioned.

My study of the young Marx in *The Development of the Marxian Dialectic* attempted to show how and why Marx moved from philosophy to political economy. Subsequent attempts to adapt Marx and his successors to contemporary politics proved frustrating. The attempt to discover an "unknown dimension" that would avoid the totalitarian consequences of Russian and Chinese versions of Marxism as well as the sterility of scholastic and dogmatic orthodoxies in the West was often interesting, sometimes fruitful, but ultimately unsatisfactory.[2] The negative results were expressed in the *The Marxian Legacy*, on whose cover I insisted on reproducing Bruegel's painting, *The Blind Leading the Blind* instead of the editor's choice of a scene from a demonstration during May 1968 in Paris. May 68, in which I participated, means something different to me. I tried to express it positively in a twelve-hour lecture series at Duquesne University in 1978 under the title, "The Return of the Political." That manuscript began with a review of the path "from Kant to Marx"; several versions later, it has taken the reverse direction. Definition of "the political" called for a systematic, not a historical, argument.

The Marxian tradition is structured by a duality that resembles the distinction I have drawn here between *genesis* and *normativity*. The genetic option insists on the priority of class struggle and the formation of class consciousness. The normative approach points to structural necessities that make the oncoming revolution inevitable or obligatory. These structural orientations can lead to opposed practical options. The genetic orientation can lead to reformism, which asserts that the class is not yet ripe enough to control its own destiny. It can also lead to revolutionism, when the distinction between economic struggles and political class consciousness is introduced by Lenin. Similarly, the normative approach may be invoked to justify the refusal to take risks because the conjunture is unfavorable, as in Kautsky's reformism. It can also serve the revolutionists to guarantee that, despite apparent difficulties, structural necessity guarantees ultimate success. These two structural movements are found not only within a single movement; they are often present in a single life and action. Their most acute effects are seen in the tragic figure of Rosa Luxemburg.[3]

The presence of this same structural polarity in the *Critique of Pure Reason* suggests the need to transcend the Marxian framework. Kant's intention was to call the twin errors of what he called opportunism and dogmatism before the court of the critique. Application of Kant's critical method to Marx's theory reveals its conditions of possibility. Marx's politics is dependent on a reduction to a pregiven, external economic infrastructure. But a revolution founded on the economic civil society to which Marx reduces politics could only realize what is implicit already in the capitalist relations on which it depends. To paraphrase Lenin, Marxist revolution would be only the highest stage of capitalism. The Kantian critical question can be asked again here. Is it really capitalism as a system of social-economic relations that defines our modern present? What is the origin of capitalism? The critical theory of Jürgen Habermas seemed to offer an orientation. His *Legitimation Problems of Late Capitalism* demonstrated the manner in which economic crisis tendencies are countered by administrative methods, which in turn suffer from a rationality deficit due to their inability, in the long run, to legitimate the actions needed to preserve the system. Legitimation and political possibility are tied together in this proposal by the qualification that we are living in late capitalism. Habermas did not explain what he meant by *late*. He has gone on since then to formulate his own foundational system.[4] My own questions took first a historical detour.

Historical research into the origins of capitalism led back to the eighteenth-century political structure known as enlightened despotism. This contradictory system can be interpreted as the cohabitation of a genetic and a normative structure similar to that encountered in the history of Marxism.[5] Despotism would generate activity in the unenlightened; their subsequent enlightenment would validate the imposition. The separation of the state from the citizen meant that its action would be necessarily despotic. The French Revolution only apparently breaks this duality. Its phases can be interpreted as the failure to mediate between the genetic and the normative poles without threatening the existence of the one or the other. Overemphasis on the one or the other—on praxis or on the institutionalization of its gains—calls forth a reaction in kind. Similar suggestions can be made regarding the development of the American Revolution or the failure of the Prussian variant of enlightened despotism.[6] The implication is that "the political" and enlightened despotism share a common structure, whose eighteenth-century manifestations differ, just as its twentieth-century appearances will not repeat the details of the earlier patterns. The rise of capitalism—or what the philosophers call "civil society"—provided the missing mediation in the nineteenth-century. Capitalist civil society is the unification of the poles of private and public affairs, of genetic action and normative legitimation. The sphere of economic relations replaces the political questioning symbolized by the paradoxical formulation of enlightened despotism or the unstable process of revolution. This is why Marx's *Capital* can claim to be a political theory as well as a theory of social relations among individuals. This means, however, that the crisis of capitalism engenders a "return of the political."[7] The political was the Kantian "condition of the possibility" of the rise of capitalist civil society. Political action returns to the agenda when its economic ersatz proves inadequate.

The political overdetermination of the historical development of civil society explains the increasing meaninglessness of labels like left and right, progressive and reactionary, even liberal and conservative. These labels presuppose a logic of history that replaces particular historical action. They eliminate the novelty of the new by reducing it to mere manifestations of the linear historical logic that they take for granted. Judgment is replaced by (purported) knowledge of what the situation really demands. The result is the destruction of the political sphere. The loss of political labels is no loss.

The most controversial claim of the systematic approach to politics is the priority of republican over the democratic institutions. These terms have suffered misuse and abuse during the reign of capitalist civil society and its Marxian critique. The only preliminary to their reconsideration is the insistance that the priority of the republican over the democratic form does *not* mean that the citizens are denied participation in the decisions that affect daily life. The republican form does not exclude democracy; democracy alone, however, does exclude the forms of *representation* central to republican politics. The political is public, in contrast to activity in and from the private sphere.

The difference between what are usually called left- and right-wing political positions appears in their attitudes toward democracy. The Right is antipolitical; it wants to privatize the relations of civil society to insure the rule of law and order. This antipolitical attitude explains the peaceful coexistence of apparent opposites: technocrats and religious fundamentalists, fearful petits bourgeois and arms salesmen, used-car millionaires and old wealth drinking the last profits from dying primary industries—all agree that politics should be kept from the hands (and eyes) of the public. In this they do not differ materially from their enemies across the iron curtain.

The twenty years of political experience that I try systematically to elucidate in this essay belong to what is called the "New Left." I've tried frequently over the years to define its newness. The most important feature of the New Left has been its attempt to redefine the political *as a question.* Not the answers it offers but the questions it asks define this politics. It began with the civil rights movement which combined a demand for justice, a quest for fraternity, and a near-anarchist love of liberty. Unifying this politics was its concern with the law. Its tactics tried to bring others to an awareness of the exigencies of the law. Its strategy was significant. Particular actions, like sit-ins, freedom rides, or voter registration drives, created the scene for a public debate about the universality of the law. The goal was not participation for its own sake, nor the creation of universal equality. The goal was to articulate particular instances in a manner that forced the citizen to recognize in them the universal demands of living in and as a society. In this, the New Left was "Kantian" and republican: it sought to create the space for the public exercise of judgment.

The New Left was threatened from without and from within. The urgency of the Vietnam War focused energies on a problem for which an immediate solution was necessary. The price of a solution was the loss of the political questions that had at first sensitized the New Left to the war. The result was the inability to think about the nature of the regime in North Vietnam and the inevitable disillusionment with antiwar "politics" when the war ended. The New Left expressed its questioning in the notion of the politicization of everyday life. Institutions were rejected. A we/they situation was created. Politics became immediate and emotional. The public process of enlightenment was abandoned in the intensity of personal inwardness. The rhetoric of direct democracy replaced the republican concern with the law. The result of transforming the personal into the political was the destruction of the individual foundations necessary for any politics.

Can one talk of a return of the political today? It is appropriate to close this preface by addressing that question to the new social movements that in their diversity, seem to be replacing the classical Marxian proletariat or the liberal pluralist regroupings of interests.[8] The peace movement that has grown rapidly since 1981 presents features that recall the civil rights movement; its growth, the forms of its public appearance, and its concern with democratic participation are familiar. Two criticisms that can be addressed to this movement suggest its possible direction. Stress on the mere physical right to life—what Castoriadis calls "zoological politics"—does not have the same implications for public enlightenment and debate as did the demand for justice, fraternity, and liberty in the civil rights movement. The right to life is neither a civil nor a political right. Its protection does not have the same institutional implications. This becomes a serious problem in the light of the second reproach, which criticizes the tendency to unilateralism and the suggestion that since "we're over here" we have to criticize and change our government, leaving aside the nature of the others'. This neglects the importance of the republican guarantees in Western democracies; it forgets—as Andrew Arato puts it—the differences between having an empire and being an empire. The future of the peace movement or the new social movements depends on their ability to articulate *particular* instances that demand public and republican participation, which will permit them to grow beyond mere interest politics. The systematic argument presented here suggests that the conditions of *receptivity* that would insure the success of such a politics are present in modern society. The challange to the political movements is to discover its institutional forms.

June 11, 1984

CHAPTER 1

Introduction

Marx generally is thought to have posed the modern form of the theory-practice problem. This approach supposes that Hegel had completed the systematic philosophical project inaugurated by Kant's "Copernican revolution" which returned philosophy to her place as Queen of the Sciences. The post-Hegelians then had to confront a dilemma described vividly in Rudolf Haym's 1857 *Hegel und seine Zeit*:

> I am certain that many contemporaries still remember the time when all of the sciences nourished themselves at the rich table of Hegelian wisdom, when all the departments paid court to the philosophy department in order to benefit to some small degree from the sublime vision of the Absolute and the flexibility of the famous dialectic; when you were either a Hegelian or a barbarian or an idiot, a backward and despised empiricist; when even the state imagined itself more secure because the old Hegel had demonstrated its necessity and its rationality; and when it was for this reason nearly a crime in the eyes of the Ministry of education not to be Hegelian....One

> must recall this time in order to understand the pathos and conviction with which the Hegelians of the year 1830 asked themselves in bitter seriousness what indeed could constitute the further content of World History now that the world spirit had come to its goal of full self-knowledge in the Hegelian philosophy.[1]

The young Hegelians' revolt against the Hegelian system proceeded from systematic premises. The principles of the overthrow of the Hegelian system were taken from within the system itself. If the system were fully rational, and yet the world was a place of suffering, unhappiness, and irrationality, could one not conclude that the task before the new generation was to give the dialectic another "turn," this time toward the real world? Theory had to become practical, praxical, political.

The theory-practice problem, which apparently questions philosophy's self-sufficiency, comes into being because of the imperative that philosophy be systematic. The purported completeness of the Hegelian system leads, paradoxically, to its own overcoming. The classical transcendental turn is replaced by what I call an "Originary turn" which takes into account the immanent relation of philosophy to the world. Calling this relation "immanent" draws attention to the necessity of philosophical involvement with the world. That necessity must be grounded. The immanence of the justification of philosophical involvement means that the grounds will be double—from the side of philosophy and from the side of the world. The necessity of philosophical involvement must be demonstrated from within philosophy *and* from the nature of a world that needs and is receptive to rational imperatives. This was seen most clearly by the young Marx; it appears also to have motivated Hegel's early development. The philosopher and the revolutionary both solve this early problem. That, to put the matter paradoxically, is the problem from which the present investigation begins.

The recurring paradoxes with which modern theory and modern politics are confronted are described here by the neologism, *originary*. This category is intended first of all to replace the notions of cause or beginning, effect or solution. These more common usages are inadequate for two related reasons. The relation of cause to effect, beginning to end, or problem to solution cannot be shown to be *necessary*. Other causes, beginnings, or problems might well lead to similar effects, ends, or solutions. The lack of a necessary relation is due to the *externality* of the categories to one another. The same difficulty holds for the relations of theory to practice, or of practice to theory. The practice for which theory is said to call, or the theory that claims to justify a practical activity, cannot be contingent, external, or arbitrary. To show that a practice is necessitated by theory, or that a theory is the necessary expression of practice, demands that they be related *immanently*. The immanence, however, does not mean that the two are identical. Theory is not practice; practice is not theory. This structure of immanent relation or of copresence is expressed by the concept of the *originary*. Origins in this sense are neither cause nor beginning; my conceptual innovation is intended to stress the novelty of the structure imposed by the demand for immanent necessity.

The originary turn is based on the systematic imperative brought to its fullest expression by Hegel and by Marx. The originary is inherently paradoxical because it is the copresence of the double demand that theory demonstrate its immanent relation to the world, and that the world express its receptivity to the theory. In its most direct form, the paradox is that the completion of the system demands a practice that is apparently external to the system; and that practical activity calls for a theoretical complement in order to justify itself. The direct expression of the paradox recurs repeatedly within the articulations of the systematic theory and in the structure of the practice seeking its legitimation. The relation of Hegel's phenomenological approach to his logical system illustrates the systematic difficulty. The practical problem is presented by the political question whether Hegel demonstrates the consoling presence of Reason in History or rather articulates the historical and therefore changeable nature of systematic Reason itself. Similarly, but in inverse order, for Marx the practical paradox appears in the relation between the class struggle, which is supposed to provide the foundation of historical development, and the (self-contradictory) logic of *Capital*, which is said to make revolutionary practice legitimate. The theoretical expression of this paradox is found in the relation between the logical theory of alienation and the phenomenological description of the constitution and transformation of the world by the laboring subject.

The copresence of the theoretical and the practical imperatives within an immanent systematic unity can be expressed more abstractly. The categories of *genesis* and *validity* (or *normativity*)[2] are generalized expressions of Husserl's fundamental insight that the act of knowing entails both a *noetic* and a *noematic* component without whose copresence the knowledge is either incomplete or illegitimate. This Husserlian insight transforms the theory of knowledge into a theory of judgment. It is taken a step further in Merleau-Ponty's early *Phenomenology of Perception* which demonstrates that the apparently genetic noetic aspect of knowing can be shown to function normatively, just as the apparently normative noematic validity claim can operate genetically. This reversibility is made possible by the systematic immanence of the two moments within the unitary act of knowing. Genesis is not causality; norms are not essence. An orientation that concentrates on the genetic can argue that its results acquire normative legitimacy by virtue of their genesis. Similarly, a normative approach can demonstrate that valid results are generated by the necessity of obeying logical norms whose function is to govern their expression in the world. What cannot be asserted, however, is that the normative or the genetic component alone can explain the result. The temptation to separate one of the copresent moments is built into the originary structure.[3] Giving in to this temptation would violate the systematic immanence from which the demonstration began. This explains why Merleau-Ponty's later work, especially *The Visible and the Invisible,* turned toward ontology. The categories of genesis and validity (or normativity) are to be understood in this ontological sense.

The paradoxes induced by the necessary copresence of the genetic and the normative moments are originary. Within this unity ontology in the traditional sense is complemented by politics. The result transforms both. Their interdependence within the immanence of the systematic demand means that each is a moment of the other; each depends on the other without being reducible to it. Two consequences follow from this structure. Neither ontology nor politics provides answers, solutions, explanations, or resolutions. The temptation to treat them in this manner parallels the general temptation to explain genesis by normativity or normativity by its genesis. Maintaining the tension constituted by their copresence means that the task of the philosophical and of the political is to pose problems—to provide new questions and not the solution to old problems. This is not the task for theoretical speculation; the originary structure demands a methodological mediation between the copresent moments of the philosophical and the political. The method too is oriented toward questions not answers, the new and not the preconceived, problems instead of solutions. The peculiarity of this methodological mediation is perhaps the most important innovation suggested here. Mediation does not mean the homogenization of unlike moments; it does not mean the hermeneutic translation of the one into the other; it does not provide an external link between them. Originary method mediates by preserving the difference, articulating the polar moments, stressing the interrogative structure of the originary. This means that the method itself will have the dual structure typical of the originary. Each of its moments will contain implicitly the question that the other articulates explicitly. This, again, expresses the paradox of the originary.

Neither Marx nor Hegel articulated a separate methodological moment in their systematic theories. Indeed, both insisted that such a separation of method from theory was invalid. The ground for this refusal is that both Marx and Hegel present fundamentally historical systems. Despite evident differences in their theories of history, Marx and Hegel articulated the modern systematic immanence of a world in constant self-transformation. The premise that unites their approaches is expressed by the difference between the German terms *Historie* and *Geschichtlichkeit*. Hegel's introduction to his *Philosophy of History* will be seen to express thematically what Marx's *Communist Manifesto* demonstrates polemically. *Historie* presupposes a given framework or tableau on which events are painted. The framework gives the events their "historical" character. The relation of the events and the presupposed framework is external, accidental; it is fundamentally ahistorical because the framework alone cannot produce the event, nor can the event constitute its own framework. The alternative, *Geschichtlichkeit*, presents an immanent copresence of the framework to the events, and of the events to the framework. The resulting structure parallels those that have been defined as originary. The framework may function as normative or genetic, as may the events; what was once a norm can operate genetically, or the inverse. Only in in this context does revolution become a question, for theory as for practice.

The question of revolution explains the fundamental role of Kant in the present argument. Kant can be read as the author of a philosophical critique that is the culmination of classical philosophy, or as the originator of a transcendental philosophy whose ultimate conclusions are drawn in the systems of Fichte, Hegel, and Marx. Kant no doubt undertook the former project; but there is also no doubt that his results drew him increasingly to the systematic orientation. Even at the outset, in the *Critique of Pure Reason*, an uncertainty concerning the status of philosophy can be demonstrated. It is not enough to allude to the external evidence of the progression through the *Critiques*; evidence of systematic intent must be shown internally. Such an external demonstration will be seen to be based on a systematic methodological error that is repeated by Hegel and Marx. Kant's "Copernican revolution" has to be shown to develop necessarily toward the political question of revolution; conversely, his political interrogation of the French Revolution has to be shown to lead back to the systematic critical philosophy. This dual movement from the philosophical to the political and from the political to the philosophical characterizes Kant's system as originary. More important, it stresses the interrogative and modern quality of his critical philosophy.

The movement from Marx to Kant remains to be justified. A pedagogical and a theoretical explanation of the anachronism can be suggested. The young Marx makes explicit the dual character of the originary demand as it emerges from consideration of the Hegelian system. Marx can be interpreted as having remained faithful to this insight, just as Hegel's system itself will be shown to appeal implicitly to the same criteria. But a close reading, guided by the originary imperative, shows that both Marx and Hegel violate their own achievements. The structural "temptation" immanent to the originary is illustrated by their error. The same interpretative framework applied to Kant yields more satisfactory results. The claim is not that this was Kant's intention; nor is it argued that Marx or Hegel were working from this explicit political or philosophical interrogation. The anachronistic suggestion permits the use of Marx, Hegel, and Kant to demonstrate the nature of an originary theory. Beyond this pedagogical justification of the anachronism is its systematic grounds. These point to questions that transcend the framework of this systematic study. The structure of the originary system is based on an imperative of immanence which characterizes the modern. The theoretical justification of the movement from Marx to Kant is that the originary Kantian system permits a more adequate understanding of modernity than either the Hegelian or the Marxian systems. Illustration of this claim is provided by the interplay between the theoretical and the political through which the system progresses.

The priority of the modern formulation of the theory-practice problem has a political implication which the present articulation of an originary system can only suggest. This limitation explains also the form in which the originary system is presented here. The three parts of the book illustrate the independence and the interdependence of the philosophical, the political, and the originary method that mediates their relation. An asymmetry in their relation and an inversion in the order of presentation beginning with Chapter 6 need explanation. Chapter 2 explains the need to move beyond classical philosophical formulations; chapter 3 illustrates the originary structure that results from this imperative. Chapter 4 explains the "constitutive temptation" that results from the failure to articulate a separate methodological mediation. Chapter 5 proceeds to formulate the moment of methodological receptivity which corresponds to the imperatives of philosophy. All of these chapters demonstrate the originary argument by an exposition of Kant, then Hegel, and finally Marx. With Chapter 6, the progression is inverted. The methodological moment of particularity depends on the concept of the political. The order of illustration is reversed both in Chapter 6 and 7 because of the claim that it is Kant whose theory most adequately presents the originary political structure. The justification of that claim is *only* philosophical here. This explains the second asymmetry. If the originary argument were to be fully developed, part 3 would have three chapters, paralleling the three chapters in part 1. A practical difficulty made such a presentation impossible. Either the three new chapters in part 3 would have to make their case with illustrations from political theorists comparable to Kant, Hegel, and Marx; or they would restate the materials already adduced from these three but placed now in the context of the political. The latter solution would have introduced too much redundancy; the former would have been the basis for a new book, one which, this time, would have had three chapters treating the political and only a single presentation of the philosophical. The only other option would have been an ungainly syncretism.

This presentation of the systematic structure of originary philosophy ends with the claim that the Kantian republican politics is more adequate to the conditions of modernity than either the Hegelian normative state or the Marxian revolution. The basis of the argument is the concept of civil society as modern. The originary and *geschichtlich* structure of modern civil society poses questions. Capitalism, in its Hegelian or Marxian variant, can be understood as one answer to those questions. As an answer that closes off the questioning, capitalism violates the originary modern structure. The Kantian republic can be capitalist, but it need not have that economic priority as its basis. Other structures of republican civil society are possible. It remains for another book, the presentation of an originary politics, to demonstrate the necessity of this possibility.

CHAPTER 2

From Transcendental to Originary Philosophy

THE STRUCTURE OF THE MODERN

Cartesian doubt usually is considered the beginning of modern philosophy. But this doubt is only a beginning. It does not fully determine the structure of the modern, nor does it explain how modernity became possible, in fact or in theory. The doubt has deepened as modernization and rationalization have spread horizontally to new domains at the same time that their vertical penetration has increased. This is not the place for a sociology of knowledge. Suffice it that by the end of the nineteenth century, modernization appeared to be a method for increasing the social good. At the same time, from the cognitive point of view, the substantive, *modernity* came to indicate a structure driven by an internal crisis. The doubt that produced positive social and political accomplishments turned on its own products, and turned too against itself. The critique of traditional forms of life and thought gave way to self-criticism.

Sociological and historical grounds are often adduced to explain the transformation of the Cartesian theoretical doubt into a crisis-laden self-critical modern civilization. Most interesting have been the results of the Frankfurt school's attempt to join together the insights of Marx, Weber, and Freud. The historical-theoretical (and pessimistic) conclusion of this orientation is Adorno and Horkheimer's *Dialectic of Enlightenment.* They suggest that the traditional attitudes subjected to corrosive doubt were rationalized out of existence. The modern forms that have replaced them are now themselves the objects of critical doubt. Doubt becomes self-doubt; the critique loses its self-confidence; its justification can no longer be taken for granted. The result is a loss of anchorage and a "crisis" of the modern sciences. The second-generation Frankfurt theorist Jürgen Habermas has confronted this crisis in a series of works whose summation is the two-volume *Theory of Communicative Action.* Habermas joins a theory of social action and a theory of the social system by means of a theory of social evolution that mediates between the two. The theory of social action is genetic; the theory of the social system is normative. The status of the theory of social evolution that links the two is the key to the project's success. To escape from the self-doubt of modernity, Habermas must be able to show that this theory explains not just the possibility but the necessity of the modern crisis of rationality. The solution must not, however, be so strong as to eliminate the problem from which it originates. Facile invocations of a "post-modernity" only confuse the issue.

Modernity is not defined only by the rationality crisis whose necessity is immanent to modern theory. The crisis presents a problem. At the same time, it constitutes a temptation that induces to self-misunderstanding and to error. The problem is that of beginning; the temptation is that of ending. Fixed beginnings would eradicate the doubt that is fundamental to the critique; a fixed point would assure certitude, destroying the foundation of the doubt. An end or solution to the crisis would have the same effect. The question of beginning is not simply epistemological; the temptation to conclude is not merely sociological. Both approaches are possible, but their results are limited.[1] The old-fashioned philosophical concern with ontology and the priority classically accorded to the political present an alternative. Recourse to these "premodern" concerns may appear paradoxical in an attempt to clarify the nature of the modern without violating its self-imposed imperative of immanence. The point is not to "apply" lessons from the tradition, nor to invoke its solutions to resolve the crisis of the modern. That would be an unmodern appeal to an external guarantee of certitude. The paradox is only apparent; the classical question will be seen to reemerge as the process of modernity penetrates the life-world. If the modern is not simply arbitrary or accidental, it does not have a beginning but an origin. The nature of an origin is to be ontologically prior and actually copresent in the structure it originates. The epistemological and sociological concerns are subordinated to the ontological and political questions on which they depend for their methodological place. This avoids the vague descriptions of modernity, sometimes pictured as a process with a beginning and an end, sometimes as a substantive result with a determined content. It suggests also that the culturally contingent relation between the beginning (and the end) of capitalism and the origins of the modern world depends on the priority of the latter.

The problem of beginning and the temptation of ending did not exist in traditional, premodern modes of life. Various forms of external legitimation told the individual what to do, when and why to do it. Two types of external legitimation should be distinguished. In its most simple form, society as a whole is regulated by an external, pregiven, and unquestionable teleological myth. More important than its function in guiding the behavior of the individual is the theoretical status of this telos. The external legitimation functions as a norm that explains both the beginning of the society and its destination or end. As social complexity increases, a second type of external legitimation appears. Independent spheres of social action each generate their own logic with which they can treat the specific factual problems that confront them. The external world grows more sharply differentiated as complexity increases; new facts appear and generate in turn new and independent life-spheres, which in turn generate new logics. The result of this process of differentiation and specification is a growing loss of meaning of the social totality. Particularity becomes its own norm.

The transition to the modern, and the nature of its crisis, can be described by these two structural aspects of premodern external legitimation. The normative telos, which gave meaning to the simple social totality, stands opposed to the generative external world of fact that governs the logic of the separate spheres. Faith competes with science, sacred with secular law, custom justifies revolt against new types of political authority in a quarrel of the ancients and the moderns. Recourse to the one seems to exclude the other. At this point, the doubt that founded the development of the particular sciences is transformed into a principle. This principle demands that justification be immanent. The implication of this imperative of immanence is that the modern does not have a beginning, an external cause, or a telos. Because it is a principle, the immanent doubt implies the philosophical claim that the modern has an origin. More strongly still, because the transformation of the particular doubt into a principle was shaped by a structural necessity, the modern itself can be defined as originary. An originary structure is characterized by the immanent copresence or tension of the demand to explain genesis and the imperative to legitimate normativity. The history of the modernization of the modern world, in each of its sociological aspects and in its temporal rhythm, can be analyzed across this conceptual framework.

The principle of immanence explains why the temptation of ending is simply a variant of the problem of beginning. Unable to appeal to an external standard, philosophy has two options. The immanently experienced sense data can be defined as the ultimate basis from which the coherence of the world is reconstructed. This assures the validity of arguments about that world by means of a genetic reconstruction of the constitution of what is asserted. Genesis can be said to determine validity in this case; the assertion of fact provides by definition the normative justification. But this apparent preservation of immanence unintentionally retreats from the modern principle. The genetic fact loses its status as immanent when it becomes the normative standard which legitimates scientific claims. What was an immanent genetic fact becomes an external standard against which to measure and to validate the claims of experience. This is, in a word, the dilemma of empiricism. The same paradoxical situation appears when philosophy opts for the primacy of the normative in various forms of rationalism. The normative is opposed implicitly to the genetic, against which it stands as judge or measure. The unintended implication is again the emergence of an externality that the modern project was intended to overcome. In both cases, philosophy escaped the uncertainty imposed by the immanence of the modern by absolutizing one or the other pole. Seeking a solution, philosophy designated arbitrarily a beginning or a norm that is supposed to be beyond doubt. The critical originary principle is replaced by a foundation that is supposed to guarantee certitude. Ontology is replaced by epistemology. The beginning is transformed into an end by the immanent structural logic that defines the modern.[2]

This originary modern structure recalls Kant's description of the condition of philosophy before his "Copernican revolution." The implications of the empiricist position fall to the side of genesis; the rationalist argument belongs with the normative approach. Kant's philosophy was treated by his successors only as a beginning. The structural dualism that Kant articulated seemed to demand resolution into a single, foundational unity. The various attempts to transcend Kant in this manner all run the risk that their proposed foundation falls back into the status of externality. The foundation becomes a cause or a beginning. Its "effects" are then said to be generated by the foundation. The difficulty is that there is no way to demonstrate the necessity, and hence the validity, of these specific effects without an implicit return to the empiricist beginning. The other option is to treat the foundation as an essence or norm that governs its "appearances" in the empirical world. In this case, the fall back to externality takes the form of a reduction of the appearance to its essence in a movement that denies implicitly the reality of the appearance itself. A further problem emerges if such subjective idealism is avoided by appeal to a systematic interaction among essences and appearances. The systematic whole that is reconstructed itself becomes the external—and only—

givenness. The result of this variation is the elimination of growth, learning, or change. The solution amounts to the end of history, and with it the end of philosophy and politics. More successfully than the other post-Kantian systems, Hegel and Marx confront and articulate the nature of this difficulty.

Hegel and Marx articulate a further implication of the principle of immanence that characterizes the modern. Hegel is of course the philosopher of *system*.[3] The term requires definition; the demand requires justification. Systematic philosophy is self-contained, self-referential, and self-justificatory. Its reflexive structure makes each of its facets now the source of another, now the implication of another. The whole is in the parts, and the parts in the whole; the end is in the process of its accomplishment, and the accomplishment is possible only because of the preexistence of the end. These characterizations—and the many other formulations that will reappear in the following pages—are nothing other than the expression and result of the modern principle of immanence. System is destroyed only when recourse to externality is invoked. That externality gives system the closure that eliminates growth, learning, or change; it eliminates the possibility of history, philosophy, and politics. This is as true for Marx as for Hegel. Marx adds to the Hegelian systematic philosophy a second implication of the principle of immanence. The system must be complete, and it must be able to demonstrate (reflexively, i.e., immanently) its own completeness. Marx expressed this demand for completeness in his early critiques of Hegel's supposedly rational system that, he thought, could not be satisfactory as long as it left an unjust and hence irrational world outside itself.

These structural implications of the modern principle of immanence suggest that Kant be treated not as the beginning but as the *origin* of modern philosophy. The distinction is not simply verbal; its implications go beyond the history of ideas. The usual reading of the "Copernican revolution" portrays Kant's questioning the "conditions of the possibility of knowledge" as a renewal of *transcendental epistemology*. This portrait is not false, but it is not complete. Hegel, for example, pointed out that Kant spoke also of the "conditions of the possibility of experience." This suggests that Kant founds a *transcendental ontology*, whose articulation must be systematic and complete. It also leads Hegel to express wonder, criticism, and often disdain when Kant draws up short of the full expression of this systematic implication. In Marx's "revolutionary" transformation of what Kant originated, philosophy—as epistemology or as ontology—tends simply to be ignored, only to return unexpectedly and without explicit invitation to hinder, or at times to help, the expected systematic transformation. Both of these readings treat Kant as the beginning of a movement that has a determined end toward which it must move. However modern they themselves may be, they mistreat Kant as a premodern relic. The "Copernican revolution" is not the beginning of the crisis of modern rationality; nor is Kant's critical philosophy its end. As originary, Kant's theory is simply an articulation of the structure of that crisis. This suggests the necessity of a specific reading of Kant's philosophy as governed by the modern principle of immanence.

Treating Kant's philosophy as originary reveals another implication of the structure of the modern. Modernity is immanently *historical*. The historical character of modernity differs from the traditional portraits of a series of events ordered successively on and by a framework that is pregiven and unquestioned. This framework can be portrayed spatially or temporally; it may be both spatial and temporal. Even in this latter case, it remains an external frame. It resembles the tableau on which the historian paints the symbols and myths that give sense to his world. No philosophy of history is possible or necessary in this framework. The problems that appear retrospectively as its equivalent were posed at first as mythology, then as theodicy. These traditional styles of historiography can be designated as normative. When concern with the event itself, and then with its genetic role, replaced the normative concern, the linear temporality of theodicy was replaced by a spatial frame in which interaction takes on a new importance. This new framework can be designated by the German term *Historie*. Its framework is still tabular, but it permits the formulation of a nontheological orientation to history, alongside a theory of (international) politics and natural law. The transition to a history in which the events and their framework of meaning are created together is suggested by the originary modern structure. Its result is a *Geschichte* in which the philosophy of history must include also a theory of politics.[4]

The originary structure of modern history and its relation to politics distinguishes traditional transcendental philosophy from the originary philosophy articulated best by Kant. Another of Kant's supposed errors provides further illustration of this distinction. Kant's epistemology is said to postulate a "monological subject" who is always self-identical and who can be replaced by any other human subject. Kant's concern is said to be the description of the conditions in which the validity of an experiment is checked by another investigator who repeats the same process in the same conditions. This subject is "monological" because any unique individual can replace any other. When it comes to the moral, and then to the social and political world, this formal and abstract monological subject poses problems. It seems necessary to introduce a "dialogical subject" who changes and learns through interaction with others and with the world. Two solutions are proposed at this point, corresponding to the options for the normative or the genetic. The "hermeneutic" approach asks how a subject can understand an object unless the two share already a common framework of meaning. The subject is not an independent, self-created atom separated radically from the equally isolated and independent object. The two interact within a structure which is said normatively to constitute them both as the specific beings they are. This normative structure—in the form of culture, society, history, *Geist*, or language—then becomes the object for analysis. But if this normative context is treated as the principle explaining the knowledge generated in the hermeneutic relation, the modern principle of immanence is violated. The framework of meaning which constitutes the subject and the object is separated from them and prior to them. This explains why hermeneutic analysis functions most effectively in traditional contexts. The genetic variant tries to avoid this traditionalism by inverting the relation of constitution. The action of the subject on the objective world transforms that world. The transformed world, in turn, reacts back on the subject. The result is a "dialectic" between the two poles. The implication of this dialectical interaction is that the world becomes more like the subject as the subject becomes more like the world. In the end, subject and object are said to become identical with one another. This suggestive picture repeats the familiar problems. The active subject is portrayed apart from its object. Translated as either a "class" subject or as "humanity" or "Spirit," this subject becomes an essence determining the appearances that are reduced to the status of empty manifestations. If this idealism is avoided, the subject as actually separate from the world on which it works becomes an empirical cause whose effects on the world cannot claim necessity. Or, if the dialectic is in fact assumed to reach a conclusion, the relation of the subject to the object achieves a transparency such that the growth of knowledge ceases, history comes to an end, and so too do philosophy and politics.

Kant explained only the beginning, not the origin, of his critical philosophy. He did not explain the immanent necessity that motivated the new philosophy.[5] The movement from transcendental to originary philosophy must itself be originary. The one is not a beginning, the other its end. Originary philosophy does not complete what transcendental philosophy began. The transformation of beginning into origin is best articulated by Hegel; the transformation of end to origin is clearest in Marx. This was not the explicit goal of either. What is treated here as a virtue was for them an inconsistency or a youthful uncertainty overcome in maturity. They did not intend to elaborate an originary philosophy, nor did they. The modern philosopher who returns to their work reads it differently, with a shock of recognition. This has been less true in the case of Kant, who is only now beginning to excite among our contemporaries that same shock from which modern philosophy originated. Rereading Kant in the light of Hegel and Marx permits a reinterpretation of the critical project. Inconsistencies and difficulties in the Kantian text take on a weight that they might not otherwise bear. Concerns that seem anecdotal or external to the philosopher are integrated into his oeuvre. The first step is simply to formulate the problems. A second chapter will draw their systematic implications.

CRITIQUE AS ORIGINARY

Kant's *Critique of Pure Reason* has been commented traditionally as the renewal of classical transcendental philosophy. More recently, it has been treated from the standpoint of epistemology, or methodology in the philosophy of science. Both interpretations are founded in Kant's distinction between the *quid juris* and the *quid facti*. Kant's questioning the "conditions of the possibility" of a given world or fact builds from his "Copernican" turn that renounces as vain the attempt to constitute a factual world from either the deliverances of the senses or the givenness of rationality. Kant assumes the givenness of the facts; he questions the conditions in which they—or, for the epistemological reading, our knowledge of them—can be claimed legitimately to exist. Two approaches are suggested by the first (A) and the second (B) editions of the *Critique of Pure Reason*. After the sensible manifold of intuition is homogenized a priori by the Transcendental Aesthetic, the "Transcendental Deduction" of the A edition pictures a threefold synthesis that operates on this homogenized givenness in order to subsume it under concepts. The "Transcendental Deduction" of the B edition moves from a different direction in its central paragraph 16. The "transcendental unity of apperception" or the "I think that must accompany all of my representations" becomes a transcendental condition of the ontological givenness of the world. This ontological reading in the B edition is called into question, however, by Kant's revisions in the remainder of the B edition which did not excise the presentation of the Schematism of Pure Reason. That doctrine of an "art hidden in the depths of the human soul" performed the necessary transcendental unification of the three syntheses in the A edition. The B edition assigns the unification to the "transcendental unity of apperception." If Kant's revisions were consistent, he would have had to drop the schematism from the B edition.

The inconsistency between the two editions of the *Critique of Pure Reason* suggests the need for a redefinition of the critical project itself. A mediation between the two approaches is suggested in two brief political essays that Kant wrote in 1784, after the completion of the *Critique* but before its revision. The structure of the modern political state and the dilemmas of its politics parallel the questions posed to the critical philosophy. The preface to the first edition of the *Critique of Pure Reason* (1781) had announced triumphantly that only a "small but concerted effort" will be necessary to achieve "such completion as will leave no task to our successors save that of adapting it in a *didactic* manner" (A,xx). Kant's 1784 essay, "What Is Enlightenment?" begins from another, apparently contradictory remark in the preface. Kant characterized his times as an "age of criticism" (A, xi, note). He added that it was not yet an "enlightened age" but rather an "age of enlightenment" characterized by the growth and spread of Reason. Kant qualified this description politically, speaking of his age as the "century of Frederick." The remark is surprising. Kant neither admired nor followed the political model of the French *philosophes.* He did not think that the spread of enlightenment depended on the kind of influence Voltaire thought he exercised on Frederick, or Diderot on Catherine. He did, however, participate in the general spirit of the Enlightenment. Drawing the implications of his remark will suggest theoretically the kind of "completion" his *Critique* expected; it will suggest practically the kind of "didactic" task that the critical system requires.

The rulers who created the modern nation-state could have subscribed to the lines with which Kant prefaced the first *Critique.* They were building a structure whose administration would demand eventually no more than to be adapted "in a didactic manner." The basis on which they built is implicit in an italicized citation from Frederick by which Kant explains his praise in 1784. "Argue as much as you like and about whatever you like, but obey." This split between obedience and freedom, between the public and the private, is the structural feature by which the modern state is identified.

Kant was not so naïve as to believe that guarantees of private personal freedom were the product of the monarch's enlightened free will. Reason of state led the freethinking Prussian monarch to welcome the Jesuits after they had been banned by the Catholic monarchs of Europe; reason of state sought to wipe out superstition and dogmatic authority; reason of state tried to eliminate the traditional feudal and customary barriers to individual self-assertion. In destroying external barriers, reason of state constitutes a citizenry subordinate to itself alone. Private freedom and public obedience to the state depend on each other, in history and in theory. This structure is modern; nothing external to the state can stand in its way. But in this movement that creates the modern free citizen, the state sets itself apart from the private individual whose only relation to it is obedience. The state becomes external to the society. Creation of the modern citizen produces a new political problem that puts the modernity of the state into question. The implications of this paradoxical structure will return frequently in Hegel and Marx.

The problem for the philosopher, as for the monarch, is defined by the separation between the public and the private, the universal and the particular. The temptation is to operate from the stance of the universal or public authority whose task is to impose its stamp on the private and the particular. This structure is what the apparently contradictory term *enlightened despotism* seeks to capture.[6] Leonard Krieger's analysis of this political and intellectual structure suggests that it functions as a "schematism" or an "idea of reason" that speaks in the "conditional mode" and expresses "a political principle in the special language of political action."[7] Krieger's Kantian language is not unmotivated. There are ample suggestions in Kant that follow this pattern. The goal is to make compatible the universal (law, state, concept) and the particular without destroying the unique individuality of that particular. The problem recurs in Kant's consideration of revolution in his last published work, the *Conflict of the Faculties*. He observes that progress can come only "from the top downwards,...not [in] the usual sequence from the bottom upwards." This one-sided assertion is put immediately into question on the next page, when Kant recalls the problem of who will educate the educator.[8] It is not enough for the philosopher or politician to impose a common space from which particularity is banished. The concepts or laws under which the particulars are subsumed must themselves be necessary and rational if they are to be effective and legitimate. That demonstration, which is the "education of the educator," demands the overcoming of the externality of the relation of the state and the individual from both sides.

"What Is Enlightenment?" appears at first to propose a solution that ignores the separation of individual and state. Kant begins by defining the task as "man's release from his self-incurred tutelage." He explains himself vigorously: "If I have a book that understands for me, a pastor who has a conscience for me, a physician who decides my diet, and so forth, I need not trouble myself. I need not think, if only I can pay—others will readily undertake the irksome work for me." The refusal of any kind of external authority satisfies the requirements of modern philosophy. At the same time, however, it recalls the fact that the philosophers always have had less difficulty once they arrived in the land of Reason than they have had in guiding the uninitiated to that land. Kant's problem is that he has no way to show the necessity that will bring the individual to realize the need for, and then actually to achieve autonomy. Kant is aware of the dilemma. He offers different, often contradictory solutions in the course of his political reflections. The difficulty is rooted in his theoretical premise.

The preface to the B edition of the *Critique of Pure Reason* explains the positive result of the negative critique in the famous assertion that "I have therefore found it necessary to deny *knowledge* in order to make room for *faith*" (B, xxx). The faith with which Kant is concerned is not the acceptance of an external standard. It is a belief in the autonomy of moral will which makes free action both possible and necessary. Morality is made safe because it does not "require that freedom should be understood, but only that it should not contradict itself." In this way, the "doctrine of morality and the doctrine of nature may each, therefore, make good its position" (B, xix). This dualism poses theoretical problems. It is also unable to solve the practical demand that the autonomy of enlightenment be in fact realizable. This theoretical and practical problem is at the origin of the epistemological dualism for which Kant is usually criticized. By not requiring that "freedom should be understood," Kant leaves himself open to the objection that he has invoked freedom as an external norm. That would contradict the modernity that makes possible and necessary the critique. Freedom must be understood, as a norm *and* as the genetic source of autonomous enlightenment.

"What Is Enlightenment?" recognizes the need to give a rational content to the formal autonomy from which it begins. Kant introduces an argument from Rousseau. "The touchstone of everything that can be concluded as a law for a people is that the people could have imposed such a law on itself." This definition takes one positive step beyond the abstraction of Kant's unknowable ethical will.[9] A further step in the same essay adds an additional specification: "a contract made to shut off all further enlightenment from the human race is absolutely null and void even if confirmed by the supreme power, by parliaments, and by the most ceremonious of peace treaties.... That would be a crime against human nature, the proper destination of which lies precisely in this progress." The appeal to Rousseau's republican theory of law, coupled with the insistence on the public debate that accompanies any contract, are crucial to Kant's later political theory. At the present stage, when the critical adventure had barely begun, they can be read only as his recognition of a gap in the argument. More important, these passages testify to Kant's rigorous application of the principle of modernity. The autonomy of enlightenment will get a content, but not from an external source. For the moment, however, the political parallels have to be left aside for purposes of exposition. They will return.

The philosophical difficulty has its roots in the ambiguity of the critical approach itself. The "Copernican" hypothesis was expected to return philosophy to her throne. Reason was no longer to follow experience and to depend on nature. Now reason would give its own a priori laws to the world. One implication might be that the Queen of the Sciences finds herself in the position of the enlightened despot. Such an interpretation must be avoided, however consonant with Kant's text it may occasionally appear. The "Copernican" hypothesis permits two other readings: either philosophy is given a radically new content or philosophy becomes merely method. Both interpretations can be justified from the text. For example, Kant describes his work as "a treatise on the method, not a system of the science itself. But at the same time it marks out the whole plan of the science, both as regards its limits and as regards its internal structure" (B, xxii). The two sentences seem to support both arguments. Looking more closely, the first preface seems to justify speaking of the *Critique* as method when Kant insists that it establishes a "tribunal" before which claims are to be brought (A, xi). Yet this same first preface promised the substantive completion leaving "no task to our successors save that of adapting it in a *didactic* manner" (A, xx). The second preface seems to lean more toward the claim to be the content of science. It refers to the creation of a system (B, xxxviii), and a work to "bequeath to posterity as a capital to which no addition can be made" (B, xxiv). Yet this latter citation continues by stressing that the Transcendatal Dialectic limits the pretensions of unchained reason. Kant seems to vacillate between an interpretation of the *Critique* as substantive or normative and the presentation of a critical method whose task is to generate valid knowledge.

The source of the ambiguity can be traced to the very title of Kant's project. The genitive *of* in the *Critique of Pure Reason* can be read as either subjective, objective, or neutral. Who or what does the criticizing? Who or what is criticized?

1. If the subjective interpretation is proposed, pure reason is the active agent doing the critique. In this case, justification for the claim of pure reason to function as "tribunal" (A, xi) must be provided. Otherwise, Kant would be guilty of the very dogmatism that he condemns on the ground that it proceeds "without previous criticism of its own powers" (B, xxxv, emphasis omitted). He would be appealing to an external standard in violation of the modern principle of immanence.

2. Reason's claim to be "pure" might be taken as the object of Kant's critique. This interpretation fits both the goals of the Transcendental Dialectic and the famous assertion that "Thoughts without content are empty, intuitions without concepts are blind" (A 51; B 75). But the next two *Critiques* show no concern for the problem of purity. More-

over, if this were all Kant could demonstrate, he would not have rescued Reason's throne. He would have proven only the unreasonableness of philosophy's pretension to be Queen of the Sciences.

3. The most plausible suggestion is that pure reason itself is the object of the critique. This leaves open the question of who is doing this criticism and with what legitimation? Kant claims that critique alone "can sever the root of materialism, fatalism, atheism, freethinking, fanaticism, and superstition....as well as of idealism and skepticism" (B, xxxiv, emphasis omitted). Having eliminated its enemies, pure reason stands alone, judge and party to its own case. Immanence is maintained, but at the risk of arbitrariness or tautology. Pure reason falls into the same dilemma as the enlightened autonomous individual. If it is not to be arbitrary, it risks being empty. Epistemological reflection on method must be replaced by a more traditional ontological orientation if the principle of modernity is obeyed.

These philosophical dilemmas parallel the political problems. Kant cannot escape by returning to an external or premodern structure. The ambiguity is built into the project itself. It might be argued that Kant overcame these difficulties only after he had applied the critical method to the traditional domains of nature and morality, and then finally to itself in the *Critique of Judgment*. The preface to that third *Critique* announces that it is the end of the "critical business." Kant proposes to pass to the elaboration of a "doctrinal" philosophy. The methodological section of this volume (part 2) will center around the meaning of these two terms for Kant. From the point of view of a modern philosophy, Kant's oscillation between the methodological and the more substantive interpretation of his "revolution" is an expression of the originary structure that defines the modern project. The Kantian work as a whole, and in each of its parts, concentrates at times on the new continent discovered by the critique, at times on the method that permits its exploration. Kant was aware of this peculiar structure, to which he calls attention in the "Transcendental Doctrine of Method" which concludes the *Critique of Pure Reason*. Kant describes an "Architechtonic of Pure Reason" in which "the diverse modes of knowledge must not be permitted to be a mere rhapsody, but must form a system" (A 832; B 860). He goes on to oppose this "organized unity" to an "aggregate." Finally, he compares it to "an animal body, the growth of which is not by the addition of a new member, but by the rendering of each member, without change of proportion, stronger and more effective for its purposes" (A 833; B 861). This description recalls the *Critique of Judgment*. It also indicates the reason that Kant's historical and political writings are part of his originary project.[10] Kant does not begin those essays from the transcendental *quid juris* which presupposes the existence of an object whose validity claim he will examine. This does not mean that Kant did not begin his questioning from the traditional transcendental form. However, the fact that he was driven beyond it has to be integrated into an understanding of his philosophical contribution. That interpretation begins in chapter Two's discussion of the originary turm.

Phenomenology and Logic as Originary

The tension between the public and the private, the universal and the particular, is not unique to Kant's philosophy. The development from the young Hegel to the author of the *Phenomenology of Spirit* and finally to the creator of the encyclopedic System began from the same interaction. Hegel's attempt to understand "spiritless" Germany's inability to make its own French Revolution returned to an earlier revolution that originated the Christian community, and to another that brought an end to the classical Greek polity. He stresses the paradoxes to which this movement opens. Like Kant, Hegel assumes that Reason is the only authority that can be accepted among the enlightened. This holds for the religiously enlightened as well. Like Jesus, they must rebel against institutions which are authoritarian because they deny rational self-determination. The Jewish religion can be criticized because its God is an external force decreeing laws whose validity it is forbidden to question. At the same time, these institutions of the Jewish people are nonetheless those of an authentic community. Even if they are imposed externally by an abstract and authoritarian God, the result of Jesus' rebellion against the external element in Judaism can therefore be only a private religion that rejects the public forms and forum of the Jewish community. It will not be the rational "folk religion" by which Hegel hoped to found a community like the Greek model built on free public institutions. Put differently, an institutional public freedom can only exist within the framework of law. It must be able to resort to force. This means that it places itself apart from the individual, recreating the problem. The conclusion can only be antinomic, however Hegel twists and turns. An enlightened, rational, but private religion is incompatible with a public institutional folk religion. As with Kant, Hegelian reflection thrives on such incompatibilities.

When Hegel published the *Phenomenology of Spirit* in 1807, the violence of the French Revolution had given way to the triumphant empire. Tension and opposition apparently had been overcome. From this standpoint, the *Phenomenology* is a modern theodicy. Its famous preface, completed at midnight before the battle of Jena, reads as a world-historical, philosophical-political epiphany. System had been achieved on the evening when the fate of Germany was decided. Hegel demonstrates the parallels between the progress of the individual toward Reason, the development of the species in the same direction, and the unification of these two processes in a development through the community of religious representation to attain Absolute Knowledge. The *Phenomenology* is a compendium of humanity's ultimate achievement. The unity of the development of the individual, of the species, and of Spirit itself leaves nothing external to itself. Contingency is exluded from this dialectical progress. The implication is that just as Napoleon had destroyed the traditional Germanic world, so Hegel puts to their final rest the presuppositions that have misguided philosophy. The anecdotal conclusion to this picture portrays Napoleon riding by on his white horse as Hegel comments that here is the *Zeitgeist* on horseback. The system is the result of the genetic action whose dialectical climb finally achieves unity and necessity. Such a view is plausible, but problematic.

The systematic approach oversimplifies a philosophical work whose structure recalls the literary genre of the

Bildungsroman. It could well have taken as its motto Wilhelm Meister's *Ich muss scheinen, bis ich werde.* As in the novel, we wonder about its author, his relation to the material described, why he is telling us the story. We also worry about verisimilitude. Did the story necessarily take place as described; could the narration have taken a different path; did the narrator learn from the experience which therefore is presented in a reflected (or distorted, or rationalized) form? Does the author return elsewhere to reflect on this work, perhaps to reject or to alter it? All of these questions have been raised by interpreters of the *Phenomenology of Spirit.* Hegel's student and editor, Michelet, sees it as part of Hegel's psychological path to discovery but not one of the discoveries. Another student, Gabler, who succeeded Hegel in Berlin, argues that its first part is a necessary beginning for philosophy, but he admits that a logical and a historical beginning are also possible and perhaps necessary. Hegel's first biographer, Rosenkranz, suggests that it represents a crisis in Hegel's development from which the author emerged safely. Later scholars have treated the text as if it were incomplete working notes—with some notes finding their way into the final volume, others dropping out, still others appearing elsewhere. A more literary criticism studies the articulations of the text, finding in some cases small inconsistencies, in others significant ones. For example, Haering's "palimpsest" theory stresses the two souls dwelling in an epistemological project interspersed with or perhaps transformed into a cosmological, world-historical treatise. Finally, there are the literary detectives. Ironically, it is they who set us back on the right track.[11]

The literary detective finds two documents that call into question the systematic progression through a beginning, middle, and conclusion to the Bildungsroman. The first is the letter to Schelling of May 1807 that accompanied a copy of Hegel's just-published work. Hegel's apology for his literary style may be noted in passing. More important is his insistence that the *Phenomenology of Spirit* is the "first part, which in fact is the introduction" to the System. These words take on more weight when we learn that the printed volume (which Hegel never revised or reprinted, as he did with many of his other works) exists under two different titles. Hegel himself apparently was responsible for this change of titles, which has important implications for the originary structure of the work. The one title is *"First Part: Science of the Experience of Consciousness."* The second title is *"I: Science of the Phenomenology of Spirit."*. The two titles agree that the work is the first part of a broader project and that it is a "science." The nature of the science and of the project to which it is the introduction depend on whether phenomenology and experience are identical, and on the relation between spirit and consciousness. Analysis of these two relations presents the originary structure of the science. At the same time, the relation between the science and the system becomes the focus of the next stage in Hegel's development. This clue from the detective provides a device for sketching briefly this first phase of the Hegelian project.

A further piece of evidence points back to Kant. When Schelling replied to Hegel some six months later (November 1807), he apologized for having had time to read only the preface. Even though Hegel's goal, and his own, was the creation of a System, Schelling felt that a serious problem separated their endeavors. In what sense, he asks, does Hegel oppose concept to intuition? By concept, he notes, "you cannot mean anything else than what you and I called Idea, namely that whose nature is precisely to have one side that is concept and one side that is intuition." This was the last letter the former friends exchanged. Hegel did not mean the kind of hypostatized unity to which Schelling was referring. Such a unity makes the foundationalist error that violates the originary structure. The origin becomes an essence determining manifestations whose independence is illusory. Schelling correctly feared that Hegel had turned back toward Kant. Hegel's account builds from a significant duality in the *Critique of Pure Reason*. What are the conditions of the possiblity of experience? What are the conditions of the possibility of knowledge? The *Critique of Pure Reason* asks both questions without drawing attention to their distinction. The answer offered in the "Transcendental Analytic" is the same for both. The implication of this duality is that epistemology and ontology are not distinguished. This suggests that experience and knowledge (or science) are identical. The task of the *Phenomenology of Spirit* is to demonstrate this identity. This is the sense in which the work is a "science of experience." This first solution needs now to be supplemented by further detective work.

Hegel's insistence on the introductory nature of the *Phenomenology* is a first clue toward explaining the relation of spirit and consciousness in the two titles. The second clue also concerns the relation to Kant. Hegel returns to the domain he calls "phenomenological" in the systematic *Encyclopaedia* (Para 415 and note). Phenomenology is a subordinate science within the system because its object, consciousness, is determined externally. It is not self-determining, immanent, autonomous. Hegel adds that Kant's philosophy is typical of the weaknesses that result from such a situation. It "treats Spirit as consciousness, and contains only determinations of the phenomenology and not of the philosophy of spirit." The description is *only* phenomenological because consciousness is determined externally. This external determination means that consciousness is dependent. This implies that it cannot demonstrate relations of necessity or account for freedom. Spirit—and by implication philosophy—is self-determining. A phenomenology of spirit must be the process by which spirit determines itself, presents itself, and comes explicitly to know itself. This is precisely what the introduction to the *Phenomenology of Spirit* promises. Its object is said to be "only the presentation of appearing knowledge....the path of natural consciousness that strives toward true knowledge...the path of the soul through the series of its forms...to Spirit...in that it passes through the complete experience of itself and comes to the knowledge of what it is in itself." The *Phenomenology* is introductory in the sense that the medium into which science is to enter is spirit. Guided by the philosopher who already scouted the way, the reader follows the "experience of consciousnesss" as it becomes self-aware and thereby scientific. This relation of spirit and consciousness explains the first title of the book.

Hegel's own introduction to this phenomenological introduction to philosophy stresses the relation between genetic consciousness and valid (normative) science. He begins from the attitude of common sense which pictures a subject in relation to an object. This relation of subject to object is called knowledge. Knowledge can be conceived either as a tool bringing the object to the subject or as a medium through which the object is presented to the subject. Both conceptions pose problems. The tool transforms the object while the medium refracts it. Neither presents the object as it truly exists in its otherness. It is no help to try to eliminate the effects of the tool or the medium in order to avoid distortion. That only returns to the starting point. Common sense suggests a different approach. This time it distinguishes between a true science whose validity it presupposes and the experiental knowledge that an individual consciousness has. This new dualism again makes true knowledge impossible. The presupposed dualism excludes by definition the result at which it aims. This dualism is none other than the Kantian premise. Hegel describes the dilemma concisely in his *History of Philosophy*:

> To investigate the faculty of knowledge means to know it. The demand is thus the following: One must know the faculty of knowledge before one has knowledge.— It is the same thing as wanting to learn to swim before getting into the water. The investigation of the faculty of knowledge is itself a knowledge. It cannot arrive at what it seeks because it already is what it seeks; it cannot come to itself because it is already with itself.[12]

The implications of this passage point back to the literary reading of the *Phenomenology of Spirit*. Hegel needs a development or *Bildung* so that the skepticism that could result from the frustrations of common sense does not turn into a nihilism with no content. His novel must illustrate the "self-completing skepticism." The introduction stresses that the result of the experience is not Nothing but rather a "determinant negative," which has a content and moves dialectically. Yet, if the story "cannot arrive at what it seeks because it is already what it seeks," then the effort of telling the tale was not necessary. The foundationalist philosophical structure replaces the originary account; essence is presupposed as determining existence. More than this is implied in Hegel's argument.

A further reflection in the introduction shows that Hegel is aware of the need to maintain the originary stance. Common sense seeks a measure that makes possible the comparison between the consciousness of the object and the object itself. Hegel immediately rules out the traditional image that "we" philosophers are or possess that standard. He rejects any additional external input (*Zutat*) from the philosopher, who is allowed only to observe (*Zusehen*) consciousness. The structure of consciousness is dual: it is conscious of an object, and it is conscious of itself as knowing the object. This means that consciousness is itself structured as a comparison or examination. Consciousness is therefore its own measure. Consciousness must change its knowledge if there is no correspondence between the consciousness of the object and self-consciousness. Changing its knowledge means changing its object, since its knowledge can be only the consciousness it has of a pregiven object. Hegel concludes that neither the object nor self-consciousness is fixed and permanent. Neither can serve as a pregiven valid measure. The measure, rather, is consciousness itself which is nothing but the dialectical relation Hegel calls "experience." The result is that the introduction, which began from a criticism of Kant, in fact concludes as a vindication of the "Kantian" identification of the conditions of the possibility of experience and the conditions of the possibility of knowledge.[13] Consciousness and experience thus have identical structures. The title change suggests that their articulation is spirit's phenomenological appearance. But the title change also suggests caution, as does the originary structure. A philosophy of spirit needs a normative guarantee that each step proceeds with necessity and that the demonstration is complete. The detective work takes on a philosophical dimension.

The phenomenological project must meet the paradoxical demand that the path to science is itself scientific. Hegel's literary approach avoids the difficulties that caused Kant's oscillation between the stress on philosophical method or on substance. The two titles point to the copresence of the genetic and the normative. The phenomenological description of the experience of consciousness must be at the same time a philosophy of spirit. Hegel portrays three figures in his story: the reader undertaking the voyage to learn philosophy, the consciousness at which he simply looks (*Zusehen*), and the already initiated author. The acting consciousness is a "naïve" consciousness that represents the commonsense view of knowledge. This actor is moved to doubt, indeed to despair. As mere consciousness, it depends on external factors over which it has no power. It has experience. It measures the inadequacy between its self-knowledge and the knowledge of the object. It seeks to move forward by means of the determinant negation of its failed past experiences. But what keeps it from moving on to simply another variant of the same structure? How is it to find the new and to know it as new? Either this consciousness is not an individual but a species consciousness, in which case the *Phenomenology of Spirit* is a retrospective description of the real evolution of humanity where, as the older Hegel says, "World History is the Court of the Last Judgment." Or there has to be a *Zutat* from the philosopher who has already made the voyage. But that *Zutat* from the knowing philosopher supposes that he himself has experienced the truth which he now communicates. Such knowledge is only possible by means of a normative assumption that begins to pull apart the originary structure and point toward Hegel's next phase. The assumption is that the experience of consciousness was in fact structured by scientific rationality. This explains why Hegel replaces *experience of consciousness* in the first title by *phenomenology of spirit* in the second. The apparently genetic stress in the one account gives way to the normative orientation that was pointed to in the *Encyclopaedia's* distinction between autonomous self-determining spirit and externally determined content. The shift is not without significance in assessing Hegel's articulation of the philosophical principle of modernity.

The literary detective work is nearly complete. The *Phenomenology of Spirit* owes its vitality to the constant pressure exerted by the competing genetic and normative demands whose copresence defines the work as originary. A final detail reaffirms this interpretation and suggests a transition. Hegel began to revise his *Science of Logic* in 1831. He returned to the question of the introductory character of the *Phenomenology* in a brief note. Now that the entire system had been elaborated in the *Encyclopaedia of the Philosophical Sciences,* Hegel asserts that the *Phenomenology* is not to be seen as the "first part of the system of science." This brief comment resolves the last of the problems raised by the title change. There remains one peculiarity: the term that remains constant throughout is *science.* It passes from the phenomenological period into the "science" of *Logic,* and into the "philosophical sciences" that are the content of the *Encyclopaedia.* Its definition cannot be given precisely because the path to science must itself already be scientific, and "it cannot arrive at what it seeks because it is already what it seeks." The next phase of Hegel's work will show that science and what is here called "origin" have identical structures.[14] This reciprocal relation is, once again, testimony to the modern imperative animating the Hegelian system as a whole.

Once the *Phenomenology of Spirit* is no longer seen as the introduction or first part of the system, the problem of a beginning returns. Rationality appears omnipresent when self-determining spirit is both subject and object of philosophy. This explains the caricatural Hegel who asserts in the preface to the *Philosophy of Right* that "What is rational is actual and what is actual is rational." Hegel replies to the critcs of this identity in a Remark added to paragraph 6 of the *Encyclopaedia.* There is a difference between existence (*Dasein*) and appearance (*Erscheinung*). The accidental (*zufällige Existenz*) is not the same as the actual (*das Wirkliche*), since it is only a possibility (*ein Mögliches*) not a necessity. Hegel refers the reader to the *Logic* for further details. The same issue returns in paragraph 16 of the *Encyclopaedia.* The order of the sciences presented there must be necessary and immanent, not external and aggregative. Disciplines such as heraldry, based on arbitrary beginnings, are ruled out even when they present the apparent rigor of science. The empirical aspect of science is distinguished from the necessary rational element with which philosophy can deal. For example, the science of government contains rational principles determining that there must be taxes; but science does not make the decision how high these taxes should be. When that empirical decision is made, it is justified by giving reasons (*Gründe*) as opposed to a conceptual (*begrifflich*) philosophical demonstration. Similar strictures apply to the historical sphere, where accident and externality coexist with immanent necessity. Finally, the source of knowledge must be considered. Anthropology, the study of internal intuition and external experience, are all based in feeling, faith, the authority of others, or mere immediate experience. They do not belong to the philosophical system. With what, then, is that scientific or originary system to begin?

Hegel's discussion of the place of the history of philosophy as one of the sciences within the encyclopedic system suggests an approach to the apparently normative science of the *Logic*. The way this historical development is brought into the system presents an interpretative framework for dealing with those mixed domains where the empirical and the rational coexist.[15] Hegel explains that although it is external, accidental, and based on a variety of different principles, the history of philosophy "shows in part one philosophy presented in different levels of development and in part that the particular *principles* that ground one system are only branches of one and the same whole" (13). The next paragraph insists that his own philosophy gathers the fruits of this development as the Idea or Absolute which can exist only as system. "A philosophizing without system cannot be scientific," he continues, since each part is justified only by its immanent existence within the whole. Outside the system there is only accident, presupposition, subjectivity. The system itself is a system of systems, a "circle that circles in on itself," a "circle of circles" each of which is necessary to the others. These images recall the definition of Spirit that permitted the distinction in the *Encyclopaedia* of *philosophy* from mere *phenomenology*. If they are taken as its beginning, they entail a foundationalist reduction of the originary system to an ideal essence. That is not Hegel's path. The *Encyclopaedia* begins in fact with the presupposition of a logic. The development of the genetic phenomenological position to a full philosophical science does not account alone for the encyclopedic system. The normative contribution of a philosophical logic cannot be neglected.

The starting point of the *Logic* can be clarified when attention is paid to the distinction between science and system. Hegel titles his book *The Science of Logic*. His argument shows that the two categories are interdependent. The section "With What Must Science Begin?" warns against two errors. The beginning cannot be something that is mediated, determinant, or real (*Daseinendes*). In each of these cases, the putative starting point becomes in fact the result of some presupposition that mediates, determines, or interacts with it to give it its character. Beginning, insists Hegel, must be radical, pure, and immanent. The implication is that the beginning cannot be constitutive of what it begins. It is not a (real) cause. The starting point is not a kind of active principle working on an objectively given otherness which it transforms. Such a beginning again introduces an external presupposition. The beginning that Hegel proposes in the *Logic* is the unity-in-difference of Being and Nothing, which displays itself as Becoming. His demonstration is straightforward, although its implications are far reaching. As pure immanence, the beginning can only be self-relatedness. Self-related thought is that Absolute at which the *Phenomenology of Spirit* had arrived in its systematic fullness. Hegel insists here in the *Logic* that the journey of initiation is not necessary. The beginning can be made from immanent conceptual necessity without the phenomenological interaction with the accidental external world. Purely immanent self-relation is the structure we normally call Being. But such self-related immanence is also absolutely without content and undetermined. From this point of view, it is what we normally call Nothing. The result can be described simply: it is what it is not and it is not what it is. This is the structure we normally call Becoming. The *Logic* unfolds this starting point as the "circle of circles" that can claim completeness and necessity because the immanence of the beginning guarantees the copresence of the genetic principle and the normative standard. This structure guarantees its claim to science.

The difference between science and system appears when the *Logic* and the *Phenomenology* are compared. The beginning of the *Logic* makes possible a structural development that guarantees the necessity needed for the phenomenological *Zusehen*. At the same time, the beginning of the *Logic* and the conclusion of the *Phenomenology* manifest the same structure of absolute, immanent self-relatedness. The difference between the two is captured by what Hegel calls the "speculative proposition" (*Satz*).

> All that is necessary to achieve scientific progress...is the recognition of the logical principle that the negative is just as much positive. What is self-contradictory does not collapse into nothing, an abstract nothingness, but essentially only into the negation of its particular content. In other words, that such a negation is not negation in

> general but the negation of a specific subject matter which resolves itself. Consequently it is a specific negation. Therefore, the result essentially contains that from which it results—which strictly speaking is a tautology, for otherwise it would be an immediacy, not a result.

The triadic structure of the *Logic* proceeds immanently, whereas the phenomenological determinant negation and "self-completing skepticism" depend on an external presupposition. This implies that the scientific status of the *Phenomenology* depends on the normative *Logic* which guides the *Zutat* to the genetic orientation by recourse to the speculative proposition. Symmetrically, the *Logic* entails a "phenomenological" moment in the movement to Becoming as articulating the determinant structures of Being. This does not mean that the *Logic* presupposes either the voyage of initiation or the theoretical contents of the 1807 work. The success of the normative claim in the *Logic* depends on an immanent genetic phenomenological moment, just as the genetic *Phenomenology* depends on a logical normativity.

Hegel's claim to unify science and system depends on this interrelation between the phenomenological and the logical methods. The systematic unity of the two manifests the originary structure typical of modern philosophy. Like the scientific character of the *Phenomenology*'s introduction to science, the scientific character of the *Science of Logic* can be justified only on these grounds. This argument makes evident a dimension of the originary structure that was not apparant in the Kantian philosophy. The problem for the interpretation of Kant was whether the *Critique* is method or substance. The notions of genesis and normativity were applied there as opposing the processual to the structural, action to system. This presentation of Hegel's beginning makes clear that the genetic and the normative are themselves to be defined in an originary context. The normative has a genetic function and the genetic has a normative component. The originary identity that Hegel demonstrates between science and system permits that articulation because it brings together method and substance. This is why Hegel can encompass the Kantian revolution within his encyclopedic ontology.

Anthropology and Economics as Originary

The first section of the *Communist Manifesto* is a vibrant evocation of the wonders of modernity.[16] Marx combines an excited welcome of capitalism's destruction of traditional barriers with a violent disgust at the new forms of exploitation it develops. Capitalism is both positive and negative. This ambivalence structures the entirety of Marx's theory. The young Marx tended to accentuate its negative implications in his elaboration of a radical anthropological critique whose basis is that "for man the root is man himself."[17] The mature Marx argues for the necessity of socialism by drawing the positive implications from his study of *Capital*. The voluntarist politics of pure will and the determinist expectation that necessity will force action form the poles that are always present temptations in each phase of Marx's development. This holds not only for Marx's own politics. He sees the same polarity in the modern bourgeois world. For example, the preface to the second edition of the *Eighteenth Brumaire* rejects the one-sidedness of Hugo's voluntarist interpretation of Bonaparte's coup as well as Proudhon's determinist reading of the same event. Marx's own analysis, to which chapters 6 and 7 return, builds from the philosophical structure revealed by the modern. This is why the controversy concerning the "two Marxes" can never be resolved. Marx's contribution to an originary philosophy begun by Kant and Hegel demonstrates that not only philosophy is structured by the immanent demands of the modern.[18] Modern reality itself presents the identical originary framework. This is why the early philosophical concern remains present in Marx's politics. Politics cannot impose its imperatives from outside any more than philosophy can impose its categories on reality. Marx's recognition of this structural problem explains the parallel between the tasks of modern philosophy and the modern Prussian state that Frederick was trying to construct, to which the discussion of Kant referred already.

This portrait corresponds to the goal Marx had already set for himself at the time of his doctoral dissertation. Marx rejected the young Hegelian attempt to *apply* the lessons of Hegelian rational philosophy to the transformation of the world. He formulated his own project in a lengthy note to his dissertation. His editors have titled his note "On the World's Becoming Philosophical and on Philosophy's Becoming Worldly." The post-Hegelian moment in Marx's thinking is seen first in his stress on the need that the world be structured in a way that accepts rational philosophy. Philosophy will be transformed in this interaction in which it no longer stands apart from the world with which it is concerned. Marx does not elaborate the nature of this transformed philosophy in the dissertation. The next three phases of his early development articulate its originary character. The first step remains the premise of the other two. This stage is marked by the discovery of the primacy of civil society over the political and by the notion of the proletariat as the "solution to the riddle of history." The second phase draws the implications of this discovery from the anthropological perspective, which argues at first from a normative stance in the theory of alienated labor, and then from the genetic orientation in the constitutive approach to the theory of ideology. The final phase combines a theory of class struggle with a reconstitution of the crisis-ridden structure of capitalist society as a whole. Both the anthropological theory of human nature and the economic account of the social system remain within the principled framework of the modern.

Two essays written in 1843 for publication in the *Deutsch-Französischre Jahrbücher* of which Marx was coeditor sum up his initial stance. The polemical "On the Jewish Question" demonstrates the priority of civil society over the separate and therefore ideological spheres of religion and politics. The major lines of Marx's argument are simple. Merely political change no more transforms social relations than does the elimination of the idea of religion from the world of ideas. Social transformation must be concrete and material. Its locus is civil society, to which Marx then turns in "Toward a Critique of Hegel's *Philosophy of Right* Introduction." That essay begins with the declaration that the critique of religion, which is the presupposition of all critique, has now ended. The times call instead for an "irreligious critique." This new critique is to be built on a constitutive anthropology. The first step is the denunciation of religion as "the opium of the people." The constitutive moment appears in the assertion that it is in fact "man" who makes religion. The constitutive orientation is reinforced by Marx's definition of *radical* as "going to the root" which "for man is man himself." Yet Marx seems aware of the problem inherent in this reduction, which supposes a distinction between ideas and a real world to which they are but an external correlate. He had already stressed that "Man is the world of man" and supported this assertion concretely with reference to contemporary conditions. His denunciation of the religious opium, moreover, was accompanied by the positive observation that religion is also an active protest against social conditions. The resulting "irreligious critique" is not constitutive but fully immanent. The critique must "make these petrified relations dance by singing before them their own melody." Neither the "theoretical party" nor the "practical party" has understood this imperative. The realization of philosophy without its elimination is no more possible than the elimination of philosophy without its realization. "The critique of the weapons cannot replace the weapon of the critique. Material power must be overthrown by material power. But theory itself becomes a power when it grasps the masses." The masses must be shown to need and to want to grasp the theory; theory must have a structure that they can grasp. The relation is not constitutive; it is originary. Treating religion as both rebellious and yet alienated preserves the tension that unites the norms asserted by religion with the conditions of its genesis. The consequences of this structure are drawn at the conclusion of "Toward a Critique."

Marx's essay introduces the notion of the proletariat as a structure within, and finally as determining the form of, civil society. He asserts abstractly that there must exist a particular class that can make justifiable universal demands. Such a class will be able to say "I am nothing and I must become everything." Turning to German reality, Marx does not find such a class. His argument returns to the structural level. He speaks of the "formation of a class with *radical chains*, a class of civil society that is not a class of civil society, an estate that is the dissolution of all estates, a sphere that has the character of a universal because of its universal suffering, and has no *particular* claim to rights because no particular wrong but general wrong [*Unrecht schlechthin*] is done to it" This class is the proletariat. Two aspects of Marx's presentation are crucial to his further development. He begins the definition by pointing to the formation of the proletariat. He continues with the assertion that such a formation is now underway in Germany. This formation is then designated as an "artificial" (*künstlich*) as opposed to a "natural" (*naturwüchsig*) development. The motor of this artificial development is the specific economic system whose domination over civil society will become the next object of Marx's concern. The structural tension analyzed in the modern critique of religion takes on a sociological orientation, pointing to a new phase in Marx's development.

The introduction of the proletariat achieves for Marx what Hegel had to accomplish when he transformed the phenomenological description of the experience of consciousness into a philosophy of spirit. Marx has shown the necessarily rational structure of the world; in his terms, he has shown reality straining toward thought. The resulting position is not yet complete. The transformation of philosophy that the Note in the dissertation demanded in order to permit philosophy to become worldly has not yet been demonstrated. Marx's implicit awareness of this lack appears at the conclusion of this essay. Even if the proletariat were to come to exist in Germany, what will transform it from the passive product of the economic conditions into an active agent freeing itself from tutelege? The image of the irreligious critique singing its "own melody" before the petrified relations might be invoked. That is still an external relation whose necessity cannot be explained. Instead, Marx suggests that emancipation will occur when "the lightning of thought strikes in this naïve soil of the people." He does not define how this lightning functions. Modern marxists define it as the formation of class consciousness, but they are hardly more precise about its conceptual structure. At this point in Marx's work, reference to the Hegelian science as a "circle of circles" is more helpful. The proletariat is the path and the goal, the theory and the practice, the nothing that can become everything. The difference is that Marx's structural account claims at the same time to be the presentation of a *real* actor that will bring about the real unity of subject and object, genesis and normativity, politics and philosophy. The result would be the end of history, the "solution" to its riddle. Before coming too rapidly to this conclusion, which he shared with the young Hegelians, Marx attempted radically to rethink the nature of philosophy and its relation to politics.

Most of the material written by Marx (and Engels) during the years 1844-1846 is governed by the attempt to work through the implications of the first phase. Little of it was published at the time, often for good reason. At the most general level, the so-called *1844 (Paris) Manuscripts* attempts to explain the "lightning of thought" by a normative argument whose axis is the theory of alienation; the 1846 *German Ideology* attempts to solve the same problem by accenting the genetic toward an anthropological theory of constitution by laboring man. Elements of both approaches are interwoven in the often fragmentary explorations of the moment. Two well-know examples provide a counterpunctal illustration. The genetic theme appears in the third of the *1844 Manuscripts* when Marx praises the "greatness of the Hegelian *Phenomenology* and its final result...that Hegel grasps the essence of *labor* and of objective man, true because actual man, as a result of his *own labor.*" Marx's stress on the phenomenological Hegel is surprising in a work whose logical orientation is evident in its announced effort to derive the entire capitalist system from its beginning in "alienated labor." Marx seems to recognize that the revolutionary theory cannot be merely a contemplative *Zusehen*. On the other hand, the *Theses on Feuerbach* appended to *The German Ideology* show that Marx did not expect the lightning to come as a result of a natural evolution in which labor transforms nature and transforms itself in the same movement. The third thesis asks, "Who will educate the educators?" Its implication is that just as the Hegelian phenomenological movement needed either the initiated guide or the material *Zutat*, Marx's genetic presentation of the stages of human history in *The German Ideology* needs the moment of normativity explaining the necessary transition to a new form. This normativity, which is the lightning, cannot be taken for granted by a theory of genetic constitution. A closer look at these two works shows the persistence of the modern dilemma.

The *1844 Manuscripts* begin from working notes that demonstrate, with the aid of citations from the classical economists, the necessary "formation" of the proletariat. Marx turns then to the "artificial" character of this social formation in the account of alienated labor. A demonstration of the mutual interdependence of alienated labor and private property justifies the conclusion that the abolition of the one will entail necessarily the disappearance of the other. Alienated labor is the key to this transformation; its structure must demonstrate the necessity of its abolition. Marx conceptualizes alienation in the Hegelian language of determinant negation which demands logically its own negation and *Aufhebung*. His account begins from a new criticism of political economy for treating private property as an unquestioned presupposition. An immanent presentation would treat it differently. Marx proposes to analyze its implications as "greed, the division of labor, capital and landed property, trade and competition, value and devaluation of man, monopoly and competition, etc." The manuscript breaks off without completing this attempted transcendental account of the real conditions of the possibility of private property. The internal reason for the failure can be understood by a comparison with the fragmentary second manuscript. Parallel to the Hegelian phases, Marx seems there to be attempting a phenomenological approach, which he then abandons, as if he had realized that the conditions for its success are the copresence of a logical guarantee. The relation among the manuscripts thus repeats the Hegelian principle of immanent modern philosophy.

The first manuscript had shown at least a necessary relation or mutual interdependence between (alienated) labor and private property. The second manuscript draws the logical conclusions from this structure. At first, the two relate positively to one another. The action of each (unintentionally) improves the lot of the other. Capital's search for greater profit increases the productivity of society as a whole; labor's demand for higher wages forces capital to invent new and more efficient machines. This nonreflective identity breaks apart in the second moment, when each realizes that its relation to the other makes it dependent on something external to itself. Each then seeks to affirm its independence. Capital becomes greedy and exploitative; labor engages in industrial struggle. Such self-affirmation is condemned structurally, since each side *is* nonetheless dependent on the other. Pretending to independence, each denies and acts against what it in fact is. Each is thus self-contradictory. The self-contradiction leads to a third moment of collision which is logically necessary because the real independence that characterized the first moment is still present. The partners act out the contradiction expressed in the second moment against the interdependence of the first moment. Marx's manuscript breaks off at the point where the logical necessity of the antagonism and collision has been shown. Presumably, the move to a new stage beyond capitalism would have followed. Marx never criticizes this type of logical argument to which he occasionally returns, but he seems to have been unhappy with its implications. When he and Engels describe a similar pattern in *The Holy Family*,[19] they make their political argument by pointing out that the capitalist is satisfied in his estrangement whereas the proletariat is driven to action from its need. This is a polemical variant of the more genetic approach of *The German Ideology* whose roots can be seen already in the third manuscript. This rejection of logic is related to a rejection of Hegelianism which, however, is more verbal and rhetorical than philosophically accurate.

Marx appears to overcome his debt to Hegel in the third manuscript. After praising Hegel's greatness, he turns to the error vitiating his system. Hegel's stress on the positive side of labor neglects the negative, the alienated labor that Marx finds central. The ground of this neglect is that Hegel was concerned only with mental labor. The result was Hegel's smooth climb toward the self-related Absolute. The negations and otherness encountered could easily be overcome because they were only thought-negations, not external realities. Marx proposes to do in reality what Hegel did only in thought. "The entire so-called world history," explains Marx, "is only the creation of man through human labor and the development of nature for man." In this process, new needs are created. These new needs spur a further interaction and transformation of the world into a being-for-man. "One sees how the history of industry...is the open book of man's essential powers." A further implication is that "natural science will lose its abstract tendency and become the basis of human science." The result of the series of lyrical passages in this third manuscript is that "communism as the completed naturalism = humanism and as the completed humanism =

natualism is the true resolution of the conflict between man and nature and between man and man. It is the true resolution of the conflict between existence and essence, between objectification and self-confirmation, between freedom and necessity, between the individual and the species. It is the riddle of history solved, and it knows itself to be this solution." Marx's rejection of the supposed Hegelian idealist pretention to the Absolute ends with a materialist variant of the same claim. Marx is treating the question of origin as if it were a *real* solution. The result is that the premises—civil society—are eliminated. The origin is transformed in this collapse of its poles. The materialism that results is based either on a mechanical causality or on an idealist essentialism. Its foundation is an anthropology; its goal is the transparent relation of subject and object, thought and being, theory and practice.[20]

This phase of Marx's development culminates in *The German Ideology* (and the *Theses on Feurerbach*). Marx seems to imagine a grand historical pagent in which man-the-laborer develops from the animal world through stages of need formation and productive satisfaction until the ground is prepared for the final reconciliation in communism. This communism serves as a logical telos permitting the construction to claim necessity. At its worst, this represents a fall into the tabular enlightenment picture of historical progress. At its best, it calls for the kind of activist orientation stressed in the *Theses on Feuerbach*.[21] The *Theses* caricature a traditional philosopher whose neglect of activist imperatives can be castigated. They close with the famous assertion that "The philosophers have only *interpreted* the world in various ways; the points however is to *change* it." The inadequacy of this activism to the problems posed by the lightning of thought is evident. More important, Marx had made any solution impossible in the preceding tenth thesis. He insisted that the standpoint of the "old materialism"—civil society—is to be replaced by the "standpoint of the new *human* society or socialized humanity." The abandonment of the primacy of civil society from which the Marxian project began leaves only an activism that cannot justify itself theoretically. The "new materialism" and "socialized humanity" are a logical petition of principle. The "standpoint of the new *human* society" is separated by definition from the present. Its assertion is as premodern as the religious opium (or utopias) criticized earlier.

Marx's attention returned to the analysis of the structure of civil society during the years that led to *Capital*. He did not write a study called "communism" or "socialism." The normative telos had to be shown to be immanent to capitalist modernity. Marx explained the new form of his project in a letter to Lassalle, which notes that rereading Hegel helped him in organizing his materials. His theory, he says, will be "a presentation, and through the presentation a critique of what is presented." The external standpoint is rejected explicitly. *Capital* is civil society's self-critique. It presents the originary structure of capitalist society in a manner that satisfies theoretically the demand of the eleventh thesis. Success would mean the recoupling of politics and philosophy in the kind of originary structure from which the Kantian position was seen to begin. Marx never completed this project, nor did he adequately describe his method. Combining his rereading of Hegel with the return of the primacy of civil society suggests an interpretative framework consistent with the analysis to this point.

Capital combines a genetic analysis of the process of class struggle in civil society with a normative account of the production and reproduction of private profit within a framework structured by equal contractual exchange. The genetic component is apparent in the long chapter (in Vol. 1, Ch. 10) describing the struggles over the length of the working day. Success in this struggle has consequences at the level of the system's logic of reproduction. Capitalists are forced to innovate in order to produce more than the "absolute surplus value" that comes from direct exploitation of labor power. A new system logic results with the forms of indirect production of "relative surplus-value" (in Vol. 1, Ch. 12). Productivity is increased by labor-saving inventions, or by new forms of work organization like Taylorism. Marx traces the historical development by which society moves from simple cooperative work to the division of labor and manufacture, and then to machinery and modern industrial production. Each of these stages is reached under pressure from the struggle of the working class. The stages are the results of the tension between working-class demands and the structural systematic imperatives of the moment (Vol. 1 Chs. 13-15). At the same time, however, *Capital* is also a normative account of the asymmetrical and ultimately self-contradictory logic of the capitalist system. Two normative readings are possible. The theory may be treated as a "phenomenology" of class struggle. In this case, the structural economic analysis is interpreted as demonstrating the necessary breakdown (or crisis) of the system that guarantess the triumph of the revolution (Vol. 1, Ch. 25). The political consequences of this view are problematic and dangerous, as will be seen. The theory may also be read as a "logic," demonstrating that the necessary class struggle is structured by a movement in which the self-interest of each participant blinds him to his own structural position (Vol. 3, Chs. 13 and 14). This second approach would open Marxism toward a theory of history and politics, but it would not recommend any specific political orientation.

The same originary structure can be described from another point of view. *Capital* begins from a lengthy and minute description of the structure of the commodity, the exchange of commodities, and the phenomenon of money. After nearly 150 pages, Marx finally permits the reader to leave "this noisy sphere, where everything takes place on the surface" to enter the sphere of production, on whose threshold is written "No admittance except on business." This is a move away from "a very Eden of the rights of man. There alone rule Freedom, Equality, Property, and Bentham." The new sphere of production is the "revealed secret" of the asymmetry of social relations of exploitation concealed by the apparently normative free contractual exchange. The labor theory of value and the famous demystification of the "fetishism of commodities" open access to a capitalist civil society where the system's normative functioning is contradicted by the genetic relation of capital to labor on which it is based. Each stage in the analysis can be understood as the working through of this contradictory unity. This normative analysis of the logic of capital once again points to the necessity of the genetic component.

Capital lends itself to innumberable interpretative variants because its object has the structure of an origin. The temptation toward a material explanation in the form of the primacy of the economy (and its breakdown) is always present, as is the inverse tendency to attribute primacy to the class struggle. Citations can be found for each position. If *Capital* remains relevant today, it is not as a handbook of political economy or as a guide to revolution. It can be read with profit today because it is above all a theory of the originary structure of modernity.

CHAPTER 3

Originary Philosophy as Political Philosophy

WHAT IS THE POLITICAL?

The substantive use of "the political" instead of the usual concern with politics points to a problem whose theoretical structure becomes clear only within the principled immanence of modernity. Philosophy has been troubled since its Greek origins by its relation to the political sphere. The paradoxical nature of this relation is expressed in the pedagogical imperative that the philosopher (and his public) leave the everyday world of appearance to enter a more real or true landscape. The legitimation of this pedagogical necessity must be made explicit. Kant's question of enlightenment, Hegel's already scientific path to science, and Marx's "lightning of thought" express this classical dilemma. The modern stress on the principle of immanence draws the implication that the problem must be resolved not only from the side of the subject. The classical "transcendental turn" is not only subjective,[1] as Kant's "Copernican revolution" seems to imply. That first moment leaves an unintegrated external givenness that escapes the imperative of systematic immanence. A fully modern philosophy must show also a transformation on the side of the objective moment. Marx's insistence that the world must become philosophical as philosophy becomes worldly calls attention to this point. Kant and Hegel confront the same difficulty without, however, explicitly naming it.

The substantive formulation suggests that the political is structured by the double demand for subjective and objective transformation. The political is the systematic formulation of this relation within the framework established by the modern principle of immanence. The relation can be expressed generally by means of the relations of necessity and completeness which related to each other as normative and genetic. The "originary turn" makes explicit and founds rationally methodological categories that articulate these philosophical criteria concretely. These will be considered in part 2 as the categories that demonstrate the receptivity of the world to the universals of philosophy, and those that articulate the particularity that generates this intervention. First, the manner in which the originary turn draws philosophy and politics necessarily into relation must be elaborated. This necessary relation explains and articulates the legitimation of the pedagogical imperative that classical philosophy could only assert without justification. The specific character of modern history and its necessary relation to the political become explicit once again in this movement.

The originary turn that orients philosophy systematically toward the political is not the result of a decision by the philosopher, nor is it the reaction to a constraint imposed by the world. Such a picture of the motivation or explanation of the originary turn reintroduces a premodern externality. The substantive formulation of the political stresses this distinction. Politics as a form of subjective action on the world, or as a reaction to real external pressures on the subject, is threatened by the double temptation to which the originary structure is open. It may become a constitutive approach that cannot justify the particular norms it seeks to impose on the world any more than it can be certain that the world will in fact be receptive to these norms. Or, it may react to the apparent reality with which it is confronted by adapting blindly to its imperatives without measuring their rationality or the rationality of its own reactive behavior. The political structure toward which the modern directs philosophical attention is neither an enlightened despotism nor a kind of plebiscitory or anarchic democracy that abolishes the state. Its public and republican structures, and its representative character, are elaborated in part 3. Kant provides the most explicit demonstration of this systematic structure, which appears for a moment in Hegel and Marx, who, for inverse but structurally identical reasons, then reduce its specificity. This time it is Kant's success that casts light on the reasons for their failures.

The criteria of necessity and completeness apear to clash with the imperative that philosophy turn toward the political. This appearance is the result of the premodern picture of politics as action taking place on a canvas provided by the tabular conception of historical development. The actor is portrayed as standing apart from the object on which he acts. The object is treated as if it obeyed its own logic, which the actor seeks to understand in order to assure maximum success in his goal-oriented intervention. The difficulty arises not only from the separation of actor and object, each with its own logic whose necessary coordination the picture can only assume. More important for the present phase of the argument, the assumption that the object (the world) has its own inherent logic is the expression of a premodern enlightenment view that is only apparently historical. The tabular framework or canvas on which a succession of events is portrayed can show either (causal-empirical) necessity at the expense of completeness or (rational-normative) completeness at the expense of necessity. The tabular vision of history was first overcome by Kant's movement beyond history to *Geschichte*.[2] The logic of this Kantian development explains why his historical writings do not constitute a "fourth *Critique*" but a theory of the political.[3] The same logic accounts for the criteria of necessity and completeness. Philosophy must be able to explain not only the (transcendental) conditions of its own possibility but also the (originary) conditions of its necessity. This latter demonstration can be offered only by a philosophy to which its object is not external but immanent. The necessity of philosophy is motivated by the structure of its object. The object must demand the philosophical complement in order to attain its own completeness (and therewith its own necessity, as opposed to its merely contingent existence). The Hegelian categories of the "in-itself" and the "for-itself" express this same imperative, which Marx's Note to his dissertation adumbrates in a more "political" direction. The presence of such an object shows philosophy's necessity. The philosophy that develops is the articulation of the completeness that makes the object truly exist as this particular being necessarily in this particular relation. This is the first step toward the demonstration of philosophy's political orientation. It explains the necessity of philosophical involvement with the world. The kind of involvement is not yet specified.

The image of a world (or object) that demands and justifies the necessity of philosophy seems to return to a position of externality that makes politics only a reactive reflection of existent conditions. The image seems to imply that the political serves as the normative legitimation of an order whose establishment it must preserve. Politics would be the universal that gives meaning to the particulars which are subsumed under it. Politics would be what Marx was sometimes (inaccurately) to call ideology, and which he (erroneously) equated with Hegel's concept of the modern state. This specification of politics draws attention to another aspect of the Kantian dilemma concerning the content of the enlightened consciousness, the Hegelian problem of the manner in which science relates to the partially scientific, and the Marxian inability to specify the nature of class consciousness. A structure that is capable of learning, growth, and interaction with others is necessary for each of these projects. When the political is structured in this manner, its relation to the world that occasioned its necessity is transformed. That world cannot reduce history to a succession of events on a flattened and constant canvas. An immanent temporality is necessary. A world that needs philosophy in order to assure its completeness must itself have the kind of open and interactive structure designated by the concept of *Geschichtlichkeit*. The completeness that comes through the incorporation of a temporal and interactive structure itself takes on the dimension of growth, learning, and interaction. This means that the political has the necessary task of preserving precisely that openness that originated its necessity. The political is not constitutive action on a pregiven "real" problem. The political and the structure of its problems arise together and depend on one another. Politics does not seek to eliminate the world by making it identical to its own norms, nor does it simply react to concerns generated outside itself. Both formulations are premodern.

This specification of the relation of philosophy to the political abstracts explicitly from the content of both. It makes only the general observation that philosophy's political role is to preserve the conditions that make it both possible and necessary. The type of interaction between the world and philosophy can be elaborated as a theory of representation. The tabular framework of the traditional history seeks an adequation of the representation to the represented. That would mean, among other things, the death of politics and the end of history. The originary turn points to two problems that must be resolved. Philosophy and politics, each in its own way, have to be able to determine *what* is to be represented. The actual has to be distinguished from the merely accidental. Not every particular object demands the political demonstration of its completeness and the philosophical articulation of its necessity. Second, philosophy and politics must themselves present a representation that is adequate to the designated object of representation. The representation is not imposed but *received*. This was most clearly suggested in Marx's insistence that the world must be shown to want philosophy. Lawful philosophical universality or political representation cannot be imposed on domains or interests to which they are foreign. Given the modern premise, this representation can work only when it entails the kind of temporal learning permitted by modern *Geschichtlichkeit*. The details of the methodological articulation of this structure are presented separately in part 2.

The practical implication of the modern representative structure gives content to the formality of the political. There is a genetic and a normative element to this content. The two depend on and complete one another. The originary historical structure demands action that does not abolish the tension that needs the action for its own completeness. Such action can only be a public and communicative interaction. The necessity and the validity of this public action depend on its representative character. Modern political action represents right (as the unity of particular justice and universal lawfulness). The political form of this representation defines both what is permitted and also what constitutes the individual as human. The right that modern politics represents has the originary character that joins together necessity and completeness in a movement where first the one, then the other plays the role of genetic impetus or normative measure for a continual process in which rights are created, preserved, and renewed. The resulting political form is what Kant describes as republican. Its content is right, both as what is to be represented and as the form of this representation itself. The details of the Kantian demonstration will be presented in chapter 7, which will illustrate also the way in which Hegel's *Philosophy of Right* reduces the properly political moment of this structure to its philosophical moment, while Marx errs in the opposite but symmetrical direction.

The relation between philosophy, political philosophy, and the political can be summed up for the moment from the side of philosophy. The definitions presented here appear to transform philosophy into political philosophy and then to equate political philosophy with the politcal itself. There is an important sense in which this appearance is justified. In traditional societies the political is separated from the social because there is no public process in which its representativeness could be put into question. In modern formations, the political is integrated into the social fabric. This appears to contradict sociological theories of modernization which portray an increasing differentiation of the political steering mechanism as societies modernize. But the political common to both the traditional and the modern society does not designate a function or an institution. The political is the manner in which, explicitly or implicitly, a society defines or represents itself to itself and to others as a social unity. This is the sense in which Greek politics dealt with the "Good Life in the City." The Good Life defined the City as such; and the City in turn had to define the Good Life. This "political" structure is only infrequently made explicit in modern democratic societies. Its existence and its weight are felt at those times of national identity crisis that transcend the everyday of politics-as-usual. Were the philosopher to turn activist while still claiming philosophical justification, his task would be to bring to explicit debate this implicit structure. To the extent that the philosopher does turn activist, he is only being consistent with the demands of modern philosophy, which can demonstrate how and why philosophy must be drawn to the political if the systematic task is to be completed. This does not mean that political philosophy sits in judgment over the other particular sciences as a kind of caricatural Hegel. The implication is only that philosophy and the political are themselves defined together as an originary structure.

The systematic relation of the philosophical and the political permits beginning from either pole. The necessity of the relation is demonstrated from the side of philosophy, its completeness from the political. Kant's development presents the purest case study. Once the modern imperative of immanence and its correlative demand for system is accepted, the progress through the critical philosophy toward the recognition of the necessary place of the political follows rigorously. The critical method does not, however permit what Kant's *Critique of Judgement* calls the "doctrinal" articulation of the politics whose necessity is demonstrated. Hegel presents a different picture. The author of the System confronts the question of the rationality of History. Is Reason in History, or History in Reason? The modern political state suggests one answer, the traditional state another. The System only apparently permits its author to have it both ways. Marx was only too aware of the Hegelian difficulty. He appears to opt fully for the priority of the political—expressed in the economic relations of production—in the past as in the present. The result is Marx's misunderstood theory of ideology. The politics of that theory can imply the reduction of appearances and institutions to their "real" foundations. But that implies that ideology is, like religion, a premodern form. The principle of immanence points to the philosophical premise that underlies Marx's position and permits a more positive interpretation. Marx discovers ideology as the structure of the modern world. The politics that follows from this philosophical discovery differs from the politics usually attributed to the revolutionary as philosopher.

KANT'S PATH TO THE POLITICAL

The formal structure of *Critique of Pure Reason* can be interpreted as an originary attempt to demonstrate the possibility and the necessity of scientific knowledge. The "Transcendental Aesthetic" presents the way apparently contingent sense data acquire an a priori spatial and temporal form that makes them susceptible to being incorporated in valid knowledge. From the side of rationality, the understanding supplies a set of a priori categories under which the now a priori manifold of sense data can be subsumed validly. The resulting picture of the homogeneity of the subject and object demonstrates only the possibility of knowledge. Kant must show further how the homogenized manifold that is subsumed under the categories is unified and is recognized as mine. This demonstration can be either genetic or normative; or it can use one approach for one task, the other for the second. The difference between the first and second versions of the "Transcendental Deduction of the Categories" shows that unification and mineness are not identical. The connection between sense and understanding must be established from both sides. This calls for a further step in the argument. The understanding must be shown to impose its categories with necessity; from the other side, the receptivity of the unified manifold to the categories must also be necessary. With this step, the systematic structure of knowledge is established.

The presentation of Kant's theory of enlightenment showed the analogy of Kant's argument to the moments in the formation of a polity. The demonstration of the a priori form received by the accidental sense data is comparable to the classical stoic attitude that all men are members of a common unity because all must pay obedience to the same natural necessity. The externality of this "citizenship" is overcome when the understanding adds to this common necessity the formulation of specifically rational laws that are human products. These rational laws have then to be refined into a unitary structure in which the citizens recognize their particular goals and customs *(Sitte)*. The unified aggregate which recognizes itself in common and rational laws must also be certain that these laws will actually function equally for all cases. From the other side, the laws must be shown to correspond to the actual needs of the polity so that their effectiveness is legitimate. Now that the unified group has ceased to be a traditional formation, the modern organized pattern articulating rational rights and duties is present. This modern form brings a new turn to the classical difficulty. Good laws make good men, and good men make good laws. The problem of the beginning of the polity cannot be solved by the appeal to an external lawgiver who will constitute (despotically) either the good laws or the good men. Nor can "nature" be counted on to produce this happy result. The theory must pass first through the practical lawgiving of each to himself. From the theory of nature Kant will move forward to a theory of ethics.

The theoretical dilemmas faced by Kant can briefly be illustrated with reference to the last two phases of his argument. The homogenized manifold of intuition that is subsumed under the categories must be shown to be unified and must be explicitly mine. The first (A) edition of the *Critique* offers a genetic account of this process while the second (B) presentation tends toward a more normative orientation. The A edition elaborates a threefold synthesis in which an "apprehension in intuition" is followed by a "reproduction in the imagination" and then a "recognition in concepts." This synthetic procedure assures the unity of the manifold at the level of possibility and of necessity. The synthetic machinery generates a homogeneity between the subjective and the objective aspects of the process. The necessity that this synthesis occurs is guaranteed in its final moment, which is the statement of the explicit self-reflection or unification of the subject and object as identical. The difficulty is that this normative telos appears as a presupposition that is not fully integrated into the system. The transcendental *quid juris* presupposed the givenness whose validity it seeks genetically to reconstruct. The unification comes from the outside, from the presupposed object whose rational necessity cannot be distinguished from accidental givenness. Kant's reformulation in the second version seems to be a recognition of the problem. The structure of the B edition is more complex and often confused. Its central paragraphs (16, 17, 18) show a relative unity and novelty whereas the other sections of the text (for example, 24) contradict them with assertions recalling the A edition. The B Deduction can be taken as a normative argument. The central passages stress the "I think" that must be able to accompany all my representations. This Transcendental Unity of Apperception is that without which even the unities produced by the mechanism of the A edition would not be valid. The normative serves to explain how and why the synthetic machinery must be set into motion. It is the immanent telos that unifies the genetic categorial processes of the understanding and justifies the claim to completeness that the deduction needs. The problem in this version is that the machinery of the A Deduction is taken for granted; it is a psychological presupposition that is not integrated into the system. At this stage, Kant has given no explanation of A's normative telos which sets the machinery to work, or of B's genetic activity which provides the representations for the company of the "I think." This lack explains the next moves.

The two most widely debated concepts in Kant's *Critique* are the notion of the schematism and the distinction between the noumenal and the phenomenal. Both doctrines are present in both editions with only minor changes. A consistent interpretation can be proposed by treating the schematism in the context of the A edition while noumenal/phenomenal distinction can be treated alongside the B version. The first implication of this distinction is negative. If Kant were in fact pretending to give a strictly normative account in the B edition, he would not have needed the generative action of the schematism. The task of the "Schematism of the Pure Concepts of the Undertaking" is to explain why the three fold synthesis must take place necessarily. The schematism insures that the pure categorial structure of the understanding will in fact (i.e., necessarily, not just possibly) enter into the synthetic relation with the a priori purified sensible manifold. The structure of the argument is clear, but its details become problematic. The schematism must be pure, spontaneous and not receptive—a form of *inner* sense that guarentees the generation of a relation to the external. The difficulty appears when Kant describes this schematism as "an art concealed in the depth of the human soul" (A 141; B 180-181). Such an assertion hardly can be accepted within systematic philosophy! Kant needed a component insuring necessity for his categorial machinery of the A Deduction. Treating the schematism as a *real* agent makes an illegitimate presupposition. The fact that Kant maintained it in the B edition demonstrates the need to maintain the originary structure which the treatment of the schematism as a real but mysterious "art" violates. Interpretation of the schematism in the context of the A edition makes it into a psychological reality. This realism is a problem that will return when Kant recognizes its negative implications for a political theory. A different reading of Kant's philosophical argument here is suggested by the B edition.

The phenomenal/noumenal distinction can be interpreted as replacing the mystery of the schematism (although it presents other difficulties with which the originary account cannot deal at the present level of abstraction). Whether there is a thing-in itself or whether there are things-in-themselves can never be demonstrated since experiential knowledge is by definition phenomenal. Whether the noumenal is a domain of objects only, or whether it also contains the spontaneously free acting "I think," can never be clarified for the same reason. What can be shown is the systematic place of these concepts within the originary scheme. If the noumenal/phenomenal distinction is treated as replacing the schematic function, it serves to explain the origin of those materials that are to be unified and made mine by the Transcendental Unity of Apperception. This means that the "I think" does not have to be conceived as an (external) actor constituting a synthetic manifold. Its role is normative, not genetic. The originary structure is not replaced by an apparently constitutive activity or by a real or psychological schematizing function. (Of course, the A edition seems to need this distinction in order to develop its "Transcendental Dialectic." It can be noted, however, that there is no reason why the spontaneous and pure action of that "art hidden in the depths of the human soul" could not, for example, permit a solution of the crucial third antinomy which asks how pure freedom can function causally in the phenomenal world.)

Kant did not make these explicit suggestions, which are presented here only to show the structure of the problems confronted by the critical philosophy. Kant's presentation moves toward a solution at the level of ethical theory. The third antinomy of the Transcendental Dialectic in the first *Critique* demonstrates that the idea of a causality of freedom and the idea of a fully causal mechanical universe are both correct, and yet they do not contradict one another. The demonstration has recourse to the phenomenon/noumenon distinction (and, to this extent, it does not "solve" the problem completely). Rigorous mechanical causality rules the phenomenal world, where free action is not possible. But the moral action from the free rational will may be assumed to have its place in a noumenally free actor. The results of this free action will appear to have been causally determined since they occur in the phenomenal world. Still, a deeper freedom can be assumed to exist behind the appearance. This noumenal freedom might be none other than the "art hidden in the depths of the human soul" from the A edition. Or, it might be the "I think" from the B edition to which the material representations are now brought. In either case, the solution of the problems of the theory of knowledge is assumed to lie in the domain of ethics.

The third antinomy presents the possibility but not yet the necessity of a "causality" of freedom. It shows that morality and science do not contradict one another. This proves that morality is possible. It does not demonstrate the necessity that would make morality binding on the individual who is conscious of it as duty. This incompleteness may be due to the temptation to think about freedom in an external causal manner that slides toward a constitutive approach. Such a noumenal causality of freedom would be private and particular, since the specificity of the noumenal is lost when it enters the space-time world of intersubjective phenomena. This contradicts the structure of morality that, even though the actual moral decision and responsibility remain individual, must be valid intersubjectively. This is why the 1784 essay on enlightenment insisted on the *public* use of reason. A year later, before revising the first *Critique*, Kant's *Foundations of the*

Metaphysics of Morals drew a further consequence from this imperative. He replaces the constitutive causal temptation by an explicit stress on the normative aspects of ethics.[4] The *Foundations* can be summarized briefly: Moral demands cannot be satisfied by any external criterion such as happiness because the external is variable, accidental, particular, and not universal. The only thing that is universally and unequivocally always good is the "good will." This good will stands systematically in the place of the "I think" from the B edition. Its ethical elaboration is the "categorical imperative" whose three variants explicitly fit the demand that morality be systematically necessary. Formally, the moral must be shown to be universalizable. Its maxims must be valid for everyone at every moment. Materially, the moral must treat man always as an end. Treating another person as a means or object violates the systematic demand that the world be receptive to the rational (or moral) imperative. Finally, morality must harmonize with a possible realm of ends which is not yet actual but may be actualized as a result of moral action. This latter argument, coupled with the parallel of the good will to the normative B deduction, suggests the problem that the next phase of Kant's philosophy will have to overcome. The first two formulations of the categorical imperative show its intersubjective character and the reason for which it can be accepted by the human world. The third formulation must show that completeness that guarantees the necessity that men will in fact act from ethical duty.

Another formulation of Kant's difficulty in the *Foundations* permits a more concrete illustration of the systematic modern structure. The normative approach can never say that I have fulfilled my duty. The good will can claim only to have acted from duty. The noumenal status of the good will means that the actual results in the experienced phenomenal world can never be assumed to correspond to the pure good will that intended them. The systematic completeness that would demonstrate ethical necessity must provide this guarantee. From this point of view, the crucial addition to Kant's ethics made by the *Critique of Practical Reason* is its "Transcendental Dialectic," where Kant introduces the "practical postulates" of God, freedom, and immortality. The argument is presented antinomically, as in the first *Critique*. The third formulation of the categorical imperative insisted that practical reason must aim at the "highest good" where happiness and morality coincide. Striving for the highest good is necessary only if the soul is immortal and God's existence serves to guarantee ultimate phenomenal success to noumenally free actions since perfection is not possible in the finite phenomenal world. Moral striving alone cannot claim necessity without such a guarantee. A moral imperative that demands something that cannot be achieved is senseless, and therefore it is not binding. The "Postulates" as postulates are still an unsatisfactory solution whose presence only testifies to Kant's systematic intention. After the first *Critique* had shown that it is not contradictory to believe in God, freedom, and immortality, the second *Critique* now adds that the morality articulated in the *Foundations* even recommends such a belief. This is the "faith" that the preface to the B edition, a year later, claimed to have preserved by "eliminating knowledge."

The ethical and epistemological problems are presented in a different form in the *Critique of Judgment*. It is tempting to assume that the political could be that domain where the coexistence of the two spheres is possible. That is not, however, Kant's suggestion. The political will emerge only after the philosophical system has been systematically elaborated. The preface and the two versions of the introduction to the *Critique of Judgment* stress the systematic character of philosophy. Pure, a priori philosophy can deal only with two domains: nature with its theoretical reason and morality with its practical reason. This leaves the object of the third *Critique* undetermined. Kant's concern might be with the anthropological level where the two forms of philosophy could be joined. His frequent lectures on anthropology, and their published version, contain divisions that could be placed parallel to some of those in the *Critique of Judgment*. This suggestion could be refined if the anthropology is seen as an "analytic" section to which *Religion within the Limits of Reason Alone* is the "dialectical" correlate. That unity would explain how ethical action can claim to be both theoretically necessary and assured of success in a world where the realization of the highest ends is not impossible. An "existential" moment from the essay "What Is Enlightenment?" could be added to this construction. The "courage to use your reason at all times" would guarantee the transition from an ethical anthropology to a theory of history and, finally, of politics. The difficulty with this construction is not only philological. The proposed political translation of the ethical goals remains only a formal possibility whose subjective necessity and objective realizability have not been demonstrated. The systematic motivation for the leap to the political needs the mediation of the material provided by the *Critique of Judgment*. Politics is more than "existential" courage.

The political solution to the difficulties of the first two *Critiques* cannot simply invoke the existence of a new, external domain of objectivity. Neither anthropology nor history can be introduced to solve dilemmas that are immanent to the philosophical project. On the contrary, the place of these types of objectivity has to be shown systematically. Kant's title makes use of the ambiguous genitive in the critical project. Critique is immanent self-critique. Although there are still moments when the originary position is not self-consciously assumed,[5] the positive gains are more significant. Even if the ethical project (or suggested "political" shortcut) had been successful as an abstract synthesis, the objection raised previously against the formal enlightenment consciousness would still be valid. The categorical imperative insures intersubjective validity only by treating the subject as a monological atom abstractly indentical to all other atoms. Particularity, content, growth, and change are irrelevant to such a formal subject. The source of the difficulty is Kant's acceptance of the judgmental form applied in natural science. His goal, like that of the scientist, is to subsume the particular material under an a priori valid universal law. This is the assertion that a universal predicate is applicable to the particular subject. For the account to be materially and systematically complete, morality must also show how, and why, the particular is receptive to this lawful structure. The private moral decision must be supplemented by a public self-legislation that insures that the a priori law is intersubjectively legitimate because its necessity is immanently justified for each individual. The demonstration of the necessity of this movement from the particular to the universal is the major contribution of the *Critique of Judgment.* The transition to the political can be made only when the implications of this form of "reflective judgment" have been made explicit.

The peculiarities of the articulation of the *Critique of Judgment* make clear the systematic goals of this work whose preface announces that it is the completion of the "critical business." Kant's concern is to show that, and how, the laws of freedom are realized in the causal phenomenal world. The two major parts of the book treat Aesthetic and Teleological Judgment. The relation of these two sections is not that one treats laws of freedom while the other is concerned with Nature. Within the analytic of Aesthetic Judgment, Kant distinguishes the account of the beautiful from that of the Sublime. The beautiful is defined as the experience of a "lawfulness without law" or a "purposeless purposefulness." Kant's formulations stress that this is the experience of the realization of the laws of freedom in a natural world. The purposelessness and lack of a law imply that this specific phenomenal experience does not depend on a natural causality or an intentional actor separated from the object of action. Causal Nature does, however, enter the analysis in order to assure systematic completeness. This explains the place of the Sublime. The experience of sublimity comes from a direct encounter with the brute givenness of Nature. The result of this experience is the recognition that there exists a greatness, force, and completeness in Nature to which the subject cannot attain. A feeling of moral respect which correlates with a dissatisfaction with mere self emerges. A new awareness of the Ethical Task and a recognition of the humanity in one's own person arise. Causal Nature in its sublimity guarantees that the free moral subject whose experience of the beautiful demonstrated that its laws possibly can become real in the phenomenal world learns the necessity of in fact acting according to these principles of freedom. The two moments of the Analytic of Aesthetic Judgment serve together to insure that the systematic completeness needed on the side of the free subjective actor is present. The further element will be added by the account of a teleological nature that is receptive to the free moral actions.

Kant's account of Teleological Judgment is only apparently a failure. His goal is not to eliminate the natural lawfulness of the world which the first *Critique* demonstrated. The laws of causality are not replaced by a (romantic) theory of organic Nature that ultimately conflates the objective and the subjective world. Nor is Kant's aim to provide still another presentation of the "dialectical" compatibility or coexistence of laws of nature and forms of freedom. The *Critique of Pure Reason* had shown that it is not contradictory to think of Nature as having a teleological organization. The advance in the *Critique of Judgment* is to formulate explicitly this noncontradictory thought. The aim is not to prove that Nature is really a teleological structure—the form of judgment that asserts teleology is a "reflective judgment." As opposed to the "predicative judgment" by which science or morality subsumes a particular under a priori laws, reflective judgment begins from the particular to search for a law that fits its particular structure. The laws at which reflective judgment arrives cannot have the same form of validity as the universal laws of nature and freedom because the particular from which they begin is an empirically given that remains external to the law. The validity claim of the reflective judgment is established discursively. The implicaton is that the material complement needed to guarantee the external receptivity to the laws of freedom does not come from a teleological nature but from the process by which the validity claim about this natural teleology is demonstrated. In this process of discursive validation, the public self-legislation that makes the private moral decision intersubjectively legitimate finds its proper place. The possible coexistence of causality and teleology that the first *Critique* showed to be noncontradictory is now seen to be necessary.

The structure of the *Critique of Judgment* suggests that the "critical business" it concludes is not the end but the beginning of a specific kind of philosophy. The discursive process by which reflective judgment establishes validity claims moves beyond the formal monological subject. Reflective judgment obeys the imperative to "think in the place of the other." It implies the existence of a common, and ultimately a communal, sense that permits this interchange. These two criteria preserve the originary structure. The explict immanent self-reflection proposed by the *Critique of Judgment* presents that objective world that needs philosophy to demonstrate its own completeness and necessity. This same immanent self-reflection is the philosophical structure whose articulation permits the assurance that the objective world will be receptive to the philosophical system. This structure is no more tautologous than the Hegelian demand that the path to science be scientific, or the Marxian quest for a world that is philosophical and a philosophy that is worldly. The discursive process by which reflective judgment goes beyond the formality of the monological subject is a first guarantee. But Kant does not stop with this assertion. Kantian "politics" is not simply the replacement of one form of judgment by another. Kant sees the need for political content. When he announced in his preface that the *Critique of Judgment* ended the "critical business," Kant added that he would turn now to the "doctrinal" aspect of philosophy. Although he did not explain what the term meant, the only possible interpretation points to the place of political content in the system. The reflective judgment that moves from the particular to the universal cannot begin from any arbitrary given, external, or empirical particularity. There must be some way to decide *which* particulars lend themselves to this form of judgment. Such particulars are originary. Their articulation will be the task of political philosophy and of practical politics itself. Along with the preservation of the conditions guaranteeing the necessity of receptivity, the political will be the articulation of the structure of the particularity. The critical philosophy passes necessarily to the political, without giving up the philosophical critique on which the necessity of the political depends. The political is needed for the philosophical critique to demonstrate its own completeness.

THE AMBIVALENCE IN HEGEL'S UNIFICATION OF POLITICS AND HISTORY

Originary logic helps to clarify the nature of Hegel's concept of history. His historical and political theory serves, in turn, to confirm the originary intention that animated his systematic philosophy. Hegel's ambivalence has immanent theoretical grounds that are more significant than biographical accounts of his personal views. At the beginning of the *Lectures on the*

Philosophy of History, Hegel tells his students that the only compendium to which they can refer to understand better his lectures is the concluding section of his own *Philosophy of Right*. This latter text is unquestionably part of the encyclopedic system, whereas the status of the lectures has been often debated. Hegel's reference could imply that he wants to integrate history into the system; or he could be suggesting that the system is to be integrated into history. If the system is given a rational place in history, it acquires at the same time a political role. On the other hand, the integration of the historical within the systematic circle of circles implies the end of politics as well as the end of history. Both interpretations can be supported from the Hegelian texts. Both tempted the man Hegel.

The polemical preface to the *Philosophy of Right* contains a theoretical kernel pointing to its historical character. Hegel attacks the relativism and nominalism that question the validity of existing laws and institutions. He condemns the explicitly ahistorical, particularist premises of these approaches. Both treat the existent state, which in fact makes possible their critical stance, as if it were an accident. They act as if the world were only waiting for their new philosophical truths in order at last to begin correctly to create history rationally. The relativist and nominalist approaches forget their own historical situatedness. After condemning this "atheism of the ethical world," Hegel seeks to explain why such an attitude could come to be important. The nominalist stance has a positive aspect which it itself does not understand. It demands that laws and institutions that claim legitimacy not be imposed by force from outside. Valid laws must have a rationally understandable form. The implication of this position is shown by a comparison of laws of nature with laws of right. Laws of nature simply are. Their existence cannot be opposed or criticized. Error is the fault of the judging subject, not that of external nature. Because the standard of nature's laws is external, knowldge of them adds nothing to nature. Laws of right are only partially similar to laws of nature. As posited, or positive, social law is external and empirical. But its claim is to incarnate rational criteria about which there can be debate, dispute, and dialogue. This means that laws of right can change. The debate, dissatisfaction, and even disobedience have an effect on the law itself. As opposed to the law of nature, the law of right is essentially historical. This necessary historical debate points also to the possibility of politics.

Hegel's preface downplays the theoretical foundations of his polemic in favor of more pragmatic implications. The changeable nature of laws of right means that a *Philosophy of Right* is important to the state.[6] After a swipe at Kant's influence, which is said to teach that the true cannot be known, Hegel attacks the replacement of conceptual philosophy by appeals to the heart, feeling, and emotion. He cites the recently fired professor, Fries, whose picture of laws emerging directly from the people, expressing a living sociality and the holy chains of friendship, is apparently radical and democratic. The problem is that these romatic and immediate intuitions are given no rational form. Appeal to such a subjective foundation is dependent on the accidental and external world. This loses the rich architechtonic that makes possible and necessary a whole and harmony from what were only isolated individuals accidentally brought together. The subjective orientation can by its very nature never find fulfillment in any legal structure or political institution. Its subjective freedom is a negative self-relatedness that retains its identity only by excluding otherness. Its intuitionist basis may become arbitrary because it recognizes no external legal necessity. Once again, the polemic has a positive theoretical conclusion. Hegel stresses the need to avoid the overreaction, typified by the Platonic Republic, which attempts to eliminate this troublesome free subjective individuality that poses a threat to the harmony of the Polis. A polity cannot remain fixed by its external institutional structures. Continued rational existence for a polity, like freedom for the individual, demands that its structure be open to the historically new. A polity is structured by immanent and public laws of right, not by external accidental or subjective. The "debate" integrates subjective particularity into a positive whole.

Hegel does not develop these historical and political implications in the preface. The polemic instead takes a contemplative and resigned tone when Hegel turns to the role of philosophy itself. He develops the implications of his famous assertion that "the actual is the rational and the rational is the actual." Philosophy cannot leap beyond its time. Even if the period is empty and shallow, philosophy's task is not to transform but only to understand it. Philosophy can say only what is, not what ought to be. Hegel's first explanation of this limit is based on a rejection of philosophy as constitutive. He mocks Plato's recommendations on child care or Fichte's attempt rationally to construct passport regulations. He goes on to the positive challenge that is posed by the *hic rhodus, hic salta. Rhodus* becomes the "rose" of reason on the cross of the present. Finding reason in the rosy present permits the philosopher to dance in his times. The rationalist resentiment that retreats into subjectivity and feeling manifests only hatred and self-hatred. The individual is the child of his times, as is the philosophy which grasps its time in thought. The philosophical knowledge that makes peace with its epoch is described with a resignation that does not seem to fit the combative tone from which the polemic began. Philosophy comes to paint its "gray on gray" only once actuality has completed its development. The dance with the rose of the present is replaced by a passive contemplation because "the owl of Minerva begins its flight only at dusk."[7]

The need to reject both the constitutive and the subjectivist approaches against which he polemicized does not justify Hegel's resignation. Hegel is correct to avoid these orientations which, each in its own manner, introduce an externality into the modern structure. But the conclusion that "with this gray on gray actuality cannot be rejuventated but only understood" itself depends on an external premise that Hegel has not justified. Only if history has *in fact* come to an end can the Hegelian philosopher justify such a stance. If this were the assumption, Hegel's pragmatic insistence on the place and role of a *Philosophy of Right* in modern states would not make sense. The laws of freedom would be replaced by externally developing natural laws that philosophy modestly seeks to understand.[8] This would eliminate the role of debate and rational discourse in the establishment of legitimate political laws. Hegel's awareness of this difficulty appears when he introduces finally the modern state. He returns to the assertion about the actuality of the rational in a remark to Paragraph 258. The fact that we still recognize a cripple as a human being suggests that the actualities that are rational are not entirely and wholly penetrated by rationality. Such is the case for the modern state. This is why the philosophical debate comes to interact historically with the specific modern historical conditions. Hegel's point is not that history does in reality what philosophy only then reflects in thought. Nor does philosophy present that rational kernel or essence that shapes and nourishes the manifestations and events of history. Both of these views introduce an externality. Their copresence in the preface suggests that neither stands alone as a definition of what Hegel means by history. Their copresence suggests that the originary structure of history is the underlying premise of Hegel's construction. In short, Hegel ought to have told students of the *Philosophy of Right* to consult his theory of history! We, on the other hand, need to try a different approach.

The fundamental methodological insight of the *Phenomenology* seems to imply that Hegel's system is inherently historical; the fundamental methodological insight from the *Logic* apparently points to the opposite conclusion. Determinant negation implies that the process of rational development includes the phases through which Spirit had to pass in order to arrive at its present status. The past is not simply overcome and forgotten. The past becomes a moment of the present. Because the present evolved from and is involved with its past, it is itself open to further change and growth. Every stage necessarily will reflect, and reflect upon, its own historical character because the presence of its past is essential to what is has now become. Knowing that it has become means that it knows too that further change is possible. The speculative proposition from the *Logic* enters at this point. Because further change is known to be possible, the *Phenomenology* is a way of doubt, anguish, and despair. The direction and kind of change, and the necessity that guides its realization, must be shown. This transformation of the path of skepticism and despair into a positive self-completing logical development may mean that each of the moments in the process was in fact only illusory. History then would be the realm of appearance, where events are meaningless and action is vain. Or, history could be a vast moral panorama from which the subject learns the lessons needed to reach adulthood. Both of these patterns substitute an essential idealism for the skepticism and despair of Hegel's phenomenological history. The logical structure of history has a different measure that must be examined before one can understand the specificity of modern history in Hegel's presentation of his own *Philosophy of History*.

The combination of a phenomenological and a logical method that could articulate the structure of the historical must be shown to be systematically necessary. Neither method alone, nor their combination, is applied to a pregiven object or placed on a pregiven framework. The results of the determinant negation seem fated either remain random or to demand an external frame to give them a coherence and sense. Such a framework is the tabular history that serves as a canvas on which the developing scenario can be painted. But development and history are not synonymous. The tabular framework permits the observer to distinguish phases that can be ordered in a before-and-after sequence. This presupposition of an outside observer and a pregiven canvas means that the development is only apparently historical. Its sequence cannot be shown to be necessary. Neither of the external factors is affected by the supposedly historical development. The historicity of this development is only *historisch*; it presents external succession or accidental conjunction. Addition of the speculative proposition advances a step by articulating explicitly the interaction between the development and its framework. This movement presents a self-engendering and self-justifying *Geschichtlichkeit* in which necessity finds its place. But the fact that history is still a presentation implies the preexistence of a spectator or judge who remains outside of and unaffected by the appearing history. Necessity in this *Geschichtlichkeit* is not assured fully. The external instance can not be equated with philosophy. That would also reduce the genetic process to a mere appearance with no independence of its own. The full presentation of history will have to involve at once, and in one necessary process, all three of these moments: the events themselves, the canvas on which they appear, and the instance before which they appear. If the resulting interaction is not to be accidental, the presence of History in Reason—and thus in philosophy—will have to be shown. The philosopher's *Zutat* will no more suffice than that of the politician.

The process through which *Historie* becomes *Geschichte* and posed the question of the presence of Reason in History is sketched in the introduction to the *Philosophy of History*.[9] Hegel proposes to demonstrate historically what his theoretical philosophy already showed. He does not stress the philosophical ground of his choice of the starting point for the demonstration, which fits with the criteria we have just developed. Examination of the approaches to the writing of history provides a manner of portraying the unity and necessity that brings together the events, their self-conscious *Geschichtlichkeit*, and the narrative instance. Hegel deliberately rejects forms like legend, ballad, and tradition because of their accidental, nonreflective character. He begins from a form of historical consciousness that is called "original" (*ursprünglich*). Narrator and narrated share a common spirit that has produced and molded their attitudes and gestures. The two sides solicit and are solicited by one another in a process of mutual self-definition. Original history is naïvely self-confident, untroubled by question, doubt, or reflection. The self-relatedness that guarantees its autonomy by excluding doubt or otherness becomes a weakness when it is forced to reflect on its own premises. The story it tells is only one story among many others. New persons, conditions, and events come into being; original history becomes merely a particular history among other particular histories. This weakness conceals a strength that appears when history becomes "reflective history." The narrator now knows that he is speaking of one among many possible histories. The relation among the histories and the justification of the choice of one or the other have to be presented for debate. The result will be a further development since the justification must have immanent grounds in the historical object itself. This last imperative is met by what Hegel calls "philosophical history."

Hegel distingishes four types of reflective history whose immanent dialectical relation moves them toward philosophical history. *Universal history* emerges first. The material events of the past are treated as having led necessarily to the formation of the spirit from which the author is writing. But this material progression toward the present neglects too much of what was important to the actors of the previous history. Reflection then suggests the notion of a *pragmatic history* whose self-conscious goal is to make the past present through didactic portraits that will affect decisions in the present. Necessity is presented now explicitly from the narrative standpoint of the historian. "But," remarks Hegel, "what experience and history teach is this: that peoples and governments have never learned anything from history or acted on teachings that could be deduced from it."[10] If necessity is presented from the standpoint of the author, each period will have its own models and its own sequence. One pragmatic history will succeed another, each insisting on the validity of its own spirit. The reflective result will be a *critical history* which relates the different histories among themselves. This critical history can advance to considerable refinement in its cross-checking of the forms of necessity advanced. The difficulty is that it can neither justify the general point of view from which it assembles its own critical position (and therefore risks becoming only another form of pragmatic history), nor can it guarantee the factual material that the different historians present to it (and therefore it risks the naïveté of the universal historian). The transition to *philosophical history* passes through a kind of necessary evil which liberates the historian. Partial histories treating specific ideas or institutions lose the subjective generality to which reflective history had risen. They are compensated by the return of the empirical concern lost by the critical history that preceded them, while at the same time they can integrate legitimately the partial histories into one totality, which is the necessary presuppositon that made possible the partial history itself. This points forward toward the philosophical goal: a history of spirit itself.

The progressive "phenomenological" development toward philosophical history is oriented by an immanent "logic" which creates its own framework. This logical structure is suggested first by the fact that Hegel's examples are chosen from different temporal moments. Among the writers of original history are included Herodotus, Thucydides, and Guicciardini as well as statesmen of antiquity, monks of the Middle Ages, and memoirists in the French tradition. The rejection of forms of immediacy like legend or tradition is a further demonstration of the same intention. The structure of original history is implicitly reflective; the stages of reflective historical presentation are simply the full development of this reflective structural necessity. Philosophical history adds the further articulation that makes the account complete. This is the crucial addition. The self-reflection achieved by reflective history is now complemented by the explicit presence of a similar structure in the external world. The demonstration of this systematic necessity presents a logical *Geschichtlichkeit* which is fully independent from external accident because it is wholly self-determining. This is the sense in which philosophical history and world history can coincide. This is why Hegel can assert that "World History" is the progress of the consciousness of freedom—a progress whose necessity we have to understand." More strongly still, Hegel can conclude that the "final goal" of the world is the consciousness of this freedom. Despite Hegel's explicit disclaimer of the philosopher imposing his a priori on history,[11] the ambivalence implicit in this argument cannot be ignored. A history that is itself immanently philosophical has precisely that structure that we saw Hegel identify (in chapter 2) as Kant's fundamental ambiguity. The conditions of the possibility of knowledge and the conditions of the possibility of experience are brought together in the same account. Hegel's systematic orientation has to include this duality without reducing or eliminating one side in favor of the other.

Hegel returns to the subject matter of philosophical history after the schematic presentation of the categories of the World Historical Individual and the Cunning of Reason. These two figures will be treated in chapter 4. "World History," he insists, "can speak only of those peoples which form a State."[12] Hegel does not pretend to explain the birth of the state. He admits that it is preceded by forms of conduct that may be based on an unconscious free action. He also stresses the preexistence of natural religious feelings and familial piety. These are forms of *Sittlichkeit*, but they still fall outside the domain of the rational and the historical. The birth of the state is central for their transformation. "Peoples without a state may have passed a long life before arriving at their destination; and during these periods they may have attained considerable development in some dimensions."[13] This prestately experience gives content to the various state constitutions that develop. It does not, however, explain the birth of the state itself. Hegel avoids the temptation of a constitution theory in his definition of the state:

> It is the state which first presents subject matter that is not only adapted to the prose of history, but involves the production of such history in its very being. Instead of government issuing merely subjective mandates sufficing for the needs of the moment, a community that is acquiring a stable existence as a state requires formal commands and laws, comprehensive and universally binding prescriptions. It thus produces a record as well as an interest in understandable, definite transactions and occurences which have results that are lasting.[14]

The institutional state and the reflective process by which its narrative self-consciousness is presented has precisely the completeness and the necessity that philosophical history is seeking. Hegel's stress on the interests of the community, which demand "formal commands and laws, comprehensive and universally binding prescriptions," supplements the argument that prestately periods are ahistorical because they have no "historical narratives." This interdependence avoids the image of a state that constitutes its history as something external to it and that of a state whose history is determined by outside factors. A theory of constitution of either type would leave Hegel still at the level of reflective history.

The "progress of the consciousness of freedom" that defines Hegelian history is anchored in the state. After repeating that "Historical change essentially attaches itself to the state," Hegel continues: "The successive moments of the Idea manifest themselves in it as distinct *principles*."[15] Although Hegel explictly tries to avoid it, the temptation is to reintroduce the categories from the *Logic* to portray this stately structure of history. The use of a priori philosophical concepts for the empirical historical materials is compared to Kepler's use of a priori mathematical laws for his research. Historical assertions "must be derived empirically and historically proven."[16] Because such a proof is not sufficient to give the kind of necessity and completeness demanded by philosophical history, Hegel suggests a different orientation. He rejects the comparison with natural science and the logical temptation to reduce history to a formal progression of state constitutions.

Hegel defines history now as a progression of National Spirits (*Volksgeister*). This permits a philosophical argument about the materials of history. For example, although the formal poetic virtues of Indian epopees may be equal to the Homeric, "the infinite difference in content remains, and this is the substantial importance, involving the interest of Reason, which is immediately concerned with the consciousness of the concept of freedom and its expression in individuals."[17] This content integrates empirical particularity into the return to that "consciousness of the concept of freedom" whose progress defines world history and whose realization was the final goal of history. The *Volksgeist* is defined as the expression of "every aspect of [a people's] consciousness and will, its entire actuality. It is the common aspect of its religion, its political constitution, morals, legal system and ethics; its science, art and mechanical skills."[18] The logical historical articulation of the principles founding these *Volksgeister* can claim the completeness and necessity that the Hegelian system demands.

A peculiar inconsistency in Hegel's argument explains why his theory of the historical demands a political complement. Hegel sums up his position concisely in a passage whose definition of Spirit suggests that his aim is to integrate history into the rational system.

> The essence of Spirit is *activity*. It realizes its potentiality, makes itself its own act, its own work. Thus it becomes an object to itself. It relates to itself as an objective existence [*Dasein*]. Thus it is with the Spirit of a people [*Volksgeist*]: it is determined Spirit which builds itself into an objective world, that exists and persists in a particular religion and form of worship, customs, constitution and political laws—in the whole complex of its institutions, the events and actions that constitute it. That is its work—that is what this particular people *is*. Peoples are what their deeds are.[19]

The passage can be interpreted as stressing the originary structure that makes a *Volk* at once particular and universal by generating norms of universality as well as its own self-activity. The inconsistency is that Hegel is talking about politics and constitutions at the same level with forms of worship and customs. He is speaking of peoples (*Völker*) and not states as the actors in world history. He even had spoken of "science, art and mechanical skills" as belonging to this *Volksgeist*. This explains why his introduction can conclude abruptly that "we are thus concerned exclusively with the Idea of Spirit, and in World History [we] regard everything as only its appearance [*Erscheinung*]."[20] At this point, Hegel appears as a caricatural idealist. The inconsistency in the definition of the very category that was to permit the demonstration of philosophical necessity leaves him unable to account for the "progress of the consciousness of freedom." When he describes the progression of *Volksgeister* replacing one another, he can resort only to metaphor. He tries out the image of the phoenix, and then the picture of a watch winding down once its active desire has been satiated.[21] The result is that the historical progression can be explained only with the help of a philosophical *Zutat* that cannot be justified immanently. This necessary *Zutat* points to the place of the political.

The inconsistency in the historical definition of the *Volksgeist* becomes important in the *Philosophy of Right*. Hegel's definition of *Sittlichkeit* there presents the possibility of understanding its immanently historical and political character as an originary structure. The *Philosophy of Right* is articulated logically by the immanence of the concept of will within the system. The spheres of Abstract Right and Morality are one-sided manifestations whose unity as *Sittlichkeit* is both their result and their conceptual precondtion. The *Sittlichkeit* that culminates the theory is the premise that makes possible the forms of Abstract Right and Morality whose immanent phenomenological presentation is guided by the logic of the *Sittliche*. This phenomenological structure describes an apparently historical progression, for example, in the development of forms of contractual relations or the learning of more subtle moral codes. Hegel explains repeatedly, however, that he is talking only about a logical development. He knows that in reality *sittliche* forms like the family preceded and preconditioned many of the legal and moral structures he descibes earlier in the book. At the same time, the *Sittlichkeit*, which is a logical premise, must also be a phenomenological result of the argument. The forms of Abstract Right and Morality must be shown to reconstruct the *Sittlichkeit* that made them possible. The relation between the two abstract spheres and the third, *sittliche*, moment must manifest the originary structure.

The general outline of institutions treated as *Sittlichkeit* shows already that neither the logical nor the phenomenological interpretation is sufficient. *Sittlichkeit* has three major divisions, each of which is itself a triad. The *Family* presents the immediacy of loving feeling in which the individual conceives of himself only as a member of the unity. This family needs to have material property to subsist in the external society. The external property defines it for the world and also for itself. Finally, the educated child members emerge into society as mature individuals with particular properties and needs. These individuals make the transition to the second moment. *Civil Society* articulates the way individuals relate to one another in order to preserve and develop their particularity by the constitution of more refined needs and the means for their satisfaction. The Administration of Justice serves as a counterweight that preserves the universality of law against the caprices of particularity. Its use of punishment returns the criminal to a sense of his particular worth within the community. The ill-effects that the continual quest for the satisfaction of new needs in a society where the particular cares only for himself demand the creation of institutional frameworks (the Police) and groups that represent particular interests (the Corporations). The instability of this particularist Civil Society suggests the need for a *State* that is organized to unify the two moments of immediate familial universality and mediated social particularity. This state will have a legislative, executive, and sovereign unity that both represent and defend the continued existence of the familial and particularist civil society.[22] At the most external level, Hegel does not carry through this project. His book does not culminate with the State, despite the preliminary discussion of *Sittlichkeit* (para. 157) that introduces the main text. The first actualization of *Sittlichkeit* in the Family becomes accidental once the discussion moves to the sphere of Civil Society. The individual who has been educated and left the Family is defined there as the "son of civil society." (para. 238). In like manner, the State becomes merely a transient particular (para. 347) as the book moves to its close. The system is integrated into that history that becomes the Court of the Last Judgment.

The preliminary remarks that define *Sittlichkeit* show the need for a historical dimension within the system even though Hegel seems to want to avoid it. *Sittliche* institutions are presented first as naturally given substantive incarnations of the good. "In this sense, Antigone announces that no one knows whence the laws come: they are eternal" (para. 144, Addition). The individual feels accidental in relation to these institutions which are that "eternal justice which peoples imagine as the existence of the divine gods" (para. 145, Addition). The preface had pointed already to one important feature of this relation. The apparently natural and eternal *Sittlichkeit* is not the same as the "sun, moon, mountains, and rivers" which are only singular and are external (para. 146, Remark). The individual has a "feeling of selfness" (*Selbstgefühl*) in this relation. The bond to the *sittliche* community is known to be "more identical" than merely the externality of belief (para. 147). The implication is that *Sittlichkeit* is more than just the legend, tradition, or myth that was exluded from rational consideration in the *Philosophy of History.*[23] However, the similarity to the suggestion in the preface that there can be a debate that both legitimates these *sittliche* insitutions and permits an understanding of their transformation is not developed into a political argument. The historical premise for such a public political debate needs first to be elaborated.

The historical aspect of *Sittlichkeit* appears when Hegel distinguishes duty from virtue. Systematic imperatives explain his argument. Only within *Sittlichkeit* do moral commands become actual duties. There is no guarantee in the one-sided moral sphere that the imperatives will get a content that is both necessary and realizable. Within *Sittlichkeit* duty is not a limitation on freedom as is often imagined. Duty is itself a liberation. The particular is freed from the chains of immediacy and the passions. The frustration of an undetermined formal freedom, which knows that it ought to act but cannot know how concretely to act rationally, is overcome. Hegel's polemical sweep recalls the arguments of his preface. The Remark to paragraph 150 criticizes those who continually stress the particular. They talk constantly of virtue because they cannot stand the thought of doing merely what is necessary. They feel that they must continually manifest their unique individuality. To clinch his point, which is directed at "the French" and their predilection for rambling about virtue (para. 150, Addition), Hegel compares the traditional and the modern state forms. This polemical point brings out unintentionally its theoretical importance for history. A theory of the virtues was necessary in the "old states" because "in them Sittlichkeit had not grown to this free system of independent development and objectivity" (para. 150, Remark). Pregiven, fixed forms of virtue were necessary to replace that free rational choice. The catalogue of virtues did not depend on developed *Sittlichkeit*. It was built on what the ancients called "character," and took the form of a "spiritual natural history." Since nature is the sphere of the quantitative, Aristotle rightly defined virtue as the quantitative mean between the extremes. Ancient natural virtue performs the same systematic function as modern rational duty chosen from freedom. In both cases, the *Sittlichkeit* guarantees the necessity that the systematic imperative will be realized. The modern situation, however, involves historical necessity of a specific rational kind. Hegel must explain the necessity that leads from the one to the other.

Hegel's polemical attack on his contemporaries, and his attempt to explain his relation to his classical philosophical predecessors, shows the immanently historical character of *Sittlichkeit* itself. Hegel does not press the issue further toward a debate or to politics. He hastens to return to more stable ground. Paragraph 151 explains that the *Sitte* become habit which is then transformed into a "second nature." In his marginal commentary, and in the Addition to the paragraph, Hegel speculates about the pedagogical form of this transformation. This concern with pedagogy risks introducing an external actor or source of valid knowledge. It recalls the question of the education of the educator. Hegel's Remark, that physically or mentally "man also dies from habit," shows that he sees the danger. Yet, this same image recalls the concluding passages of the introduction to the *Philosophy of History*. Hegel's difficulty appears clearly here. The death from habit and the torpor of a *Volksgeist* dying "like a watch winding down" are now treated as a solution. Hegel comments (para.

152) that precisely this pedagogical habituation defines the way the *Sittliche* becomes valid in the actually existing historical world. *Sittlichkeit* bridges the gap between the subject and its objects, goals and institutions. It gives substance to the merely formal. Hegel's inability to say more than this is clear in his Remark to paragraph 153. He cites the famous reply to the question how one should best raise one's son: make him a citizen of a state with good laws. His Addition to this paragraph is only a polemical escape. Granted, no matter how isolated he remains, Rousseau's *Emile* will not be able to escape the "scent of the world of spirit." This does not explain the historical transformation of *Sittlichkeit* which Hegel has presented in comparing the ancients with the moderns. It does not explain the historical progression of *Volksgeister* that is portrayed at the conclusion to his theory. The external pedagogue, or the silent process of the habituation, violates the modernist rigor with which Hegel has proceeded. Inconsistency like this may have psychological grounds. It surely demands systematic rethinking.

A more systematic Hegel can be reconstructed from the outline presented to this point. The *Philosophy of Right* concludes with that sketch of World History to which Hegel referred his students in introducing *The Philosophy of History*. Despite the attempt to present a *sittliche* structure that is rational and free, Hegel apparently dissolves the system into World History. This explains one aspect of the systematic *Philosophy of Right*. A form of *Sittlichkeit* that has become is presented as if it were permanent and unchanging. The modern *Sittlichkeit* makes the particularity that was merely natural in the "old states" into its fundamental principle. This qualitatively new aspect of modernity permits free rational choice to replace the heroic but habituated "character" of "spiritual natural history." This argument is perhaps justified as a reply to a weakness seen in the *Philosophy of History*. The systematic structure of the historical broke down when Hegel defined the *Volksgeist* by a *Sittlichkeit* broader than the state. He could not account for the rationality and necessity by which such a *Volksgeist* either preserves itself or is replaced. The free particular (economic) choice that he sees typifying modern civil society solves the problem. But the price of the option for particular economic rationality is an antihistorical result.

Quantitative change through comparison is pseudohistorical. The only systematic explanation of this definition of the modern form of *Sittlichkeit* is the assumption that history has indeed come to an end with the modern world. This was Hegel's unspoken assumption in the resigned conclusion to the polemical preface. The exclusion of politics and of change is the result of this integration of system into history. The stance of the philosopher can only be the contemplative *Zusehen* recommended by the conclusion to the preface.

A more consistent reading of the systematic Hegel can be presented on the basis of these same materials. In the context of the progress of the forms of understanding World History the *Philosophy of Right* itself can be treated as a kind of "reflective history." The necessity and completeness from both sides has to be demonstrated. The presentation of *Sittlichkeit* has to stress the immanently historical character of this sphere. The interrelation between the particular sphere of civil society and the political state has to develop the possibility of that "debate" to whose necessary role Hegel pointed in the theoretical justification of his polemical preface. Hegel hints at the need for such an account. A marginal note to paragraph 154 indicates the price paid for the priority of economic rationality.

> "Not merely: others have rights; I am equal to them; I am a person like them: I ought to have duties with regard to their rights—as equal to them I ought to have rights also through these duties—in other words, a connection made by *comparison*."

The standpoint of comparison is the basis of quantitative economic rationality. Comparison is contemplative judgment because it adds nothing to the objects that it subsumes under a formally universal standard. To avoid treating the relation between the political state and civil society under this form of rationality, Hegel would need to develop a theory of representation and judgment that explains the necessity of the philosopher's *Zutat*. This would be that "debate" to whose possibility the preface and the historical introduction of *Sittlichkeit* had pointed. This political addition would then permit Hegel to have a systematically adequate account of the originary relation of philosophy and history. This leads to the paradoxical conclusion that Hegel has explained the reasons that the historical world calls for philosophy. His philosophy, however, falls short of the demand whose structure he has uncovered.

THE POLITICS OF MARX'S THEORY OF IDEOLOGY

The most common interpretation of the critique of ideology is built on a paradox that points to the systematic structure that underlies Marx's argument. The common version of the theory does too little or too much. It suggests that normative projections emerge necessarily from material social relations. This implies a genetic determinism which rules out the possibility of qualitative change. All social actors are caught up in the same mystifying context. This means that there is no way to denounce the mystification. No one can stand outside of it to identify the "really real" infrastructure that ideology is supposed to hide. To say that some are deceived in one way, some in another, only introduces a quantitative relativism. A second theoretical move then suggests that the normative mystifications conceal the material reality that generated them. If rationality is defined as a structure permitting free self-conscious action, a reality that generates ideological mystifications must itself be irrational. This completes the paradox. Mystifying projections are generated necessarily by a reality of which they are the expression. In turn, they are said to cover over and falsify the way the subject perceives that reality. Finally, the reality itself is shown to be irrational. The source of the difficulty is that material conditions are treated first as genetic and then, in a second moment, as the norm against which to measure the projection. The copresence of the genetic and the normative suggests that what is being described is not a causal but an originary structure. The usual account does "too little or too much" because its determinism makes change either wholly necessary or impossible.

The systematic demand to make philosophy worldly and to make the world philosophical implies the rejection of the causal or reductionist interpretation of ideology. Philosophy must be worthy of being received by a world that, in turn, must need philosophy in order to achieve its own rational completion. Marx quickly abandoned the explicit concern with the transformation of philosophy in order to concentrate on the critique of political economy which reveals "the anatomy of bourgeois civil society." The role of philosophy is taken over by what he calls "revolutionary practice." Although it often is reduced to pragmatic or tactical concerns, the third of the *Theses on Feuerbach* suggest Marx's more theoretical concerns.

> The materialist doctrine of the modifying influence of the change in conditions and of education forgets that the conditions are changed by men, and that the educator himself must be educated. It is thus forced to divide society into two parts, one of which rises above the society.
>
> The coincidence of the changing of conditions and of human activity or self-transformation can only be conceived and understood rationally as *revolutionary practice.*

Philosophy is not a neutral or contemplative knowledge separated from society. If it pretends to play the role of educator, philosophy perpetuates the social divisions consecrated by the separation of manual and mental labor. This makes philosophy into an ideology that hinders progress. The task of the revolutionary is to make the world "philosophical" by overcoming social divisions. Revolutionary knowledge appears (in the second paragraph) to arise immediately and naturally from activity that changes both the world and actor. This is insufficient. Marx is only giving an activist twist to the reductionist materialism that the *Theses* criticizes. He has not explained the necessity that makes possible the revolutionary practice and its positive effects. The problem of the lightning of thought remains. Marx has gone beyond Kant only in his rhetoric; their problem remains the same.

Another formulation of the nature of revolutionary practice in *The German Ideology* permits a more systematic philosophical interpretation. Marx shows that he is aware of the double imperative that typifies the modern structure of immanence.

> Both for the production on a mass scale of this communist consciousness, and for the success of the cause itself, the alteration of men on a mass scale is necessary, an alteration which can only take place in a practical movement, a *revolution*. This revolution is necessary, therefore, not only because the *ruling* class cannot be overthrown in any other way, but also because the class *overthrowing* it can succeed in ridding itself of all the muck of the ages and become fitted to found society anew only in a revolution.

Revolution is necessary to change social relations as well as material conditions. A process of historical growth is required. The revolutionary class is not able to seize power immediately, by virtue of its relation to the means of production, its total alienation, or any other *real* property. It becomes revolutionary through and in a learning process. In order to "found society anew," the proletariat must throw off the "muck of the ages." This might be interpreted still in terms of the reductionist notion of ideology. Yet, more than instrumental knowledge is involved in the revolutionary practice. The revolutionary, like the philosopher, cannot assume an external point of view claiming to gain valid knowledge separate from its genetic base and object. Revolutionary practice demands philosophy; it is the education of the educator. This is the first step, but the systematic articulation is still incomplete. The double imperative has been presented from the side of the actor. The same double imperative must also be presented on the side of the world. The further move to show the necessary realization of this double demand follows only then.

The equation of philosophy with revolutionary practice can be translated into a nonreductionist definition of ideology. Ideology institutes the separation of knowledge from the process by which it is acquired. Ideology is the historically specific procedure by which one or the other pole of the dualism that separates genesis and validity is made uncritically the principle of analysis or action. Positivism is only one illustration of a more general process. Ideology presupposes that the subject is separate from and unaffected by the knowing experience. The knowing activity is treated as having no effect on the object known. Marx argues frequently in his polemics that there is no such thing as a discrete "fact" that can be known independently. Facts are contextual. They derive their sense only within a totality on which their existence depends. Pieces of paper that are exchanged for commodities are not in themselves money. They have exchange value only in a specific social context. A machine is a machine; only in historically defined conditions does it become the means for the production of profit. Sexual, physical, and even mental differences are important facts only in definite conditions; in others, they are not noticed, they do not exist because they do not "matter."[24] This first minimal description of ideology articulates the results of the process that builds division into the structure of knowledge. It does not yet explain why such a division is necessary. The definition is incomplete because the process to which it points might be merely accidental or transitory. The structure of knowledge must be shown to be not only subjective.

The move toward material necessity can be seen when Marx's argument is compared with the opening development of Hegel's *Phenomenology*. Hegel describes consciousness as asserting the truth of what presents itself to the senses immediately. The immediacy of the given is assumed to guarantee that the thing will be received in all its richness and, therefore, in its truth. But consciousness is not only consciousness of the object; consciousness is also able to reflect on its object as known. The result is the oscillation of saying and meaning. What consciousness means or points to is the immediate thing; all that it can say, however, is a series of universal and abstract categories. The thing that is presented immediately and taken as true shows itself in fact to be the most impoverished and least determinant content. What can be said about the immediate other than to identify it as a "this," which has as its properties only to be "here" and to occur "now"? When the next "now" occurs, and attention is turned to another "this," the truth of the first moment is lost immediately. The result of the movement is that what was apparently the most concrete and immediate knowledge proves to be in fact the most abstract and universal of structures. Anything and everything has the property of being a "this," which is "here" and "now." Hegel's point is that consciousness must learn to make distinctions; it must be able to distinguish a thing from its properties, and to use its understanding to find the lawfulness of their relations. Each of these further developments brings mediation by setting the thing into an increasingly complex structure of relations *and* by asking questions from the standpoint of the greater complexity to which the conscious subject has advanced. This Hegelian argument has a structure similar to Marx's first depiction of the process of ideology. His solution shows the weaknesses inherent in the option for a phenomenological approach. Marx's theory has to go further toward systematic elaboration, just as Hegel's phenomenological description presupposed a logic that had to be made explicit.

Marx's developed theory of ideology satisfies the systematic requirements of the modern. Ideology is not a set of misconceptions forced on the dominated by a ruling class. A ruling class cannot stand outside the process it controls. The illusion of an external source of power is shared by the reductionist revolutionary and the rulers themselves. Both of them assume the possibility of conscious manipulation—the one condemning, the other trying to utilize it. These mutual self-deceptions suggest a different approach. The separated subject is not the all-powerful ruling class. The transcendent spectator is condemned to be impotent. An external spectator can reflect but never alter the development that plays before his contemplative gaze. Ideological knowledge has no effect on the object known or on the knower himself. The implications of this structure are developed by Claude Lefort. Marx's enlightenment predecessors and his Marxist successors *applied* the concept of ideology. Marx did not. Marx *discovered* the structure of ideology. The difference of appearance and reality has been present throughout the history of philosophy. A critique based on this difference presupposes a hypothetical external position that separates the critic from the modern world. Marx's discovery is that ideology *is* the structure of the modern. The fault is not that of the capitalists; nor is the error that of a perceiving subject who could correct his mistakes. The structure of volume 1 of *Capital* suggests that ideology is the precondition for capitalism. Marx's decision to begin with the analysis of the commodity and to conclude with the history of "so-called primitive accumulation" suggests that fetishism and the commodity structure are the necessary logical preconditions for the emergence of capitalism. This means that capitalism is only one of the possible forms of a modern civil society. It follows that the logic of civil society must supplement the critical phenomenology of capitalism. The revolutionary must decide whether it is the logic of civil society or the phenomenology of its capitalist form that represents the "enemy." That decision will depend on tools that have not yet been developed here.

The ideological structure of modernity explains why the reductionist version of the theory of ideology is a constant temptation. Ideology differs from religion in one significant feature. Religion typifies the general form by which a community assures its identity. A transcendent norm serves to guarantee social cohesion and consistent world views. Religion serves to avoid and to control the risk of change. It eliminates the historical character of society and of personal responsibility by prescribing forms of interpersonal relations and relations to nature. Freud's description of its parallels to neurosis is completed by the data of ethnography. An external standard permits the religious community or neurotic individual to function in a structured pattern of relations. The threat of the new is avoided; otherness is integrated into a symbolic universe suffused with transcendent meaning. This externality is precisely what modernity's immanence forbids. There is no measure or norm through which modern society can define itself and its limits. This inherent fluidity explains why the same thing can function at one moment as genetic and at another as normative. It clarifies why modern society must be inherently and self-consciously historical. This specificity of ideology explains the possibility of applying the reductionist simplification. Ideology is inherently unstable because of its immanence and its lack of measure. This is why it continually attempts to assure itself a fixed structure. It can do this by absolutizing either the normative or the genetic pole. The result resembles the external structure of religion. The temptation is to treat it by means of the reduction. That is an error. The modern form of ideology demands a political complement. The reduction eliminates ideological mystification at the cost of returning the analysis to a premodern structure. The reductive critique of ideology is itself ideological. The political complement must preserve the gains of modernity and the complexity of the ideological. Lefort's suggestion that Marx discovered ideology, as opposed to the common view that he applied a critique of ideology, points also in this direction.

Although religion and ideology differ structurally, their functions are comparable. Hegel's *Philosophy of Right* showed the necessary creation of the Rabble (*Pöbel*) within a specific type of economic production. The Rabble, and the degeneracy of extravagant wealth which this type of economy produces, threaten the cohesion of society. Hegel tried to avoid this danger without opening up the political debate that his system could have permitted. This Hegelian solution is similar to the one Marx presents in his analysis of capitalism-as-ideology. Capitalism eliminates political questioning by providing a social solution. Private vices become public virtue, comparative judgment replaces public reflection, and the social division of labor is justified by its ability to deliver the goods. Capitalism articulates the economic logic of a society based on particularism. This particularist egoism suffuses immanently all spheres of social relations. The dominance of the economic within capitalism provides the same functional integration as did the transcendent norms in traditional societies. Economics and religion, politics and culture, planting and chanting, pottery and art realize a modern version of what Mauss called a "total social fact."[25] From this functional viewpoint, the reductionist base/superstructure interpretation of ideology is not so much false as it is incomplete. It accepts the self-understanding of the capitalists without wondering whether and to what degree the dominance of the economic has in fact destroyed all intermediary structures within the public space. The account of ideology should know better than to assume that capitalists can have a correct self-understanding. The domination of economic capitalist civil society is one way in which the immanent historicity of the modern can be denied. It has not been shown systematically to be the only way in which the modern world can blind itself. The elimination of capitalism does not necessarily put an end to the phenomena revealed by the critique of ideology.

This account of the systematic structure and function of ideology explains why Marx wrote *Capital* as a "critique of political economy." The book is not a scientific overview of the capitalist economy. Marx did not expect the economy to break down on its own. His politics was not just a reaction to economics. In order to avoid external criticisms of capitalism's social injustice, Marx developed the implications of a paradox already articulated by Rousseau. Bourgeois thinkers stress the past and point eagerly to the future. At the same time, they assume a pregiven and fixed concept of human nature. With Rousseau, Marx denounces their treatment of characteristics developed only in capitalism as if they were the universal character of humanity. He returns often to these "Robinsonades" that conceive of the species as small English shopkeepers, treating time as money, acting as if there is only one way to live—alone or in society. The point is not only rhetorical. This capitalist self-conception falsifies what is central to modern social relations. Treating humans as abstract particulars with fixed drives and motivations is the ideological self-image of capitalist society. It legitimates and gives the system an identity. Yet modern capitalist reality denies this self-image. Changed need structures, the declining role of family, secularization—the list is endless, and the changes continue. Modern capitalism is built on change. This same principle of constant destruction and renewal implies the impossibility of the system maintaining itself and its identity. The dilemma cannot be avoided merely by historicizing the fixed categories. That escape parallels the move to the dominance of the particularist economic rationality. The necessity of such self-misunderstanding is built into the modern structure of capitalist society. Marx's presentation of the social relations within the capitalist economy is the expression of the self-critique of an essentially divided society unable to maintain its identity. But this does not yet justify the claim that political economy is the locus of the "anatomy of civil society," as Marx puts it in *Capital*.

Capitalist social relations reproduce the system of atomized particularity dominated by economic rationality. The attitude Marx calls "vulgar economics" presents these capitalist social relations from the standpoint of the particular. The Robinsonade is invoked as a given. Profit is the result of buying cheaply and selling dearly. Crises result from bad judgment by individuals who let their stocks grow too high, produce more than the market will bear, or pay their laborers too dearly. Decisions of the consumer are the "law" that determines products and profits. This type of account is doomed because of its particularist starting point. The social totality can only be the accidental sum of individual actions whose connection can be elaborated only after the fact and on the average. This is the "anarchy" of capitalist production as a whole, which contrasts with the minute control exercized within the particular factory. Capitalism cannot be a unified totality. Failure to recognize its immanently historical structure leads vulgar economics to treat particularist ad hoc knowledge as if it gave universally valid laws. This universalization of the particular is typical of ideology. It is based on the inability to grasp the historical totality from within. This weakness explains the cult of the fact, empirical science, particular research. It also explains why each profession tends to think of itself as independent of the total social context. Each necessarily projects a specialized point of view onto the totality. The lawyer thinks that the law (the philosopher ideas, the economist production) is the Archimedean point from which to understand and move society. This universalization of the particular brings capitalism-as-ideology the full circle. The lack of any external social totality to be grasped permits a series of abuses where any and every particular tends to universalize its own stance. The society splinters into a congeries of contempting interest groups. This ironical conclusion parallels the series of historical phases that finally permitted Hegel to turn to philosophical history. Like Hegel, Marx does not draw the political implication from this development. The systematic orientation, however, permits the construction of a "Marxian" theory of the political based on some of Marx's own insights.

The theory of the political that complements necessarily the ideological structure of modern society depends on whether the capitalist economy or modern civil society is given the dominant role. Shortly after he had discovered the priority of civil society, Marx published a brief analysis of the place and the dilemmas of the political. "The King of Prussia and Social Reform" (1845) demonstrates that the normative role that state intervention is supposed to play cannot be successful. Marx's argument is based on systematic structural constraints. The state must react continually to problems posed by a divided civil society. This division prevents any adequation of genesis and validity. The state may at first leave social problems to civil society. Its own universal and normative function is said to prohibit it from intervening to aid particular individuals. The persistence of social division finally forces the state to admit that it does have responsibilities. In order to preserve its normative universality, it must blame the adminstration for misguiding the intervention that should have put an end to the conflict in civil society. The state's claim to normativity isolates it in both cases. Either it does not intervene, or it tips the social balance away from the self-regulation that the immanent legitimation of a modern civil society demands. The state is condemned to remain external. Its structural place prohibits successful intervention in a divided civil society that is unable to legitimate itself even though it knows that it risks falling victim to its immanent normlessness. Politics appears both necessary and yet impossible from the viewpoint of the state as normative complement to genetic civil society. This suggests why the stress might be placed on the economic elements of the analysis. That option, however, falls prey to the critique of ideology. A more fundamental approach is necessary.

The modern state is caught in a structural dilemma defined by the need to be at once in and yet above capitalist society. The state has to be both a genetic and a normative ingredient in the modern structure. The ongoing public debate which defines the Good Life is not what places the state above capitalist civil society. If that were its function, the state would not be a capitalist state. As capitalist, the state must be the real Total Capitalist. It must generate from within the harmonious relations needed by the particularist civil society. To do this, the state has to find a way to stand external to the divided society on which it acts. If it is only in the society, the state is a meeting place, as suggested by the famous phrase, "executive committee of the ruling class." This makes the state only a higher-level market where decisions are made in terms of the supply and demand of socioeconomic power. Such a state hides the reality of power in the cloak of formal democratic procedures. The other option for the state demands that the fundamental rules of the capitalist game be changed. The real and effective Total Capitalist must eliminate the free market for goods and wage labor. It replaces the particular free market division of labor by a Plan. Such a state is no longer "in" the capitalist society since the specificity of capitalism as a social form has been eliminated. The dilemma is complete. The Total Capitalist is either dependent on the capitalist society and therefore impotent, or the Total Capitalist must put an end to the capitalist contradictions by eliminating capitalism itself. Thinking of the political as simply a reaction to the economic system and its imperatives is doomed because of the ideological structure inherent in modern civil society.

The dilemma of the modern capitalist state permits an interpretation of the authoritarian or totalitarian forms of fascism and so-called socialism.[26] The economic base is not able to provide the legitimation needed for the social system. The role of the state tends to expand. Since the state cannot be a real Total Capitalist, it must modify capitalist civil society. The result is the normative stress of "politics in command." Every particular action is given a universal sense by being subsumed under the state's normative claims. Discrete and private aspects of life are forced into the context of the social totality. The planned society attempts to conjure away the historicity of modernity by englobing all particularity in its web. The Party is the constant incarnation of the political within every crevice of daily life. The legitimation of totalitarian society is success. It claims to have found the solution. But this solution presents it with a new paradox. The measures taken by the state claim to be "natural" or "rational." This is the ground of their immanent necessity. Yet to maintain its control, the totalitarian state must take credit for the changes it introduces. If its success is due to having found the "natural" or "rational" order of things, then its own total power should not be necessary. The meaning that it gives to the particulars it subsumes could exist without it. If its success is said to be due to its own activity, then its claim to naturality and rationality is lost. The state is then only one particular group imposing itself on a society that is essentially different from it. With the loss of legitimacy through universality comes the recourse to legitimacy through terror. The political cannot be absolutized as a norm that has to replace the ideological uncertainty of the capitalist economy with a transparent legitimacy. This is no solution to the dilemma faced by the state as Total Capitalist.

Modern capitalism-as-ideology does not call necessarily for the science of totalitarian politics as its complement. The depiction of capitalism-as-ideology does not imply that the next step is its overcoming through science. Yet, this temptation is present throughout Marx's work. There are good grounds for it, both in actual social behavior and in the theory itself. Phenomena like the "second nature" described by Lukács or the "seriality" analyzed by Sartre demonstrate the practicality of this orientation. The danger is the assumption that a "first" or "really real" infrastructure behind the illusions will act causally at the moment of crisis when, as Marx puts it in *Capital*, "the integument is burst asunder." Economics crisis alone can not wipe away the "muck of the ages." Objective change needs a subjective correlate. A different picture emerges when capitalism is treated as only one possible manifestation of the ideological structure of modernity. Capitalism universalizes the particular in order to give itself some principle for self-understanding. When this process is carried to the extreme, a pluralism of competing particularities comes to the stage. Even if capitalist economic values were at one point the dominant source of meaning for the particular, the immanently historical nature of this system shows why it must evolve beyond that stage. The totalitarian science cannot be applied to a system that is historical. Values other than the economic have to be brought to the analysis of what Lukács called the "the present as history." This possibility is present in Marx's own texts. The "Declaration of the Rights of Man and of the Citizen" may have hidden particular social relations in an abstraction that left room for the growth of capitalist domination. At the same time, the ideals of Liberty, Equality, and Fraternity present a universal yet to be realized. Marx stresses this in an often-cited passage from the *Eighteenth Brumaire*: "The social revolution...cannot draw its poetry from the past but only from the future." This positve function of ideology is not the same as religion or science.[27]

Marx has not shown that capitalism is the only form a modern civil society can adopt. He has not demonstrated the necessity of this particular economic structure as the manner in which the ideological social relations can be understood. The actual functioning of ideology that he presents through the economic analysis is not wrong. The difficulty is that there is no reason why these same structures could not be presented through the analysis of other aspects of modernity. The difficulties to which the account leads appear in the dilemma of a politics in a modern society reduced to its capitalist economic form. The political is forced to stand outside the economic. Ultimately it must destroy this economic foundation, which itself cannot stand without the political complement. This accentuation of the political is explained by the paradoxical structure of ideology which can only give itself a fixed identity by eliminating the conditions that actually called for that identity. The complementarity of Marx's stress on the political with the Hegelian tendency to give privilege to the economic is not surprising. Both start from an originary structure that brings together philosophy with the political. The difference is that Hegel is more concerned with the integration of the system into history. This explains why his politics is determined by the economic priority. Marx's desire to transform social relations makes his system lean in the opposite direction. To be theoretically consistent, Marx's politics must retain the historical openness of the modern, despite the always present economist temptation within the system. As with Hegel, Marx realizes only partially the political innovations made possible by his systematic theoretical approach to the modern.

The "philosophy" that Marx quickly transformed into revolutionary praxis before turning to the study of the "anatomy of civil society" returns to destablize his systematic structure. The account of modernity as ideological demonstrates the presence of an originary structure on the side of the world. When this structure is treated as the economic form of capitalism, the political complement that is necessary for its systematic completion fails structurally. Revolutionary praxis eliminates the immanence of ideology. It is a phenomenological approach that demands a logical complement.

The nature of the complement is determined by the imperative that the system show completeness. Only when this demand is satisfied can the necessity of the arguments be assured. Hegel was able to show the presence of this structure only by integrating the system into a logic of historical necessity. Outside the framework of economic capitalism, Marx's account permits a more satisfactory approach. The task of the political can be reformulated correlative to the need to reformulate "philosophy." The goal is not the elimination of contradiction but its integration into a structure that permits the inherent historicity of the modern to deploy itself. The goal of philosophy is not the creation of an identity between itself and the world. Politics need not stand outside of a society over which it exercises power. Philosophy must remain in an originary relation to the world. Politics must become the public dialogue of the society developing its own identity. Marx does not develop these arguments. They could emerge from his theory if the equation of capitalism and modernity is broken. The demonstration demands a *method* if it is not to remain at the abstract level of verbal promises. Hegel's historical world comes to complement Marx's account of the kinds of particularity that permit the preservation and growth of that relation.

CHAPTER 4

System Without Method

THE CONSTITUTIVE TEMPTATION

Substantive formulations like *the political* and *the modern* arouse suspicion. Is this to ontologize one's own embarrassment? Is the inability to operationalize the concept verbally transformed into a metaphysical virtue? Ontology claims that epistemological questions presuppose clarification of the foundation on which they rest. The assertion could be easily reversed. Ontology could itself be said to presuppose a theory of knowledge. The relation of the epistemological and the ontological at this level of abstraction presents yet another of the dualisms typical of the ordinary modern structure. Its reappearance only furthers the suspicions. The originary is everywhere, and thus nowhere. Hegel's attack on the romantic "night when all the cows are black" was directed at a similar vagueness. Marx's scorn for the holy "family" of contemplative philosophy and for "German ideology" has the same root. The demand for system cannot replace the articulation of a method that guarantees against the reproach of abstract tautology. This method cannot be simply the application of the system. An object to which a system could be applied stands in principle outside the system itself. It is a presupposition. Such a presupposition is not modern. The same modern structure forbids the other alternative which conceives the method as the action by which the system constitutes an object domain.[1] To leave the system simply in its self-related completeness and necessity—as "God's thought before the Creation," in the words of Hegel's *Logic*—is no solution. A mediation is necessary. Neither philosophy alone nor politics alone can provide it.

A historical-political digression will help clarify the theoretical problem. As so often in this period, history and politics pose problems that find their parallels in the theories of the philosophers. The popular battle cry in the period that culminated in the French Revolution took the theoretical form of the demand for a constitution. Two distinct arguments for a constitution correspond to the genetic and the normative approaches. The constitution could be treated as the explicit and public codification giving rational form to an already existing state of affairs. From the stance of normativity, this led to the natural-law position for which the constitution was to mirror a state of normatively valid human relations. The normative constitution would restore truths that had been distorted by vice, greed, and ignorance. This was the thrust of Tom Paine's defense of revolution in *The Rights of Man*. The position need not, however, imply revolutionary activism. From the stance of genesis, a constitution is to codify those traditional and customary rights and privileges that have made the polity the organism that it is. The genetic constitution would protect what is and what has become against intempestative abstract reason. This was the intent of Edmund Burke's *Reflections on the Revolution in France*, to which Paine was replying. The position need not, however, imply a conservative politics. Neither methodological orientation emerged explicitly in the actual historical debates. The resulting interpenetration of the two arguments and their conservative and/or radical meanings made the constitutional question originary.[2] When it became necessary to translate this structure into political method, the notion of constitution was taken literally. There were two possible approaches. The constitution could be identified with law itself. This implies that the constitution is treated as normative. Particular political action is then only epiphenomenal or secondary, since the universal norms of the constitution define the limits and objects of action Political action simply instantiates the already existing norms. Or, the particular laws are said to constitute the constitution itself. This genetic approach means that every new law in effect rewrites the constitution, with the result that government is replaced by administration. Political action loses its particularity in a society whose only law is defined by clashing interests. Neither approach is adequate, although both were attempted.

The radical Jacobin Constitution of 1793 illustrates the difficulties that theory presents to praxis. Its prologue explains that "forgetting and disdain [*mépris*] of the natural rights of man are the only causes of the evils of the world." Explaining these sacred and inalienable rights in a solemn public declaration will permit all citizens, at every moment, to compare the acts of government with the goals for which all social institutions are established. This constant recall will prevent tyranny from ever showing its face. The people will have the basis of their freedom and their happiness always before their eyes. The legislator will be always pointed to the object of his mission, and the magistrate to the rule of his duties. The logical conclusion of these premises is drawn in the final article of the Declaration:

> Article 35. When the government violates the rights of the people, insurrection is the most sacred of rights and most indispensible of duties for the people and for each part of the people.

When this final article is brought together with the first line of the first article—"The goal of society is the common happiness"—stable constitutional government is impossible. The danger is admitted implicitly when article 33 insists that the right of resistance to oppression is guaranteed, and article 34 defines oppression as occuring "when a single one of its members is oppressed." Building on an external and abstractly universal measure like happiness and defining oppression with reference to a single member produce a kind of instability different from article 28's justifiable insistence that "A people always has the right to reevaluate, to reform, and to change its constitution. A generation cannot subject future generations to its laws." This Declaration can be criticized equally by a Kantian, Hegelian, or Marxian. The Kantian rejects the external and accidental foundation of law on happiness. The Hegelian condemns the standpoint of particularly as unsuitable for a political system. The Marxian condemns the implicit universality of the political that is imposed on civil society. The course of the French Revolution justifies each of these criticisms.

The phases through which the French Revolution passed can be mapped along the lines suggested by the genetic and normative interpretation of the demand for a constitution. The constitutive temptation presents itself in either the genetic or in the normative form. The authors of the Constitution of 1793 built from a genetic approach for which action and institutions are oriented by the external quest for real happiness. The politicians who overthrew them and formed the Directory appealed to the norms of "revolutionary legality" enshrined in a new constitution. The historical details are less important than the philosophical structure they present.[3] At this level of abstraction, the structure explains why the preceding discussion of Hegel and Marx as originary philosophers concluded with pictures that fly in the face of received wisdom. The assertion that a consistent Hegel would have had to bring to prominence the implications of primacy of civil society is given further elaboration. Hegel criticized the Jacobin Terror for attempting to impose political norms on a society whose particularity it did not take into account. His own developed theory sought to remedy this default by giving civil society its due and by avoiding overstress on the political sphere. Similarly, the historical reasons that explain why a consistent Marx must assert the primacy of politics can be explained from this situation. Marx criticized the French Revolution for ignoring the ability of the economic infrastructure to determine a politics permitting it to insure its domination. The result is that Marx's politics are oriented by the need to keep particular egoistic interests under control. Hegel seeks to control the normative political moment, Marx the genetic economic action. Each political theory tries to develop the positive implications of what the French Revolution did not understand. Kant was in a different situation. He did not need to justify or to criticize the revolution because he did not interpret it as the attempt to put an end to the contradictions that drive history. Treating the revolution as a "beginning" he sought to understand, Kant could draw from it an originary political theory.[4]

The difference between traditional and modern politics is not captured by the concept of a constitutional revolution. The various natural-law theories, enlightened, historical beliefs in inevitable material, scientific, and moral progress, and eudaemonistic appeals that formed the arsenal of the French Revolution are still premodern. In each case, the relation of theory to practice was explained by appeal to a constitutive method. In each case, the goal was to end the contradictions or tensions that had called for the theory in the first place. Each of the theoretical premises has a classical philosophical structure; none has made the "originary turn." The originary has to be able to explain the conditions of possibility and of necessity from the stance of both subject and object, genesis and validity. The same holds for a modern politics. The application of theory to practice is unable to explain how and why action will be received by a world that called for it. The same reproach holds for the inverse but identical structure. It is not enough to wait for a crisis to create conditions that call for the *hic rhodus, hic salta!* This cannot account for how and why the subject will in fact be struck by the lightning of thought that explains the particular necessity of action. This systematic difficulty affects not only the French but all attempts at revolutionary theory that do not take seriously the modern imperative of immanence. The political labels "voluntarism" and "reformism" (or "opportunism") designate forms of behavior whose theoretical grounds are described by this premodern structure.

The question of method must be solved immanently to the system itself. The originary logic points to two axes around which the method is articulated. The double receptivity of the world to theory, and of theory to the world, must be demonstrated. Simple receptivity of one or the other moment would not be *geschichtlich*. The demonstration must avoid twin errors. The poles must not be in a relation of constitution or of externality to each other. This implies that their relation is not the subsumption of a particular under a pregiven or a priori universal. A reflective judgment that moves from the particular to the universal must be shown to be possible and necessary. In this way, a second type of externality, which treats the world as if it were a "really real" substratum to which theory relates, is eliminated. The inverse identical, which treats theory as if it were the "really real" essence of which the world is only an appearance, is also rejected. The account of this structure of receptivity is developed most explicitly in the Kantian theory of "critique." It can be illustrated also in Hegel's account of the structure of that *Sittlichkeit* whose particularity and historical dimension becomes crucial in the attempt to understand the rationality of History or the historicity of Reason, and the place of the political, or the state, in this context. Marx is less convincing on this score for the same systematic reasons that made him stress the priority of politics in spite of the primacy that political economy seems to have in his writing.

A second methodological criterion brings out the strength of Marx's system. If receptivity is demonstrated through the reflective judgment that moves from the particular to the public affirmation of the universal, those particulars that in fact call for this judgment must be identified. Not every object can be called beautiful. Not every injustice or unhappiness is grounds for political action. The Kantian suggestion that the critical project is followed by a "doctrinal" philosophy is the first recognition of this methodological problem. Hegel's approach is less convincing for the systematic reasons suggested by his inability to articulate the political relation of particular to universal which leads him to universalize the structure of particularity as the foundation of civil society. Marx's strength as a political thinker appears most clearly from this methodological point of view. It will be seen, however, that the methodology of particularity depends, in fact, on the structure of the political that will be presented in chapter 7. The republican political form will be seen to make necessary the expression of a particularity whose *Geschichtlichkeit* makes possible and necessary the political complement to originary philosophy. The politics of the representation of right is necessarily an originary process.

The demonstration that the system itself has the immanent necessity of articulating its methodological structures provides the justification for the substantive formulation of the political and the modern. When the system tries to give itself substance without the mediation of method, it fails. This can be demonstrated briefly for Kant, Hegel, and Marx. In each case, the attempt to eliminate an apparent contradiction by the constitution of a unity is the source of the error. This temptation is most clearly described by the Marxian notion of capitalism-as-ideology, which explains the temptation to resolve the modern tension by the options from one or the other pole. The negative proof presented here will be supplemented in part 2 by the positive elaboration of the two moments of the method. The implication is that the relation of ontology and epistemology, or that of theory to practice, is not the exclusion or domination of the one by the other. The imperative of immanence means that neither a constitutive nor an essentialist approach can be justified. Method permits each to remain immanent to the other without being conflated abusively with it. The type of receptivity and particularity appropriate to each epistemological domain or practical endeavor will be different. The method can demonstrate the resulting structure without having to reach outside to an essence or to a fact from which to constitute a unity. This is why the modern presents for the first time the possibility of articulating the political in a theoretically adequate and practically relevant form. This is what would justify the politics proposed by article 28 of the Constitution of 1793.

Kant's Failed Constitutive Theory

The systematic basis for attributing a constitutive theory of history to Kant begins from the assumption that the theoretical dualism of nature and freedom must be overcome. The third Antinomy of the first *Critique* showed the possibility of free action but not yet its (double) necessity. Kant had "eliminate[d] knowledge to make room for faith." The ethical writings that follow may be read as the attempt to give theoretical certainty and necessity to the practical possibilities asserted but not yet proven. Freedom must be shown to make its mark on the objective causal world. The subject motived by duty is portrayed as imprinting gradually the natural world with a rational and lawful pattern. Nature is increasingly humanized and rationalized in this process. From the other side, the problem from "What Is Enlightenment?" is overcome in this process. The formally free subject acquires content that can now claim to be necessary and rational. The subject and its object affect one another reciprocally in a kind of proto-dialectic.

This systematic reading of Kant's ethical theory is unable to provide the material mediation that explains how duty can take on concrete empirical content. Correlatively, it cannot explain the systematic necessity of a world whose material structure permits the realization of the ethical project. For this reason the concept of Genius and the assumption of a natural telelogical "happy chance" in the *Critique of Judgment* could be read as Kant's attempt at a solution. Their inadequacy is obvious. They cannot justify themselves rationally. The historical writings could then be introduced into the system. They show how the private moral individual acts to constitute a public world whose increasingly rational structure gradually permits overcoming of the public/private dualism on which the modern state was shown to be based.[5] The strongest support for this assertion comes from the 1784 essay, "The Idea of History from a Cosmopolitan Point of View." The date of this essay points to Kant's concern to give concretion to the formally free enlightenment consciousness. Although it precedes the second and third *Critiques*, many of its arguments reappear throughout Kant's writings. This indicates that the constitutive temptation was always present for Kant, as it is for the modern.[6]

The "Cosmopolitan History" begins with the assertion that the first *Critique* has demonstrated that all actions are subject to the universal laws that govern the phenomenal world. This presents a problem for a theory of history. Human freedom must have its place in the panorama of historical development which, as phenomenal, is governed by the laws of natural causality. History will present a regular movement amidst the chaos and confusion of particular actions. This regularity of the whole will not be seen by the individual who does not consciously will it. Yet, continues Kant, the new "state sciences" of statistics and demography have shown that

> Each, according to his own inclination, follows his own purpose often in opposition to others; yet each individual and people, as if following some guiding thread, go toward a natural but to each of them unknown goal; all work toward furthering it, even if they would set little store by it if they did know it.

Kant does not emphasize the fact that this regular, lawful development is present from the level of the state's universalizing overview of particular action. His concern is that the lawful development appears at the level of the species, not that of the individual. This presents the problem of the relation between the choices of free individual morality and the lawful regularity perceived in the development of the species. The two must be connected. Since it is not possible to presuppose purposeful action by men acting in concert, "There is no other expedient...except to try to see if [the philosopher] can discover a natural purpose in this idiotic course of things human." The problem is that the insistence on the causal lawfulness of the phenomenal world means that the "natural purpose" is exluded. The inconsistency is even more apparent when Kant concludes these preliminary remarks with observation that the person who would use the "natural purpose" to compose a universal history would be comparable to a Kepler or a Newton. Kant's proposed solution to this problem is presented in the form of theses accompanied by commentary.

The first of Kant's nine theses asserts that "All natural capacities of a creature are destined to evolve completely to their natural end." Kant's justification is that an organ of no use or an arrangement not serving its purpose would be "contradictions in the telelogical theory of nature." This is an assertion, not an argument. To call it an anticipation of the *Critique of Judgment* neglects the fact that a reflective judgment asserting teleology makes no claims about the real world. That Kant is referring to real history is evident in the second Thesis, which elaborates on the first. Man has reason only as a species, says Kant, never as an individual. Two justifications are offered. Reason grows through trial and error. Consequently, no one individual could live long enough to develop it fully by himself. Yet reason must develop, Kant continues, for the (teleological) reason that Nature would not have given it to us were she not also to prepare us for its use. The first assertion is a constitution-theoretical variant of the "practical postulate" of the immortality of the soul and existence of God in the second *Critique*. It is in fact a more adequate justification of the Postulates than that offered in the second *Critique*. Its picture of a real, positive process seems richer than the second *Critique's* negative "dialectical" demonstration. That Kant did not return to it there suggests that he had abandoned the constitutive approach presented in "Cosmopolitan History." His second justification here recalls a different ethical argument. It resembles the demonstration that the existence of freedom must be postulated if the moral law is to be valid. A law that cannot be accomplished is self-contradictory and hence invalid. If the law exists, freedom too must exist. The structure of this assertion is systematic. The natural world calls for the development of the reason that is immanent to the natural process. If it works, this constitutive historical argument would provide support for the claims that were questionable assertions in the ethical writings. It would prove the reality of the system.

The third thesis again invokes the will of Nature. We, by ourselves, are to produce what makes our lives more than animal. Our happiness must not result from instinct but from reason alone. Nature wants us to live our distinction from the animals so that what we value in life is particular only to our species. This is why she created man "exactly as if she aimed more at this rational self-esteem than at his well being." In fact, this natural plan does not assure even the individual "rational self-esteem." Rather, it is for the future of the species that the individual foresakes happiness for rational toil. The parallel to the ethics appears again in this stress on duty, on the worthiness to be happy as opposed to happiness itself, and on the species' development. But this time the ethical parallel poses problems. If nature so endowed us, free will and moral choice would be meaningless. To escape the objection by noting that Kant is here talking of the species and not of the individual is no solution. In that case, the individual, who after all is the moral agent, is left out of the picture. The problem is that Nature is treated as a real and external actor; Kant is unable to distinguish real nature from conceptual Nature. This time the actor is constituting the moral and rational humanity. The basic structure of the argument remains the same, only the terms are inverted.

The fourth thesis attempts to tie together the threads of the first part of the argument. The means Nature uses to insure the development of our capacities is the social antagonism that ultimately forces the creation of a lawful social order. Kant introduces the notion of "unsocial sociability" which balances us between the desire to follow selfish urges and the fact that we are nonetheless involved with our fellows in a society. Unsocial sociability leads to the establishment of formal rules of behavior.

> Thus are taken the first true steps from barbarism to culture, which consists in the social worth of man; thence gradually develop all talents, and taste is refined; through continued enlightment the beginnings are laid for a way of thought which can in time convert the coarse, natural disposition into definite practical principles; and thereby change a society of men driven together by their natural feelings into a moral whole.

This picture accounts for the growth of freedom that "What Is Enlightenment?" left undetermined. Kant insists that without this unsocial sociability we might live in a state of concord and even mutual affection, like the sheep we herd, but we would never reach a higher worth, never achieve our end, "which is rational nature." Hence, he concludes, Nature knows better than man: "Man wishes concord; but Nature knows better what is good for the race; she wills discord." Discord at the level of the individual produces concord at the level of the species. The result is not instinctual but moral because it encompasses the individual both as particular actor and as member of a rational species.

This first phase of the argument is vitiated by the attribution of rational purpose to Nature. Kant began from the dualist postulate of the first *Critique* which demonstrates the lawful mechanical causality of phenomenal nature. To say now that the purposive "Nature" he introduces here is in fact noumenal is to lose the real empirical content Kant is trying to give to the formally autonomous free will. The suggestion in the commentary on the fourth thesis, that the end of man is "rational nature," increases the difficulty. Kant insisted that the inateness of reason differentiates man from the animals. To account for the development of reason Kant turns to Nature in the form of an unsocial sociability, which functions providentially. This argument is justified if Kant can show that and how it is man who gives purpose to nature and to himself as natural. A purposively functioning Nature could *then* intervene rationally in historical development. This option for a constitutive practice does not succeed. Kant's invocation of a purposive Nature was to guarantee the necessity of progress. To replace the phenomenally lawful natural necessity by a choice that gives purposes to nature opens the possibility of accident replacing necessity. This explains why Kant is apparently inconsistent with his own systematic theorizing. At times he has recourse to a natural teleology in the form of migrating peoples, oceanic currents, or commercial intercourse. These references violate the reflective character of the teleological judgment. They subsume the particulars under a universal like those "state sciences" that show regular lawfulness beneath particular choices. Kant thinks he can appeal to Nature as a "great artist" who at the same time follows a "mechanical course." This makes sense only if Kant's goal is to unify in reality the two poles from which the first *Critique* begins. The remainder of his text needs to be analyzed before going further with such conjecture.

Kant seems to have been aware of the weakness of his assertions. The second part of "Cosmopolitan History" turns to more political issues. The simple subsumption of the individual under the natural species, or under the state and its sceinces, is elaborated by this new orientation. Politics here is neither the particular nor the universal. The fifth and sixth theses suggest that the greatest problem for human kind, the most difficult and last to be solved, is the formation of a civil society universally administering law among men. This is a variant on the familiar theme of enlightened despotism. In the present context, it puts into question the introductory observations that pointed to a lawful regularity shown to exist at the level of the species by the new "state sciences." The presence of such a regularity should make the problem of creating a civil society less arduous. Kant's difficulty is the one that confronts any contract theory of society. It is a simple matter to explain how and why individuals act lawfully once the society is already in fact constituted, since the first law is that there is law. The problem is to explain the origin of the first law, the initial contract, without presupposing what is to be demonstrated. Kant's insistence on the difficulty of creating a civil society under law is a sign that the simple constitution as a result of our unsocial sociability to which the fourth thesis looked did not satisfy him.[7]

Kant has to demonstrate that the mutual opposition of unsociably social humans must eventuate in a constitution guaranteeing maximum freedom for all. He does not specify further the nature of that constitution. He returns instead to Nature's mysteriously rational ways. The conflict of the passions is said to work for the general good.

> It is just the same with trees in a forest: each needs the others, since each in seeking to take the air and sunlight from others must strive upward, and thereby each realizes a beautiful, straight stature, while those that live in isolated freedom put out branches at random and grow stunted, crooked, and twisted.

The sixth thesis adds a human complement to this natural teleology. "Man is an animal that, if it lives among others of its kind, requres a master." Whence the master? It can only be another human who, in turn, needs a master. The only solution is self-mastery. Nature is no help here; human nature is in fact a hindrance. "This task is . . . the hardest of all. Indeed, its complete solution is impossible, for from such crooked wood as man is made of, nothing perfectly straight can be built." The flow of the argument breaks off at this point. The dilemma is the same as that expressed by the existential *sapere aude* invoked at the beginning of "What Is Enlightenment?" Kant apparently drops the attempt at its constitutive solution by means of the formation of civil society. One might have expected him to thematize the way human action imprints itself in the world, perhaps along the lines he suggested a year later in his essay "Conjectural Beginning of Human History." Instead, the seventh thesis takes a different approach.

Rather than demonstrate the constitution of civil society from below, Kant suggests that its establishment depends on resolving the problem of "a lawful external relation among states." States, he argues, will do as unsociably social men have done:

> Through war, through the taxing and never-ending accumulation of armament, through the want which any state, even in peacetime, must suffer internally, Nature forces them to make at first inadequate and tentative attempts; finally, after devastations, revolutions, and even complete exhaustion, she brings them to that which reason could have told them at the beginnng and with far less sad experience, to wit, to step from the lawless condition of savages into a league of nations.

Varaints of this important argument recur at different ponts in Kant's theoretical maturation before its full implications are drawn in the essay "Perpetual Peace." The uncertainty of Kant's methodological self-understanding at this point is evident in his answer to the question whether he can believe that such a "league of nations" will come to exist. He insists that this is only a belief, which is as founded as the "faith" of the first *Critique.* His justification is twofold. "Is it reasonable" he asks, "to assume a purposiveness in all parts of nature and to deny it to the whole?" To this natural teleology is added a moral complement when Kant suggests that although we are cultured and "perhaps too" civilized, we are not yet moral. Without morality, all the good that may come is "but pretense and glittering misery." The ideal solution would of course unite the teleological and the moral approaches. At this point Kant is still groping for a method permitting their mediation. The eighth thesis returns in vain to the constitutive approach. Kant asks whether the assumption that human history is "in the large...the realization of Nature's secret plan" is a utopian or even millenarian hope. He gives three answers: First, "the idea can help, though only from afar"; second, nature does, "to however small a degree," reveal traces of humanity's progress. With Rousseau, Kant concludes from this that human nature cannot remain indifferent to the possibility that it might help here. Third, it is in the interest of the state to develop the capacities of the citizens. The typical enlightenment belief in the beneficial effects of commerce are cited as support of this point. None of these assertions is convincingly demonstrated in the text. The problems of enlightened despotism remain.

The suggestive final thesis puts the philosopher on the stage of history. "A philsophical attempt to work out a universal history according to a natural plan directed to achieving the civic union of the human race must be regarded as possible and, indeed, as contributing to this end of Nature." The argument should be compared first to the precritical *Lectures on Ethics,* which reply to the same question with a plea for support of the Basedow attempts at educational reform. The critical Kant is playing now on the dual nature of Nature as phenomenal and noumenal, causal and teleological. The intervention of the philosopher is made necessary by the development of "Nature" through forms of unsocial sociability. The theory with which he intervenes is the expression of that natural development. Thus the philosopher makes explicit what was implicit in Nature. The philosopher enlightens the citizen who can now accomplish rationally what Nature previously effected behind his back and in the name of the species. The problem is solved, but at a cost. To conceive of philosophy "as contributing to this end of Nature" is to embed philosophy in a natural process in a manner that costs reason its independence. The human end of "rational nature" of which the fourth thesis spoke is here presupposed as existing from the outset. History is simply the rendering explicit of the implicit. This essentialism, moreover, is based on the noumenal. It is by its very nature undemonstrable. Kant becomes, so to speak, a "Hegelian-Marxist."

The constitution-theoretical variant of Kant's philosophy of history fails for three distinct reasons. The approach suggested by the seventh thesis is unable to bring together the material progress of civilization with the development of human morality. The weakness of the first part of the argument undermined the attempt to demonstrate this necessity by the theory of constitution. Kant was working from the universal to the particular, from the goal to the facts to be subsumed under it. A political argument has to be able to proceed from the particular; it has to be both universally necessary for the species and binding on the particular individual. The constitutive argument from the ninth thesis fails because it eliminates from the outset the problem that it was ostensibly set up to solve. Kant recognizes this in the section of his *Anthropology* which makes a corresponding assertion.[8] He suggests that the problem can only be solved when the distinction between a regulative and constitutive judgment is maintained. His third error can be explained by this observation. His constitution-theoretical approach treats what should have been a reflective judgment of teleology as if it were constitutive. The result was that "natural" providence replaced both history and politics. The Kepler or Newton who finds the "natural purpose" and writes universal history has neither made the "Copernican revolution" nor the originary turn.

HEGEL'S THEORY OF NORMATIVE CONSTITUTION

The second section of Hegel's introduction to the *Philosophy of History* examines means by which Freedom realizes itself. The reflexive formulation, accentuating the self-realization of Freedom as substantive, is not without significance, although Hegel does not immediately stress its implications. He insists that the means used are phenomenal, sensuous, and worldly. Human action results from need, interests, and passion. Ideas are of "little mass" in human affairs.[9] The power of the passions "lies in the fact that they respect none of the limitations that justice and morality would impose upon them. These natural forces have a more immediate influence on men than the artificial and tedious discipline that aims at order and self-restraint, law and morality.[10] Hegel's polemic is directed against those whose formal moralism negates the particularity of the contradictory structures of the historical world. He replies to Rousseau's complaint that historians always fasten on periods of violence, misery, and antagonism: "World history is not the scene of happiness. Periods of happiness are blank pages in it. They are periods of harmony, when opposition is lacking."[11] This assertion is consistent with the originary structure of the Hegelian *Geschichtlichkeit*. The rejection of happiness and of harmony in favor of natural force and pasion fits the thrust of the rest of his introduction.

At the same time, the inquiry into the means used to achieve the end suggests that Hegel may be adding a dimension that threatens the immanent structure of his system. His argument is sometimes highly nuanced, but at other moments it lends itself to caricature.

Hegel's polemic is developed at some length before he comes to its theoretical foundation. He attacks the attitude that hesitates and doubts the possibility of choosing the right and the good because the multitude of relative rights and goods make it seem an injustice to privilege one over the other. This attitude is the result of "laziness of mental reflection...which gives the mind so little to do that its only occupation can be to pass its time in this sort of moral self-adulation."[12] The professors of morality come under fire. After commenting on the fates of Alexander, Caesar, and Napoleon, Hegel cries out: "This fearful consolation, that historical men have not enjoyed what is called happiness (of which only private life is capable), may be drawn from history by those who need it. It is craved by envy, vexed at what is great and transcendent, striving therefore to deprecate it and to find some flaw in it."[13] This passage continues with the famous observation that if no one is a hero to his valet this only explains why the valet has remained a valet. The underlying principle on which the polemic rests was asserted a moment before:

> We draw back at last from the intolerable disgust with which these sorrowful reflections threaten us into the more agreeable environment of our individual life...we retreat into the selfishness that stands on the quiet shore from which, in safety, we enjoy the distant spectacle of "wrecks confusedly hurled." But even when History is regarded as the slaughter-bench at which the happiness of peoples, the wisdom of states, and the virture of individuals has been sacrificed, the question necessarily arises: to what principle, to what final goal, these enormous sacrifices have been offered.

The "necessity" that founds this reflection is explained by the fact that history is the field of "those great collisions between existing, acknowledged duties, laws and rights and those possibilities which are opposed to this fixed system."[14] The ground of the necessity lies in the originary structure of *Sittlichkeit* to which attention was already called. The difficulties encountered in that discussion return here in a different form.

Hegel's attempt to clarify the "principle" to which are offered the "enormous sacrifices" that are the thread of History takes him to a path dictated by the Cunning of Reason and walked by the World Historical Individual. Hegel's recourse to metaphor instead of concept can be explained, if not justified. Hegel describes the World Historical Individual as having "no consciousness of the philosophical Idea while acting" on his goals. He is a "practical and political" person who "had an insight into the requirements of the time." These requirements are specified in a nonpragmatic manner as "what was ripe for development [*an der Zeit*]." To make perfectly clear the theoretical premises of his assertion Hegel adds that this "truth for their age" was "already formed in the inner nature of that world."[15] This potential brought to realization might be interpreted along the lines of the account of the essential *Geschichtlichkeit* that the Hegelian *Sittlichkeit* attempts to concretize. The World Historical Individual brings to explicit self-consciousness the historical structure. This role is later, and more adequately, attributed to the state or to philosophy itself. Another interpretation is more important in the present context. Hegel returns to the World Historical Individual at the end of the introduction. He criticizes those who stand in the way of "that which the advance of the Idea of Spirit makes necessary." They may stand higher in individual moral *(moralischem)* worth than those whose crimes have been turned into the means of realizing the purposes of a superior principle. Nonetheless, it is the latter (persons and principle) which counts in History. Curiously, although such concerns are irrelevant to the movement of history, the World Historical deeds are even said to be justified "also from the point of view of the secular moralist."[16] Hegel does not explain this last assertion. The principle from which his argument started seems to rule out any such justification. "What the absolute final goal of Spirit requires and accomplishes, what Providence does, transcends the obligations, the imputation and ascription of good or bad ethical motives to individuals."[17] This is the point at which the caricatural Hegel appears. The addition of a "logic" of historical development elaborated across another metaphor does not help to resolve the normative idealism present in this argument.

Hegel's presentation of the Cunning of Reason complements the role attributed to the World Historical Individual. The two images might be taken as the poles of the genetic and the normative, the phenomenological and the logical. When the Kantian assertion of a lawful regularity seen by the "state sciences" is recalled, Hegel's argument appears to be only an a posteriori rationalization. A few illustrations from the body of Hegel's *Philosophy of History* show the kind of difficulty this theory confronts. With regard to the decline of feudalism, Hegel observes that "At that moment another technical means against the superiority of the weapons [of the nobility] was found—gunpowder. Humanity needed it, and so it was quickly there. It was the chief means in the freeing of man from physical power and in the equalization of the Estates. With the difference of the weapons disappeared also the difference among masters and servants." A polemic against those who romaticize the days gone by when battle was immediate and individual follows. Gunpowder demands a "modern" kind of courage without personal passion. Sacrifice in battle is now for the sake of the universal. Cultivated, modern nations do not depend on physical strength but abstract understanding.[18] These passages are not isolated instances from non-systematic texts. Hegel returns to the invention of firearms in the *Philosophy of Right* (para. 328, Remark) when he analyses the relation of the individual to the state in international relations. His justification was expressed already in the present introduction. "The particular is for the most part of too little value as compared with the universal. Individuals are sacrificed and abandoned. The Idea pays the penalty for having given itself determinant existence [*Dasein*]...not from itself but from the passions of individuals."[19] Hegel's approach is based on the image of a self-realizing essentialism that comes to know itself only through its appearance in the transitory world. This is the theory of normative constitution that tempts Hegel. It is the basis of what is usually called his "idealism." Systematic grounds can explain why this simplification tempted Hegel.

The Cunning Reason and the World Historical Individual are present although unnamed in the structure of the *Philosophy of Right*. Its introduction stresses (para. 2) that the science of right is only "a part of philosophy." This means that the definition of right cannot be provided within the science itself. The implication of this externality is drawn in the polemic (para. 3) against the historical school of law. The apparent self-limitation of the science of right turns quickly into the opposite. Hegel's first objection against the attempt to make legal norms depend on the real material conditions in which they were formulated is well taken. His sarcastic remark that many such accepted laws were in fact imposed by brute external force is factually true. The argument becomes problematic when Hegel comes to explain the principle justifying his polemic. Monasteries, for example, may have had a proper purpose and function. Time has now rendered them obsolete and no longer "right." Hegel generalizes this argument. "A particular law may be shown to be wholly grounded in and consistent with the circumstances and with existing legally established institutions, and yet it may be wrong and irrational in its essential character, like a number of provisions or Roman private law." The self-limited science of right is now sitting as the judge of World History itself. History and Reason are apparently identified. The external definition of right is transformed from a limit to a license. The science of right is integrated into the rush of World History and serves as its "Court."

The method described in the introduction to the *Philosophy of Right* parallels the structure of the *Logic*. The subject of right is the will. Will must be self-related and thus autonomous. A free will excludes determination by external factors. This autonomy is bought at the price of indeterminacy, loss of content, abstractness. Such negative freedom may contradict its own good intention, since "only in destroying something does this negative will possess the feeling of itself as existent" (para 5, Remark). Abstract freedom cannot accept particularity, difference, or institutional concreteness. In its passive form, it becomes the "fanaticism" of Hindu contemplation. In its active manifestation, it becomes the Terror of the French Revolution whose theoretical premises were articulated in the Constitution of 1793. This negative freedom of the will can have a positive character as well. Freedom defines the specificity of the human. The negative effects of its self-maintenance are supplemented when it gets content and a goal. In this second moment, the self-related will is seen to be also a particular will. Willing something involves the will in the finite, limited, and unfree world. At the same time, this act of willing makes it actually exist. Hegel presents the manner in which these poles of abstract universality and particularity are brought to explicit unification without the sacrifice of either. This is possible only if the structured institutional relation of freedom to freedom is accepted explicitly by the will. The institutional freedom in which the free will finds its realization cannot be accidental or the product of external intervention. Although such a systematic structure fits the pattern of the originary, the source of difficulty and temptation is seen in Hegel's comment, at the end of the introduction, that the place of the philosopher is merely to observe the process taking place (*wir wollen nur zusehen*, para. 32, Addition). This confirms the methodological parallel to the *Logic*. The integration of the system of right into the structure of World History results from the inability to have philosophy—and politics—play any but a passive role. There is no place for the *Zutat* that would make the system complete.

The difference from the *Logic* is that the starting point of the *Philosophy of Right* is said to be external to the system. The concept of right is redefined (in paragraph 4) as the will, whose essential nature is to be free. Hegel offers two rather different justifications of this presupposed freedom. His Remark to this paragraph refers to the *Encyclopaedia* which shows how "subjective Spirit" passes through the moments of an immediate and natural anthropology to a self-mediating phenomenology, before psychology finally shows it to be self-determining and thus free. The Addition to this same paragraph offers a different explanation. Freedom is fundamental to Spirit just as weight is fundamental to matter. This is an unsatisfactory stipulative justification of the equation of the concept of right (paragraph 2) with the freedom of the will (paragraph 4). The *Encyclopaedia's* argument is only apparently more successful. The will in "subjective Spirit" is a particular will, like the one Hegel criticizes in Rousseau and Kant. This individual will is also the subject of the Abstract Right and Morality with which the *Philosophy of Right* begins. The concrete development of these abstract moments is shown to presuppose the presence of *Sittlichkeit*. The implication is that the unnamed and unadmitted starting point of the *Philosophy of Right* is *Sittlichkeit*. This systematic structure might be integrated into the machinery of World History at the end of the theory. The other possibility, suggested previously, is that its structure in fact demands the political *Zutat* that was lacking at the end of the introduction to the *Philosophy of Right*.

The temptation toward a normative theory of constitution is never explicit in Hegel's system. Its basic structure emerges from the attempt to make sense of the metaphors of the World Historical Individual and the Cunning of Reason. The theory of history begins from the concrete, material, and passionate means by which Freedom seeks to realize itself. This corresponds to a phenomenological method. The presupposition of such a phenomenological approach is a logic. That logic is presented in the form of the Cunning of Reason. When this image proves unsatisfactory, the methodological orientation is changed. A logical approach is attempted, both in the introduction to the *Philosophy of History* and in the *Philosophy of Right*, whose problematic interrelation was examined in the previous chapter. The methodological presupposition of such a logic is a phenomenological movement to be observed. The World Historical Individual serves this purpose. The difficulties in both the historical phenomenology and the rational logical interpretation of history suggest an explicitly systematic approach. The concept of right and its stipulation as the free will appear to unite both methods. The difficulty is that this starting point has not been justified. The ground that explains the beginning of the *Philosophy of Right* is the ambiguous notion of *Sittlichkeit*. To clear up its difficulty, explicit methodological reflection is necessary. Without that methodology, the temptation is to see *Sittlichkeit* as that onrushing World History that sweeps the system into its train. This History, in turn, becomes the secular theodicy of that freedom that "realizes itself" at the price of the particular, which is "of too little value" compared to it.

MARX'S THEORY OF GENETIC CONSTITUTION

From the point of view of the system, the revolutionary theory of Marx seeks to ground a philosophical-political *Zutat*.

As with Hegel's idealism, the caricatural aspects of the materialist theory of history are not an invention of Marx's critics. The result of a systematic materialist theory of history is the opposite of what Marx intended. The *Zutat* is replaced by a contemplative *Zusehen.* The theory becomes an idealist genetic constitution. These parallels to the Hegelian structure are not accidental. Hegel's constitutive temptation had three possible forms. It might make the phenomenological presupposition of a logic that guarantees the necessity and completeness of the path it describes. It might begin from the logical approach which assumes that an active agent insures that the system does necessarily what the logic only shows to be possible. The unity of these two orientations into a system presupposes a *Sittlichkeit* whose guarantee of the nonaccidental nature of the starting point insures the completeness and necessity of the system itself. The Marxian parallel to the phenomenological orientation privileges the logic of a material infrastructure that guarantees the necessary objective and subjective conditions for the success of revolution. A second Marxian approach articulates the role of the learning process in labor in order to avoid the logical determinism to which the first orientation leads. This anthropological strategy parallels the one-sidedness of the economic assumption. The attempt to conceive their unity is expressed in the *Communist Manifesto's* "spector" haunting European history and concretized in the notion that "all history is the history of class struggle." Class struggle is portrayed as unifying the subjective phenomenological with the objective logical priorities. This conceptual framework dissolves history's particularity into the framework of a system. The parallel to Hegel's dissolution of system into history is obvious.

The preface to *Toward a Critique of Political Economy* (1859) presents a succinct statement of the theoretical logic that justifies Marx's revolutionary expectations. After a verbal rejection of the Hegelianism of his youth, Marx begins from a straightforward statement of the reductionist base/superstructure model:

> In the social production of their existence, men enter into determined relations that are necessary and independent of their will. These relations of production correspond to a given degree of the development of the material forces of production.[20]

The material forces of production engender determined and necessary relations. These determined and necessary relations act on the will from which they are independent. Subjective and objective necessity are described within a systematic structure. The definition of the "real foundation" on which intersubjectively binding institutions are built apparently is quite simple. This simplified interpretation poses problems because it withdraws from the systematic articulation.

> The totality of these relations forms the economic structure of society, the real foundation on which a juridical and political edifice is built, and to which correspond determinant forms of social consciousness. The mode of production of material life generally dominates the development of social, political, and intellectual life. It is not the consciousness of men that determines their existence; on the contrary, it is their social existence that determines their consciousness.

The systematic reading suggests that the "totality of these relations" means both the forces and the relations of production. The real foundation thus has both an objective and a subjective component. The machines, buildings, and technology as well as the social relations among the producers themselves are treated as productive factors. The advantage of this systematic suggestion is that it avoids the danger of an objectivist determinism. The disadvantage is that the determinism is nonetheless explicitly affirmed in the simple words of the passage.

The determinism that treats consciousness as a dependent variable implies that conscioúness and social existence are in an external and causal relation. Such a structure of externality cannot guarantee necessity. This is why the reductionist argument is used to account for the necessary advent of revolution. Marx develops it from an aspect of the last passage. The "social existence" that "determines their consciouness" must have a structure that leads necessarily to the desired subjective results. Without such a demonstration, subjective action would be accidental or impossible.

> At a certain degree of their development, the material forces of production of society enter into collision with the existing relations of production, or with the property relations within which they had hitherto moved and

> which are their juridical expression. Only yesterday a form of development of the productive forces, these conditions change into heavy weights. Then begins the era of social revolution.

This elaboration retreats from the systematic assertion that the real foundation includes both the relations and the forces of production. The relations of production become an external "juridical expression" that must be transformed causally by the infrastructure when the two come into conflict. The demonstration is logically unconvincing, historically misleading, and politically wrong. It presupposes that the infrastructure determines the juridical superstructure. This means that any conflict between the two must of course be decided in favor of the former. The argument is modeled apparently on a picture of the transition from feudalism to capitalism. Even if the picture were historically valid, the model of socialist revolution should be different. The carrier of that socialist revolution is not the representative of a new mode of production like the rising bourgoisie. The receptivity of the bourgeoisie to the "social existence" that determines their consciouness can be understood. Marx has not shown why the proletariat would be receptive to the same social existence. His description of the beginning of the "era of social revolution" does not guarantee the necessary success of that revolution.

An awareness of these systematic necessities is nonetheless present in Marx's text. He knows that the ideological capitalist thinks of the worker as a laboring animal calculating his interests like the vulgar economist. This permits Marx to make a methodological distinction that tries to take account of the difficulty.

> The change in the economic foundation is accompanied by a more or less rapid upheaval in all of that enormous edifice. When one considers these upheavals, one must always distinguish two orders of things. There is the material upheaval of the conditions of economic production. It must be studied in the rigorous spirit of the natural sciences. But there are also the juridical, political, religious, artistic, and philosophical—in a word, the ideological—forms in which men become aware of this conflict and press it to the end.

Reduction is now given a specific and justified methodological place in the analysis. Consciousness of a situation is distinguished from the causal scientific knowledge of its reality. Marx even gives an active, independent role to consciousness which will "press...to the end" the conflict structured by the base. Yet the next lines make explicit that this distinction is still made within the context of a reductionist definition of ideology.

> One does not judge an individual in terms of the idea that he has of himself. One does not judge a revolutionary epoch according to the consciousness it has of itself. That consciousness, rather, will be explained by the contradictions of material life, by the conflict that opposes the social productive forces and the relations of production.

The abruptness of this move away from systematic concern is not justified by the fact that Marx is describing a "revolutionary epoch." The immanent historicity of modern social relations makes them necessarily conflictual. Capitalism for Marx is always ripe for revolution. The observation that both the "social productive forces" and the "relations of production" contain a human, practical element that contrasts with the material determinism that is studied "in the rigorous spirit of the natural sciences" does not avoid the diffculty. Such a distinction is possible only from the standpoint of an external observer separated from the social relations. That assumption was seen to be characteristic of a misunderstanding of ideology.

The implicit systematic concern is the only way to explain positively the grounds of the repeated reductionist temptation. Marx's own explicit justification adapts elements familiar from both Kant's and Hegel's failed constitutive approaches. He begins with a "Kantian" suggestion. "A society never disappears before all the productive forces that it can obtain have been developed." No justification is offered for such a teleology. It appears in retrospect that old societies develop to the full before they expire. This explains nothing. By definition any further potential is never developed, since these societies have disappeared. The argument continues in a more "Hegelian" vein.

> Superior relations of production are never developed before the material conditions of their existence have arisen in the very womb of the old society. That is why humanity never gives itself any tasks but those that it can accomplish: If we look carefully at things, we see that the task always arises where the material conditions of its relaization have already formed or are in the process of creating themselves. Reduced to their general lines, the asiatic, antique, feudal, and modern bourgeois modes of production appear as the progressive epochs in the economic formation of society.

The nearly caricatural "freedom-as-the-recognition-of-necessity" is troubling in these phrases. The assertion that humanity never gives itself tasks that it cannot accomplish is either an undemonstrable determinism or an a posteriori truism. The image of changes being prepared "in the very womb of the old society" suggests the kind of structure to which Kant's constitutive philosopher had recourse in the ninth thesis of "Cosmopolitan History." Marx's concluding lines return to the systematic question of why these material conditions necessitate a "revolutionary practice" that can rid itself of the "muck of the ages."

> The bourgeois relations of production are the last antagonistic form of the social process of production. It is not a question here of an individual antagonism. We understand it, rather, as the product of the social conditions of the existence of individuals. At the same time, the productive forces that develop in the womb of capitalism create the material conditions necessary to resolve that antagonism. With this social system, the prehistory of human society comes to an end.

Social conditions and material conditions are assumed to develop parallel to one another. Their eventual revolutionary intersection is not explained. The midwife or doctor who could bring the lightning of thought that catalyzes the expected collision is absent. The kind of true history that would follow our prehistory cannot be spelled out with systematic certainty. Marx elsewhere stresses the end of exploitation, want, and self-alienation. In the systematic context of the Marxian material reduction, such a utopia can only mean the complete domination of the economic infrastructural logic over all aspects of life. But that is just what market capitalism tries, in its own way, to accomplish!

Marx's materialist reduction nonetheless demonstrates the systematic basis of his politics. The proletariat is the revolutionary subject-object whose full self-realization will overcome finally the antagonism of past history. Marx was seen to arrive at this insight after his philosophical development ruled out any external source of change. This characterized his approach as modern. A theory that tries to bring change from without is a theory *for* revoltuion. It is an instrument applied to a separate reality. This is the structure of the reductionist model, whose form makes praxis impossible or dangerous. It supposes the existence of an absolute standpoint outside the social conditions that are judged. It implies that the totality of the material world can be known. Hegel had criticized by anticipation such a "proud position":

> It is easier to discover deficiency in individual, in states and in Providence than to see positive actual import and value. For in this merely negative fault finding, a proud position is taken [*man steht vornehm über der Sache*]—one which overlooks the object without having entered into it, without having comprehended its positive aspect.[21]

From the transcendent position, the world appears as a series of interacting points that can be charted scientifically on a tableau. The implication of this standpoint is not only misleading but dangerous, as the third of the *Theses on Feuerbach* already suggested. It permits one group (scientists, technocrats, the Party) to claim to possess the truth about and for the others. The result is a despotism that claims to be enlightened. Marx tries to avoid this implication by developing a theory *of* revolution. The proletariat *is* the immanent self-critique of capitalism. Its dual nature as conscious actor and objective product of an artificial system questions the validity of capitalist relations of exploitation at the same time that it accounts for the genesis of these same relations. Such a theory of the proletariat is at once a theory *of* capitalism and a theory *of* revolution. It does not bring norms from outside, nor does it offer tools for application to a separate reality. The revolutionary wants to overcome ideological capitalism. This goal, paradoxically, is the same as the aim of the capitalist. Both are attracted to the logic of material historical development because the proletariat is central to their concerns—as threat or as hope. Their errors are complementary. The capitalist stresses the genetic, the revolutionary the normative. The result in both cases is a theory of constitution.

A different interpretation of Marx's systematic goals can be developed from the idea that the logic of revolution is based on a theory *of* the proletariat. The logical basis for the necessity of revolution then is complemented by a phenomenological stress on the learning process by which the revolutionary subject becomes capable of transforming itself and society. Determinism is avoided by a more anthropological concentration on the learning subject. This approach can be reconstructed in Marx's development from the young Hegelian cirticism of religion to the discovery and elaboration of the structure of the revolutionary proletariat. The "left" Hegelian critique of religion was ultimately more radical that the practical political liberalism of the orthodox Hegelians. The critique of religion questioned the ability of the system to account for the unity of genesis and normativity in the actuality of the rational.[22] This criticism went beyond the Enlightenment attitude typified by Schiller's assertion that "man paints himself in his Gods."[23] The Enlightenment approach suggests that the mystifications of religion have an external causal basis. It wants to eliminate religion, just as the logical Marx wanted to eliminate capitalism. The "invertive method" *(Umkehrungsmethode)* proposed by Feuerbach and applied by Marx makes necessary an activism that the Enlightenment cannot explain. Social conditions prevent man from realizing the good life his human dignity demands. The heaven he projects is the transfigured substance of his earthly need and desire. The "invertive method" reappropriates the possitive content of these projections. Marx applied it to the Hegelian system itself in the *1844 Manuscripts* when he seized for his own purposes "what is great in Hegel's *Phenomenology*." This is the first step in leaving the "proud position" for an immanent modern critique.

The application of the invertive criticism that permitted Marx's discovery of the proletariat also demonstrates why its recursive application does not lead to an infinite regress or a relativism. Marx begins from the social basis of religion, which is "the premise of all critique." A further invertive or "irreligious critique" is then based on the premise that "man makes religion, religion does not make man." This invertive turn to an anthropological foundation is followed by a third inversion based on the fact that man is not an abstract being "squatting outside the world." This returns Marx to the social world. He draws his first conclusion in a letter published in the *Deutsch-Franzözische Jahrbücher.* Feuerbach is said to be "insufficiently political." Marx's political counterproposal comes two years later, in the fourth of the *Theses on Feuerbach.* The irreligious knowledge that the secular family is the secret of the Holy Family demands the *real* destruction of that family so that the mystifying cycle does not begin anew. The necessity of this real political intervention is not yet justified theoretically. Marx, like Kant, saw the need to "educate the educators," but he had not shown how and why this education would take place. The politics in this fourth thesis are still accidental and external. The demonstration of political necessity must show why the invertive regress cannot continue indefinitely. Its premise was apparent in the invertive critique of religion. Religion was labeled the "opium of the people." But Marx added that this opiate is also an active protest against the contitions in which it arises. The positive implications of this activity are developed in *The German Ideology.* Roman society may appear to be regulated by its legal system, the Middle Ages by the Church Universal. Yet neither laws nor religion can be eaten. The production and reproduction of the means of physical existence is the basis on which all else rests. This basis is portrayed by an anthropological description of laboring production that contrasts sharply with the "rigorous spirit of the natural sciences" proposed in the 1859 preface.

The logic of the material infrastructure is given a phenomenological foundation by this invertive turn to laboring humanity as its foundation. Laboring humanity constitutes itself through a dialectical development. New techniques of labor produce new needs, which in turn call for the invention of further new techniques. A merciless polemic is built from the sometimes subtly brilliant phenomenological first section of *The German Ideology.*[24] Its theoretical kernel can be seen in an argument that points toward the future direction of Marx's work.

> As individuals externalize their lives, so are they. What they are thus falls together with their production, both of *what* they produce as well as with *how* they produce. Therefore, what individuals are depends on the material conditions of their production.

The temptation to economic reduction is evident in retrospect. The logic of the infrastructure presented in the preface to *Toward a Critique* could follow these passages immediately. Marx's theoretical innovation here appears in the stress on "how" production takes place. This could point toward the "relations of production" which ultimately become one of the systematic infrastructural "forces of production" in the preface. Yet the first lines of this passage have a phenomenological basis that points in a different direction. They give to the priority of the infrastructure an anthropological mediation that avoids an external or causal argument. The result can be seen in a passage from volume 3 of *Capital.*

> On the same economic base...innumerable different empirical conditions—natural conditions, racial relations, external historical influences, etc.—can produce an infinite number of variations and gradations in the form of appearance, which can only be understood by the analysis of these given empirical conditions.

Engels drew the implications of this argument when he rejected the reductionism of Marx's followers. The economic base is determinant, he said, "only in the last instance." The phenomenological mediation that completes the systematic logical structure gives flexibility to the apparently formal and determinist structure of the base. The reductionism is more subtle and systematic than it appeared at first glance.

The systematic imperative explains why Marx apparently left this phenomenological approach from which he began his analysis of modern civil society. The phenomenological and the logical approaches need one another in order to demonstrate completeness and necessity. The passage from *Capital, Volume 3,* demonstrating flexibility was preceded by a more determinist assertion:

> "It is always the immediate relation of the owner of the conditions of production to the immediate producers—a relation whose specific form always corresponds naturally

> to a specific state of development of the mode and manner of labor and to the social productive forces—in which we find the deepest secret, the hidden basis of the entire social construction..."(italics omitted)

This explains why Marx spoke of the "infinite number of variations and gradations" as only an "appearance." It also explains why Engels adds to the determination "in the last instance" the qualification that statistical correlations show that the priority of the economic really can be demonstrated.[25] The phenomenological approach attempts to avoid the external and causal aspects of the reductionism. It cannot replace the logical recourse to the infrastructural necessities because their force is what gives direction to a laboring learning that would otherwise be accidental or capricious. The unity of these two approaches is captured in the *Communist Manifesto's* insistance that "All history is the history of class struggle."

The advantages of the systematic theory of history are negated by a methodological flaw in its construction. The systematic structure explains many apparently ambiguous or even self-contradictory assertions in Marx's works. The model of such phrases is the beginning of the *Eighteenth Brumaire.* "Men make their own history," says Marx, but "not as they please." Class struggle is both logical and phenomenological. It is made possible by specific material conditions, which can also be invoked to explain its necessity. Class struggle also demands active perception of these material possibilities by a collective subject. The abstract level of the description conceals its weakness. The abstraction, "class struggle," is intended to designate a concrete actuality.[26] The theory of universal history built on it in fact eliminates history. The central contradicition is present from the outset. The structure of its solution is presupposed. History is a recombination of pregiven elements into apparently different figures. The stages are preordained. The motor is always the same. Lack of success is explained as a necessary phase in a process of ripening. Discontinuity, change, or irrationality are reduced to appearances of an underlying necessity. The necessity may be built logically into the material infrastructure. It may be grounded phenomenologically in the theories of alienation or laboring learning. The difference between the two approaches is only verbal. The methodological premise is that real history actually will come to an end with the unification brought about by the proletariat. The class struggle in its immanent ambivalence is only verbally the motor of Marx's theory of revolution. The real motor is the proletariat as a constitutive agent.

The methodolgocial error underlying the systematic theory of history is demonstrated in Marxian practice. The actual political difficulties need only brief and abstract mention. The pretention that the Party speaks in the name and place of the proletariat is the most familiar form. The logical justification of its claim is its greater knowledge of the real infrastructural conditions. The phenomenological position points to the Party as the subjective component that brings the logical necessity to its conclusion. A series of further figures can be sketched. The reformist belief that "conditions are not yet ripe" is the logical correlate to the phenomenological insistence that revolutionary will only be formed in struggle. The same logical insight into "conditions" can justify the revolutionist's opposition to the phenomenological stress on the reformist parliamentary learning process. More telling than the practical political difficulties is the theoretical practice of Marxism. Its central element is the theory of history. Study of the material infrastructure can proceed to dizzying detail comparable to the anecdotal remembrance of battles past. The theory must crystallize finally in the history of the proletariat itself. The methodological error presents first the obvious difficulty in establishing the relation of priority or necessity between facts and agent. This is not specific to Marxism. More significant is the nature of the project itself. *A Marxian history of the proletariat is not possible.* The proletariat is constituted logically by the material conditions and phenomenologically by its struggles with other classes. The very thought of writing its history reveals the presupposition on which, finally, the methodological error is based. A history of the proletariat is only possible if the proletariat—not the class struggle—is the agent of history. Such a presupposition implies a constitutive theory of history that breaks with the modern. A Marxian history of the proletariat can only be a history of modernity itself.

CHAPTER 5

The Logic of Receptivity

ONTOLOGY AND METHOD

Ontology and method are interdependent but not identical. Their relation can be presented from the standpoint of either. The difficulties of a constitutive theory explain the necessity of a distinct methodolgocial articulation of the structure of originary philosophy. The constitutive temptation conceals the necessary independence of methodological considerations. From the side of method, an ontological orientation presents a parallel error. This orientation treats its objects at so general and abstract a level that the specificity of distinct theoretical domains cannot be analyzed. Method is replaced by theory. Categories like genesis and normativity, the originary structure, or the modern principle of immanence cannot be imposed arbitrarily on any and every subject and object.[1] Categorical difference cannot be overlooked in the (justified) philosophical concern that subject and object be explicitly homogeneous to one another. A philosophical method must be able to articulate the grounds of its applicability and the domain to which it necessarily must be applied.

The presentation of method has two phases. The first demonstrates the conditions that ground the receptivity of the object domain to the categories proposed by philosophy. This explains *how* the application is possible. Its corollary is the delimitation of those particular objects that are not only possibly but necessarily the objects of the philosophical system. This orientation focuses on *what* method does. This second concern is present negatively within the analysis of receptivity, where it sets limits on the ontological temptation. Its presence parallels the immanence of the political in originary philosophy. The resulting method has the generality and justification of a philosophical system as well as the specificity that permits its application and adaptation to particular structures and their principles. The how and the what assure necessity and completeness. They recapitulate the phenomenological need for an active *Zutat* and the logical structure permitting the pure *Zusehen*.

The constitutive orientation conflated method with philosophy; the ontological temptation transforms method into an ontological system. This tempation appears in the philosophical structure presented by Kant, Hegel, and Marx. Kant's hesitation as to whether the *Critique of Pure Reason* is to be understood as system or method was overcome implicitly by the distinction of doctrine and critique in the preface to the *Critique of Judgment.* Kant did not himself spell out the implications of this distinction. The generalization of method as ontology is given a consciously modern form by both Hegel and Marx. The ontological foundation and its external articulation are shown to be mutually interdependent. The articulation is the necessary expression of its ontological foundation. This articulation makes the ontological foundation complete by bringing it to self-reflective transparency. This dual structure is present in Hegel's phenomenological as well as his logical approach. It reaffirms from the point of view of method the interdependence of the two orientations from which the description of originary philosophy began. A similar structure appears in Marx's repeated efforts to demonstrate adequately the necessity and possibility of modern revolution. The attempt to explain the secret of civil society through the logic of alienated labor develops toward the assertion that history is the product of class struggle. It results finally in the articulation of the immanently self-contradictory capitalist mode of production. Each phase demonstrates a necessity whose full articulation in political practice produces a reflective completeness that explains the rationality of the resulting struggle. In each case the interrelation and interdependence of the ontological ground and its articulation eliminates the need for independent methodological considerations. The basis of this rejection of the independence of method is that the ontological system remains within the framework of immanence because the ontological ground it articulates is explicitly historical. Such a dependence of method on ontology becomes problematic when a second criterion of the modern is recalled. The reduction to the presupposed external agent is avoided by means of an abusive unification that dissolves the difference instead of resolving it. This error is symmetrical to the constitutive temptation's solution to the tension of the modern. Rather than solve the problem it dissolves it. The difference between method and ontology must be maintained at the same time that the philosophical foundation of the method is preserved. This relationship of independent interdependence expresses another aspect of the structure of the modern, to whose conditions of possibility the constitutive temptation referred.

The dependence and difference of originary philosophy and its method explain why the category "epistemology" is not appropriate to describe the method. The philosophical articulation raises questions of method. It explains why and how they come about. It does not pretend to answer them. The answers do not come in epistemological reconstructions of the "philosophy of ______" a given discipline. That would presuppose that the philospher can stand outside an already constituted and finalized body of knowledge. The philosopher is not armed with a value-free vision permitting immediate contact with the really real. Nor is philosophy an unchanging normative system against which a discipline is measured (and inevitably found wanting). The process by which a field of study becomes self-reflective is typically modern. This result cannot be introduced from outside, by philosophic decision or political command. Hegel and Marx illustrate the positive form of the relation of method and its object. For Hegel, the self-alienation *(sich entäussern)* of the originary structure grounds explicitly and reflectively the necessity and completeness of the philosophical foundation. For Marx, class struggle or the activity of the Party is the external articulation that permits the conscious transformation of a "class-in-itself" to the revolutionary "class-for-itself." The relation of the external articulation and the originary basis is that of method to theory. When their difference is maintained successfully, a further danger must still be avoided. The methodological moment can be neither the dominant nor the subordinate aspect of the relation. The temptation is to opt for one or the other. This structural danger explains why the problem of receptivity is less serious for Hegel, while the problem of particularity is less difficult for Marx. Hegel tends to give priority to the philosphical over the methodological moment whereas Marx's revolutionary class struggle stresses the political aspect of the relation. Kant's distinction of *critique* and *doctrine* suggests a method that avoids one-sidedness without the reduction to epistemology.

An implication of the philosophical independence and dependence of the method on the originary structure draws it toward the political. As modern, method is not applied to a pregiven real world; nor does it constitute the domain of objects on which it acts. This means that method is inevitably engaged in and active on the world. The result is a constant tempation to conflate method and politics.[2] The intervention of a subject on an object, or the production of an instrument, not be premodern in this specific case need. The externality is only an appearance which cannot maintain the fixity and permanence typical of the classical paradigm of a premodern philosophy. The originary *Geschichtlichkeit* insures that the externality is caught up and transformed by the modern dynamic. The phenomenological *Gestalten* portrayed in Hegel's *Phenomenology* or in Marx's historical writings are misunderstood if they are treated as independent effects of (intentional or structural) actions. The inverse but isomorphic structure is presented by the logical orientation toward method. The temptation to treat method as a real intervention is the structural result of a constitutive phenomenology; the temptation to treat it as the effect of structural necessity is the result of an essentialist logic. In both cases, the misunderstanding of the originary foundation of method transforms its independent status. Method becomes political. This conflation is no more fruitful for understanding politics than it is for specifying the tasks and the nature of method. The relation of politics to method manifests the same structure of dependence and independence present in the relation of philosophy and method. The political orientation of method is still implicit and negative in the account of conditions of receptivity. The discussion of particularity makes it explicit and positive. The shift toward politics within the domain of method parallels the move within the originary philosophy in the same direction. The need to prove not only necessity but completeness threatens to transform the philospher's *Zutat* from a form of representation into an action on a reality separate from it. The account of method as independent is necessary to avoid this fall back into premodern categories.

The demonstration that and why the modern world is receptive to the categorical structure described as originary can be circumscribed and identified by the task Kant assigned the transcendental critique. The "conditions of the possibility" of an object are also the conditions that explain why and how rational categories can be applied to the empirical manifold of the sense data that comprise the domain of application. The difference from a premodern transcendental philosophy is explained by the originary structure whose immanence excludes a tabular representation of the application of categories to a pregiven neutral surface. The critical method is applied to a domain whose structure is explicitly historical *(geschichtlich).* As methodological, the critque makes explicit the originary results at which systematic philosophical reflection arrived by other means. The results of philosphy are confirmed at the threshhold of the turn to method. The difference between Kant and Hegel/Marx is significant at this level of argument. Kant's critical system uncovers the structure of historicity. This is why his historical writings are not a fourth *Critique.* Hegel and Marx begin from a real modern history that is originary. Their difficulties illustrate another way in which the ontologization of method pushes it toward the political. The originary historical foundation is treated as the real and ultimate base to which the method must be adequate. This structure becomes the ontological foundation of an epistemological "philosophy of ______." The result is the impossibility of determining the limits and the content of the domain to which the method is applicable. The relation between method and what it represents is not established. This temptation to treat method as determined by its object is the isomorphic error to the ontological presentation of method as determined by philosophy. In politics, the result is that Hegel treats the existent form of civil society as a real threat, while Marx presents it as the source of a real solution. Kant's politics are true to the modern precisely because he avoids this methodological error.

The ontological and political temptations immanent to the critical method specify a further dimension of the account of receptivity. The presentation must show how and why the empirical manifold is receptive to the rational categories. The resolution of the problem for the philosophy of science in the *Critique of Pure Reason* is epistemological and limited. Receptivity to the a priori categories of morality is not guaranteed by this approach, which can prove only that such moral categories are not contradictory to those of science. The *Foundations of the Metaphysics of Morals* and the *Critique of Practical Reason* fail to go beyond the epistemological orientation. Demonstration of only the possibility of receptivity is not sufficient systematically. Its necessity must be shown. The reflexivity developed in the *Critique of Judgment* provides the needed argument. The teleological orientation to nature and the reflective judgment that presents the beautiful and the sublime bring together two facets of receptivity that had not been specified previously. They add to the receptivity of the world and receptivity of the subject to the appeal from the world. This dual receptivity is not articulated fully in Hegel or in Marx for the symmetrical reasons already indicated. Hegel's methodology is philosphically determined; Marx's is determined politically. This explains why Hegel can account better for receptivity and Marx for particularity. Kant's explanation of this dual receptivity of the subject to the world and the world to the subject is not presented explicitly. This accounts for his temptation to an unmediated move to a theory of political from the *Critique of Judgment*.[3] Such an unmediated politics would be one-sided. Its claim is that the reflective judgment proves that subjectivity is necessarily intersubjectivity. Kant's own reflections on the problem of theory and praxis (to which Chapter 6 will turn) point to the necessary institutional mediation neglected by this claim. No more than it is independent of philosophy, method is not independent of the political. Nor are they identical.

The orientation of method to the conditions of receptivity cannot stand alone because of the structural tendencies to reduce it to ontology or to transform it into politics. The method that is valid universally is useless as a method. An account of where and how the categories are applied necessarily must be added to the demonstration that the categories are indeed applicable. This second moment of the method is separate from the first; both are distinct qualitatively from the philosophy that ultimately grounds them. The structural relation between the two moments is determined by method's mediating function between originary philosophy and the political. The account of particularity will present the political temptations immanent to its structure in the same way the philosophical ones are discovered in the account of receptivity. The Kantian theory of reflective judgment has to be supplemented by the explanation of its practical necessity. The Hegelian *Sittlichkeit* that conditions historical rationality must show also how the individual comes necessarily to experience this rationality. Marx's approach to history as ultimately revolutionary is incomplete without the actual agent who must bring its radical potential to fruition. Each of these supplementary accounts is only possible once the critical methodological demonstration of the conditions of receptivity has been offered. The relation of these two aspects of method repeats that between philosophy and its method. This means that the logical conditions of receptivity become ontological if they are not specified by the moment of phenomenological particularity. The presence of this second moment guarantees that the methodological account has an autonomous, modern structure. Method is the necessary mediation between philosophy and the political. Its two moments, which must remain separate, are united by the originary modern relation of each to the other.

The interdependence of these two moments of method clarifies the specificity and function of an originary method. The two distinct and complementary methodological chapters here parallel the distinction between the logical and phenomenological moments of originary philosophy. The adoption of these Hegelian terms here should not mislead. Kant's suggestion that the critique needed to be supplemented by a "doctrine" could have provided the categorial labels for the method. Kant's terms were avoided because their introduction would not only make too much of an unelaborated terminological distinction; it would also neglect the fact that nearly every major work of Marx is titled or subtitled "a critique." Marx had his own idea of the critical method and its logical foundation. His approach is closer to Hegel than to Kant. More important, Kant's passage from the critical to the doctrinal moves in the opposite direction from his successors. They tended to develop from the phenomenological toward a logical system that attempts to ground the particulars. This foundational orientation draws Hegel's method toward the theoretical; the same foundational concern points Marx toward the political. The basis of both of these concerns is the modern resistance to the idea that method is applied to an external and pregiven reality. Modern method cannot become either a theory of constitution or the product of an ontology. The result of either error would resolve only one aspect of the twin tasks of method. Such one-sidedness means that despite the attempt to remain within immanence, an unmodern presupposition is introduced. Thus, Hegel's system runs the risk of being unable to designate those particulars that are in fact actual and rational. His system tends to "accommodate" the existing *Sittlichkeit* at the expense of the historical structure that he himself articulates. Similarly, Marx's politics tends to be able to explain only after the fact why the world was receptive to the politics he proposes. His system tends to become a voluntarism in the present and a rationalization or post hoc justification of the past. The methodological moment must be given its independence, as Kant's path suggests implicitly.

Formulated simply, method designates problems. Solutions are proposed by theory or by politics. When either pretends to replace method, the result is either a theory of constitution or a generalizing ontology. Neither result replaces method. The correct modern resistance to a method applied to a presupposed external reality can itself mislead. This is the source of the error of Hegel and Marx. Neither theory nor politics are the totality of all that is. Each must be able to indicate explicitly its own limits. The designation of these limits is another expression of the problems method brings to explicit formulation. Kant recognized this methodological necessity by providing each of his *Critques* with a Transcendental Dialectic that points to the limits of what can be known. The foundation of Kant's Dialectic is human finitude. Man is bound to the merely phenomenal world. Philosophical Reason deceives itself when it tries to englobe reality in one sweep. At the same time, Reason must make this effort. The Kantian dualism and the epistemological approach to the *Critiques* are insufficient explanations of the independent place of methodological argument between theory and the political. The distinction between phenomena and noumena, between understanding and reason, between method and system is not elaborated satisfactorily in the presentation of the Dialectic as method. The *Critique of Judgment* is more useful in this context: The notion of a reflective judgment suggests a method that does not subject the real to an ontology or dissolve it by means of a theory of constitution. Not every particular object can be claimed as beautiful; not every effect is the product of the teleological self-maintenance of an organism. Reflective judgment limits philosophical pretensions and demands political expression. It is the key to an originary methodology.

Representation and Really Real

Kant's account of the dual nature of receptivity corrects a systematic incompleteness of the first two *Critiques.* Although the concept of a teleologically organized nature is not a contradiction from the standpoint of the first *Critique,* the necessity of this conceptual possibility must be demonstrated. Natural teleology remains noumenal for the first *Critique.* The Postulates of Pure Reason are made explicit in the second *Critique.* This sets the noumenal on the side of the laws of freedom. This shift still does not provide the demonstration of receptivity. A different approach to the ethical writings goes a step further. The *Foundations of the Metaphysics of Morals* presupposed a free moral reason whose transcendental logic it elaborated. The origin of this moral reason was not explained. Kant did not show why moral imperatives must be accepted necessarily by the individual. A similar difficulty faced the formally autonomous enlightened consciousness. The reflexive structure of the *Critique of Judgment* unites these two aspects of receptivity. It shows why the solution to each presupposes the solution to the other. The demonstration of the teleological reflexivity of nature is possible because the orign of moral concern can be explained. The origin of moral concern in turn depends on the teleological structure of nature. This demonstration avoids the reproach of tautology because its claims are limited explicitly to questions of method.

Kant's double concern is illustrated in the section of the *Critique of Judgment* that begins from the question whether things in nature can have a goalful or teleological organization (paragraphs 82-84). This discussion is located in the methodological appendix to the account of teleological judgment, as might be expected. Kant observes that the explanation why something exists can make use of the mechanical laws of the phenomenal world, or it can interpret the object as a means to achieve a goal. In the latter case, the goal explains why the thing exists. The situation is complicated, however, since men can use mechanical laws as the means to their ends. The question then arises whether there is an ultimate goal *(Endzweck)* of nature to which human goals are subordinate. The hierarchical chain in which each species serves to maintain the next higher one seems to suggest that all of nature exists for man, who is the only being capable of giving himself goals. The difficulty with this argument was suggested already by Linnaeus. The logic could be reversed: the "higher" species serves the "lower" by preventing overpopulation and self-destruction. The man who kills animals contributes to the survival of their species, which has to be paid in the coin of individual suffering. This argument recalls Kant's invocation of Nature's wisdom in "The Idea of History from a Cosmopolitan Point of View." It also recalls Hegel's Reason in History. Kant's concern with method leads him to suggest that although the concept of a teleologically organized nature is not contradictory, each instance that appears to prove its reality also can be explained mechanically. He concludes that unknowable ultimate goals cannot be demonstrated to exist. One may talk only of final goals *(letzten Zwecke).* Kant concludes that man is the "final goal of a teleologically organized nature." This demands clarification. Men posit goals. Man is the final goal of nature. The nature of the two types of goals depends on the relation of *real* nature to its goalfully organized representation.

The assumption that man is the final goal of nature can be interpreted from two distinct standpoints. The goal may be the product of nature. Its satisfaction and completeness are also produced by nature. In this case, man is simply another animal in the phenomenal world. Or, the goal could be represented as self-given, the result of autonomous, free choice. Since the notion of an ultimate goal has been eliminated, the self-given goal will not be noumenal. It is not independent from nature; yet as free, it is not wholly dependent on it. This was the structure suggested by the third thesis in "Cosmopolitan History." Nature willed that man produce what makes him distinct from the animal world. Kant proposes here to define natural goals as aiming at happiness *(Glückseligkeit).* Self-given goals are oriented to culture *(Kultur).* Kant does not reject happiness, nor does he eliminate it as mere instinct. He points to the problem, raised already by Rousseau. Happiness depends on the relation of a projected goal and its empirical realization in nature. Goals change continually as satisfied needs constantly engender new ones. There is no end to this natural dialectic. A solution depends on culture.[4] Culture is not the opposite of happiness but its completion. Culture is defined by the ability to set goals. This formal definition must be given content. The difficulty recalls the parallel problem from "Cosmopolitan History." Development is said to occur at the cost of inequalities that are "nonetheless bound up with the development of the natural capacities of the human species; and the goal of Nature herself, even if it is not our goal, is still reached in this manner." This assertion was introduced to explain the necessary emergence of a civil society and a cosmopolitan unity of states. It is inadequate as method, just as it was insufficient as philosophy.

A different approach can be drawn from these paragraphs by means of a comparison with the essay, "Concerning the Common expression: 'It's Fine in Theory But It Won't Work in Practice.'" Kant takes up the political problem of the justification of revolutionary practice.

> It will rather depend upon what human nature may do in and through us to *compel* us to follow a course we would not readily adopt by choice. We must look to nature alone, or rather *providence*...for a successful outcome which will first affect the whole and then the individual parts. The schemes of men, on the other hand, begin with the parts and frequently get no further than them.[5]

Practice must understand these "schemes of men," since Providence can neither be understood nor changed. Providence acts subsumptively, like predicative judgment. The task for practice is to develop a form of reflective judgment that will go necessarily beyond the "parts" from which its "schemes" begin. This suggests a different approach to the discussion of culture in Paragraph 83. Culture is a discipline that frees the will from the (natural) despotism of desire. This means that culture is the precondition of morality for the empirical individual. A theory of culture would explain the source of the individual receptivity to moral concern. This would in turn explain the content and the necessary growth that the formal enlightenment left undetermined. Culture makes man receptive to higher goals than what immediate nature can offer. It is not independent of nature, insists Kant, nor are the two identical. Nature does not give specific goals to culture. It does give man the ability to set goals, which is why he is the "final goal" of the natural teleology. The way nature gives man this ability was suggested by the "schemes of men." The movement from particular to universal is a reflective judgment that could provide the foundation for the desired methodology. Kant does not draw this conclusion. His next paragraph returns to the ultimate goal of nature *(Endzweck)* as the noumenal and freely willing individual. Final goals *(letzte Zwecke)* and politics are left aside. The reasons for this hesitation, and the possibility of completing Kant's account consistently, are found in the basic structure and aims of the third *Critique* itself.

Some preliminary spadework is necessary before articulating the method as such. The second introduction to the *Critique of Judgment* is titled "On Philosophy in General." Its last paragraph contains two provocative observations. Kant first distinguishes the understanding and its "legislation" from reason and its "peculiar causality." Understanding of nature gives theoretical knowledge in a possible experience. Reason, which presents freedom, gives unconditional practical knowledge based on the supersensible in the subject. These two domains can apparently coexist. Freedom determines nothing with respect to the understanding of nature. Nature says nothing about the laws of freedom. The problem is that the "peculiar causality" of freedom must have an effect in the world of nature. The supersensible must affect the sensible, although the inverse is obviously impossible.

> The word *cause* [*Ursache*], of course, when used for the supersensible only signifies the *ground* [*Grund*] which determines the causality [*Causalität*] of natural beings to an effect in accordance with the laws of nature proper to them.[6]

This cause which is in fact a ground must show both how freedom operates and the way nature is receptive to freedom without abandoning its mechanical-causal lawfulness. The methodological implication is presented in a systematic table of the faculties, the modes of knowledge that correspond to them, the a priori principles governing them, and their field of application. To the modality of knowledge corresponds the faculty of understanding based on the a priori principle of lawfulness and applied to nature. To the feeling of pleasure and displeasure corresponds the faculty of judgment, based on the a priori principle of goalfulness and applied to art. To the modality of desire corresponds the faculty of reason, based on the a priori principle of an ultimate goal *(Endzweck)* and applied to freedom. The mediate position of judgment is significant. A footnote goes a step further. "It has been found curious [*bedenklich*]," says Kant, "that my divisions in pure philosophy nearly always are triadic." Analytically, he explains, the laws of noncontradiction recommend proceeding by dualities. When the goal is synthesis, triads are necessary. Philosophy must seek synthesis, "namely, 1) condition, 2) a conditioned, 3) the concept that emerges [*entspringt*] from the unification [*Vereinigung*] of the conditioned with its condition." The triadic approach could be read as an anticipation of Hegel.[7] A different possibility emerges within the framework of the third *Critique.* The movement from conditioned to its condition is that of particular to universal. The concept that emerges in this process is precisely that "peculiar causality" that serves as a ground explaining the necessary causality of freedom. The method permitting the articulation of the originary philosophy accomplishes exactly what this ground demands.

The formal structure of the third *Critique* points to its unique content. The familiar pattern of an Analytic and a Dialectic is violated by two departures. The book contains two critiques: the "Critique of Aesthetic Judgment" and the "Critique of Teleological Judgment." These sections correspond to the dual task of demonstrating receptivity of the free subject and receptivity of nature. The analysis of aesthetic judgment presents a further distinction. Its Analytic is divided into an "Analytic of the Beautiful" and an "Analytic of the Sublime." The difference is that the experience of sublimity emerges in an encounter with the brute immensity of nature.[8] The unity of this structure of double difference is two-sided as well. All the objects treated have a teleological structure; this character is revealed by a specific kind of judgment. Teleological phenomena defy the mechanical lawfulness of nature. The goals that animate them cannot be the product of intentional action which uses the laws of nature. The syncretic coexistence of nature and freedom is not enough to establish the phenomena as realizations of freedom. A syncretic unity would be only the kind of "final goal" that was seen to be only an instance of nature's lawfulness. Kant takes a different approach. He describes teleological structures as forms of "purposeless purposefulness" and "lawfulness without law." The art work and the organism are structures in which the parts exist for and because of the whole. The work or organism sets its own goals, for which it creates the means of realization. The goals must be seen as representations that produce a corresponding reality; they are not representations of an already given reality. The distinction is crucial. This teleological notion of representation inverts the mechanical procedure. It presents a teleology to a reflective judgment. This judgment expresses the experience of an encounter with a particular kind of object. It does not subsume the object under already given, formally universal laws. The particularity of the experienced object is recalcitrant to subsumption.[9] The represented is not subsumed under or consumed by the representation. The reflective judgment has a content. It proposes a concrete universal (or whole) that is adequate to the particular. The experiential character of this judgment explains the contribution of the moment of the sublime. Sublimity involves recognition of a greatness, force, and completeness in nature to which the subject can never attain. The feeling of incompleteness that results has an ethical consequence. Encounter with the sublime Otherness brings about an awareness of the humanity in one's own person. This natural experience explains why the individual will in fact act on the moral law. Coupled with the account of the beautiful, the experience of the sublime fulfills the tasks left unresolved by the account of culture in Kant's attempt to formulate his own methodology in paragraphs 82-84.

This demonstration of the receptivity of nature confirms the independence of method from philosophy. A teleological nature can be thought even though finite understanding can never prove its existence. This is why Kant's argument can not be part of a philosophical system that is both necessary and complete. Its status and place are different. The teleological organism inverts the mechanical relation of cause to effect. The effect sought is self-maintenance. Representation of this effect generates actions in order to realize the goal. Actions produced in this way can be then analyzed mechanically, as if they were "causes" whose "effect" is the self-maintenance of the organism. From the standpoint of method, these mechanical causes are actually effects of the teleological intention that produced them. They are analogous to actions that a human being as a goal-positing organism calls into being. They are forms of freedom whose status is not the formal a priori of the moral law. Men generate actions that they, in turn, carry to completion. This ability is what Kant called culture (in paragraph 83). Kant's concern whether man is the ultimate or the final goal of nature need not be reintroduced. That question arises only if the third *Critique* is treated as the completion of the philosophical system. As method, the *Critique of Judgment* offers a different account of receptivity. The phenomenological particularity of nature's teleology or man's place in it is not central to that methodological issue. That question will return when methodological particularity is treated. It will also permit an account of the "application" of method when the relation of theory to practice is treated. For the moment, the necessary receptivity of nature has been demonstrated without pretending to have offered an account of the really real world. This is paradoxical only if method is denied its specificity as neither philosophical theory nor political intervention. This apparent paradox will illustrate further the claim for methodological specificity. Receptivity on the part of the subject must now be shown.

Kant analyzes aesthetic judgment in four moments. The first two limit the content of the judgment; the third describes the structure of the experience; the fourth presents the positive argument, which is then expanded in the Transcendental Deduction. The content of aesthetic judgment is subjective. Its orientation is "disinterested," and it proceeds without presupposed concepts under which to subsume its object. This means that the content is not to be taken as real. The experience presents itself as organic or goalfully organized without manifesting its intentional or causal source. Its structure defies the mechanical laws of science, which are based on predicative judgment. Its claim to universal acceptance presupposes a "common sense" that explains the possibility of intersubjective communication without recourse to the pregiven a priori categories rejected by the second and the third moments. The particular feeling of pleasure represents an experience of the senses or of morally good intentions. This experience cannot be only subjective. It must be shown to make a claim that is valid for all subjects. The four analytic moments are the demonstration of the universality of a particular subjective experience. The universality claimed defies the traditional assertion that ought cannot be derived from is; the movement is from conditioned to the condition and to the synthesis it implies. This general picture requires further specification.

The judgment of taste must be disinterested. If the existence of the experienced object satisfies a need or creates a new need, the universal validity of the experience cannot be maintained. The interested judgment is then bound by needs that make it particular and subjective. Reflective judgment makes no claims about the "real" objective world. This first moment only seems to clash with the insistence in the second moment that the judgment proceed without appeal to preexisting universally valid concepts. Without the universal categorial apparatus whose validity was demonstrated in the *Critique of Pure Reason,* communication among different subjects seems to be either accidental or impossible. The subjectivity treated in the *Critique of Judgment* differs from the formally self-identical monological subject (the Transcendental Unity of Apperception or "I think") presupposed by the first *Critique.* Kant's refusal of preexisting concepts insures that the determinative subsumption that destroys particularity is avoided. This second moment is then coupled positively with the disinterestedness of the first. The result is that the aesthetic judgment is a "contemplative" relation to the world wherein we "only play" (para. 5).[10] From this point, Kant begins the positive demonstration whose two moments correspond to the two aspects of receptivity that the method must articulate. These moments are related to the first two as politics relates to philosophy. Their full implications are developed only when the particular content that gives rise to the aesthetic experience and reflective judgment can be specified. Without that further step, the argument would still be accidental, not yet necessary or complete. The two chapters on methodology must be read as complementing one another.

The third moment of the "Analytic of the Beautiful" develops the structure of the particular aesthetic feeling positively. The experience is teleological in a specific sense. It presents a "lawfulness without law," a "purposeless purposefulness," which avoids the difficulties encountered in the methodological discussion of the ultimate and final ends of nature. The assertion is in part simply the elaboration of the implications of the first two moments. Lack of interest implies the absence of a subjective intention; lack of concept forbids the presupposition of a law under which the particular experience is subsumed. To claim universality, such an experience must be communicable on the basis of a necessity that is more than accidental. Kant must demonstrate the existence of some structure shared by all humans. The lawfulness and/or purposefulness introduced in the third moment are communicated without recourse to the laws of physical science or the imperatives of ethical reason. The necessity that grounds this process is called "exemplary" (para. 17). It is a universal rule whose existence cannot be presented phenomenally. Such a structure is only apparently familiar from the earlier *Critiques.* Kant gives a different account in the present context. He distinguishes a "normal idea" from a "rational ideal." He explains the normal idea psychologically. It is the result of a process of averaging that presents the mean of a series of experiences. The normal idea is not an a priori; it will differ for a Negro, a Chinese, and a European. Encounter with the normal idea pleases only because it does not clash with expectations. This is not the aesthetic or "rational idea" that Kant describes as a unique product of the faculty of imagination. It is not derived from experience but emerges in relation to the ethical good, of which it is the expression. This relation to the ethical and the rational in their purity permits the communication of the experience and explains its claim to necessity. Kant does not give sufficient ground to understand how this "exemplary" representation can function. His reference here to the imagination and his later discussion of genius are of no help. From the standpoint of method, the material needed to complete the demonstration comes in the fourth analytic moment. This judgment of aesthetic experience to the deduction of the conditions of its validity. The presentation moves progressively toward the systematic justification of the method and its place in the system. The critical system develops beyond the account of its own logical preconditions toward the discovery of the phenomenological particulars that called for the system and that are implied by it.

The connection between the third and the fourth moments of the "Analytic of the Beautiful" is apparent when Kant repeats the qualification *exemplary* (para. 18) to define the modality of the judgment. The fourth moment notes that experience of the beautiful is not merely possible or simply actual *(wirklich).* Its necessity is neither that of scientific understanding nor that of ethical reason. It commands the agreement of all, and yet it is a rule that cannot be presented phenomenally. The universal agreement concerns the particular experience, even though it is the rule that makes possible that very experience. The fourth moment attempts to qualify more carefully this exemplary structure by which a universal rule is represented phenomenally. Kant begins from the existence of a "common sense." He insists that the term be taken literally. He is not referring to the average understanding of the common man or to conceptual structures of whatever kind. The stress is on the sensible. Kant's account is at first descriptive. He wants to convince the reader of the real plausibility of such a common sensibility. This commonality transforms the subjective character on which the necessity of the aesthetic judgment is based into an assertion claiming objective validity. This shift from the subjective to the objective explains the transition to the deductive demonstration of the validity of the moments detached in the analytic presentation. The transition is complete when Kant admits that it is not possible to determine whether the supposed common sense is natural or artificial. He does comment that an artificial common sense would be a regulative principle that engenders goals superior to those of nature. This would make relevant the discussion of the role of culture in paragraph 83. It permits the conclusion that the deduction of the judgment of taste is in fact a methodological account of the formation of culture.

The "Deduction of the Aesthetic Judgment" confirms the artificial, cultural character of the common sense that guarantees the universality of the particular aesthetic judgment. Paragraph 40 is titled "Taste as a Kind of *sensus communis.*" This common sense is not the kind of "healthy understanding" attributed to the *vulgus*. It is not the sort of average of many experiences that was described as the "normal idea" as distinguished from the exemplary "rational ideal." Kant maintains the stress on the sensible particularity of this notion. From the other side, now, he adds that it is a "communal sense" (*gemeinschaftlichen Sinn*). The changed orientation of the demonstration is significant. The terms are again to be read literally. The *communal* sense will be artificial, like culture. Kant stresses that its formation is independent, a priori, like the self-given goals of culture or of the teleological organism. The process of its formation "pays attention to the mode of representation [*Vorstellungsart*] in every other person when it reflects," with the result that "its judgments can claim validity for the entirety of human reason" (para. 40).This avoids the illusion that merely private feelings can be generalized, as if they were universalized indiscriminately and immediately. Communal sense develops by considering not the actual judgments of others but their possible judgments. The particular objects that set off such a process remain to be specified. The crucial moment of receptivity learns the necessity to "put itself in the place of every other person." This avoids the accidental results due to being situated in a particular spatial and temporal location. The operation only appears to be difficult and artificial insists Kant. It is actually what each individual does automatically when he claims universal validity for a judgment. It is, in modern language, a counterfactual assertion that is based on that supersensible "rule" to which the notion of an exemplary process and rational ideal referred. The result moves beyond the monological subjectivity on which Kant's ethics was founded. This does not imply a leap to politics, although a note (to para. 40) hints in that direction when it recalls the negative maxim from "What Is Enlightenment?" that no contract can be valid if it shuts off the progress from the human race.

The concept of a common and a communal sense was invoked to explain the universal communicability of the particular aesthetic experience. This difficulty does not confront the predicative judgment. It pictures an action of the imagination and the understanding that couples concepts and intuitions into a knowledge that falls explicitly under an a priori and lawful frame. The reflective judgment cannot presuppose such lawful conceptual structures. It is restricted, particular, and sensible. The negative conditions in the first two moments of the Analytic have positive implications. The disinterest and nonconceptual structure that they present is the strongest literal claim for the "Copernican revolution" in Kant's work. The beautiful is not a thing, a concept, or a law. It is a subjective feeling of pleasure whose occasion may be the particular object, but whose "content" is the reflective play of the human faculties.[11] This play was presented at the outset of the Analytic (para 5). Its extended interpretation brings it into relation with common sense and culture to suggest the kind of "triad" to which Kant referred in his introductory reflections. Play is conditioned; the common sense is the condition; culture is their synthesis. Common sense makes play no accident. Culture makes necessary the development of a common sense. The element missing from this structure is the particularity that specifies the interrelation of each of the terms. Kant's assertion is limited to the point suggested by the title to paragraph 35. He is giving an account of the "subjective principle of judgment in general." Just as the individual imagination awakens understanding and rational freedom which it sets into the dynamic interaction, so at the level of the community (to which the judgment that teaches to "think in the place of the others" leads) there is a common sense that permits particular objects, forms, or representations to awaken identical feelings on the part of all of the members. The concept of play could be the mediator or catalyst among the three moments.

The common and communal sense needs an analysis of culture in order to avoid the twin dangers of remaining static or becoming external to the object. Overstress on sensibility makes culture simply the product of nature. Overemphasis on the artificial aspect of the communal element has the inverse effect of fixing the parameters in splendid isolation. This double structure corresponds to the familiar pattern of priority allocated to the genetic or the normative pole. The theory of culture has to transcend this one-sidedness to include explicitly the interrelation of both poles. This imperative explains why the theory of reflective judgment stresses representation that is "exemplary." It is dealing with a particular that is the phenomenal presence of an unrepresentable rule. What is represented is not a really real or ultimate foundation that the method reproduces. That which is represented as exemplary is a rational rule, whose particular form is the theory of culture alluded to in paragraph 83. Kant does not stress this point because he did not treat method separately from system. His demonstration of the double logic of receptivity in nature and in the subject points toward the crucial place that a theory of culture assumes in the account of particularity as the second moment of method. Had Kant made his arguments explicit, he would not be liable to the Hegelian criticism from the standpoint of the logic of *Sittlichkeit*. Hegel's attempt to integrate Kant's abstract particular individual with his formal moral code into a systematic theory of cultural history would not be possible. A Kantian methodological demonstration of receptivity would preserve Kant's moral and political individualism.

THE LOGIC OF CIVIL SOCIETY

Treating Hegel's account of civil society as the methodological mediation between his philosophical account of history in Reason and his political presentation of reason in History provides a new vantage point on the structure of his system as modern. Hegelian civil society is based on the principle of particularity that destroyed the immediate, substantive *sittliche* unity of the "old states" (para. 185, Remark). Hegel gives no historical account of the advent of this structure. The external intervention of Revelation to which he refers (para. 124, Remark) does not explain the role of Socrates in Greece.[12] The modern state must integrate the principled particularity of civil society into its structured unity. Hegel's account of civil society explains this receptivity.

The theory of civil society is unable to account for the particularity that is its principle. That justification has to be provided in a separate methodological moment. Separation of the two accounts avoids the illusion that one founds the other, in theory or in actual history. The particular is the basis and principle of civil society whose institutions preserve it. Particularity is defined by needs, which are a combination of natural necessities and capricious choices by the individual. Needs must be satisfied for the continued existence of the particular person. Other persons are necessary for this realization of particular needs. They are objectively necessary as purveyors of goods and services. Subjectively, the needy individual also becomes aware that other needs must be considered. Others will satisfy his needs in exchange for satisfaction of their own needs. This all-sided dependence of each on the other implies a positive system of interdependence. Hegel calls it the external state, the "state of need and of the understanding" [*Not- und Verstandesstaat*]. Particularity is assured as long as this abstract universal framework is preserved. But because the external state is still accidental, particularism can become solipsism or blind egoism. Its content is independent of its control. From the side of particularity, the newly created needs are also acidental. Their satisfaction is still contingent, not necessary. Society becomes a field of contrast between poverty and extravagance because the external universal framework of the state provides only the abstract possibility of formal unity while the particulars are left to themselves. Although the particular can understand and manipulate this lawful external structure, it still depends on it. Particular freedom is redefined as recognition of external necessity. Subjective particularity can be realized only when it is represented as its opposite, external objectivity. The positive result of this inversion is that particularity as caprice is replaced by the formal universality of knowing and willing. This is how civil society "educates" its members away from natural particularity to formal universality. The educated man, concludes Hegel, can do anything; he has freed himself from the external limits imposed by subjective natural particularity. This founds logically the formal possibility of self-conscious and free particularity. Its material necessity remains to be established.

Hegel's account parallels the task Kant assigned to the critical method. He begins from the factual existence of the logic of particularity in order to examine the conditions of its possibility. After the introductory definition of the problem (paras. 182-187), Hegel sketches the three moments that move from possibility to necessity. The "System of Needs" analyzes the emergence and multiplication of needs. It then examines the kinds of work required to produce and to satisfy new needs. Finally, it presents the structured social divisions that articulate (accidentally) the circulation of need and its satisfaction. The "Administration of Justice" then begins to remove the contingent aspect from the "System of Needs." It shows how freedom is given institutional force. The law takes account of the particularity that must persist in civil society. The action of judge and jury guarantee subjective adhesion to the system. The accidentality that the presence of particularity preserves is dealt with finally by the action of the "Police and the Corporations" which insure the objective material effectiveness of the lawful universe while protecting the particular. This protection preserves particular interests as something shared in common *(als eines Gemeinsamen).* This commonality has the same general and abstract form as the universality to which the particular sacrificed in the first moment in order to fulfill his needs. It is the "comparative" universal that Hegel rejected in introducing the sphere of *Sittlichkeit* (para. 154, marginal note; above, chap. 3, C). Hegel is aware of the paradoxical character of this "educational" experience. The commonality that serves as standard is itself particular, accidental, changeable. This commonality becomes the external "state of need and of the understanding" whose contingency must be overcome by the fully rational modern state.

The parallel to the Kantian critique breaks down when Hegel leaves the categorial level of Civil Society to seek a solution at the level of the State. The "concrete universality" of the State is supposed to integrate abstract universality and material particularity in what appears as an originary structure. The specificity of modern Civil Society is dissolved; it becomes simply a moment of Philosophy as System. The necessity of receptivity and the particularity that guarantees its completeness are not demonstrated immanently. Hegel's categorial presentation of the institutional structure of the State is only the first and therefore incomplete moment, describing immediate relations whose rationality is shown only in the succeeding moments of the demonstration. When Hegel passes from the conceptually immediate State to relations among states and to universal history, this move parallels his systematic attempt to embed the System within the reality of history. The flow of actual history remains external to the philosophical theory. Conditions of possibility cannot acquire the character of necessity demanded for systematic completeness. This weakness was present in the Hegelian theory as an originary philosophy. Yet if a logic of method, derived from philosophy, can be demonstrated, this weakness may be said not to be built into the originary system. A more adequate "Hegel" can then be constructed without violating the arguments of his text. The structural logic of Civil Society explains *how* representative relations can be understood within a society based on particularity. The difficulty is that this logic does not integrate an account of *what* particulars must be represented. Because he has no explicit account of *what* counts as particular, Hegel is led to take a historically real structure (the division of property, and later the Rabble) as a given. This explains many of the objectionable features for which he has been crticized. When the account of methodological particularity is given its independent—and political—status, these criticisms no longer prove fatal.

The logic of Civil Society is presented through a phenomenological description. The needy individual confronts other needy individuals. Comparison with the commodities they offer in exchange for others that will satisfy their needs teaches them refinement and brings new needs. This multiplication of need may cause dissatisfaction. It has also the positive result that the strength of desire is limited because no particular need is dominant. This decreases the weight of external, accidental and nonreflective necessity. Needs loose their natural and material character. Individual need is "educated" to satisfy opinion, which is not particular but social, and thus relatively universal. The particular individual learns to consider the general values of society when marketing goods in exchange for self-satisfaction. At the same time, the demand for social equality emerges from this comparison with general values. The general result is a dialectic between (abstract) social universality and the particularity whose concrete form is an unlimited multiplication of needs. This dialectic is aborted by the "absolute hardness" that comes with the recognition that the external world is the property of another will. The logical *Zutat* of the philosopher must enter to show the phenomenological will that the reason it is checked is that its particularity is only formal.

A second step follows from the intervention of the philosopher. The particular will was, so to speak, only commerical; it must become industrial. It must learn to labor in order to particularize the external world. This will overcome the "absolute hardness." The general "education" acquired in civil society is given a further definition. Learning mobility and rapidity in relating different objects permits the development of general theory. Language becomes more refined. Practical education is even more important. The subjective need and habit of working in the world are acquired. This teaches the particular to adapt to the specific material with which it is working. Similarly, as subject, he learns to adapt himself to the will *(Willkür)* of others. This dual process explains the subjective and objective conditions of the possibility of the rational division of labor in the face of external necessity in the world of need. The division of labor simplifies work. Increasingly abstract labor produces growing quantities of goods. Hegel notes the negative implications of the increased dependency brought by this simplification. However, since material dependency already existed in the accidental world of need, the rational division of labor is a progress. Making labor more mechanical even suggests the positive possibility of replacing man with the machine.[13]

The third moment of the System of Needs complements the subjective particularity from which Hegel began. Its English translation as "Capital and Class Division" is misleading. *Das Vermögen* is "that by virtue of which" a particular situation comes to exist. *Vermögen* is the material condition of the possibility of the creation of needs and their satisfaction by work. The subjective analysis of needs and labor presupposed pure and abstract economic actors. The comparative universal necessity encountered there was the law of the market. That assumption expresses the "proud position" that abstracts from historical and material conditions. The discussion of *Vermögen* returns to concrete divisions in the form of Estates whose existence is given naturally. The place of the individual in one or the other is accidental. The only necessity is that the Estates be unequal among themselves in order to complement each other in a unified whole. Hegel portrays them as corresponding to the logical need for immediacy, particularity, and concrete universality. The landed Estate lives the life of substantive immediacy. The business class accounts for the particularity. It is subdivided among artisans who do concrete work for others, factory workers who do abstract work for general social need, and commercial workers whose reflective activity exchanging singular objects takes place by the mediation of the abstract universal means of exchange, money. The universal Estate is occupied by the executive and administrative functions.[14] The accidental character of particular membership in one or the other Estate means that it is not important to which of them the individual belongs. It is important only that each have a particular material place in the logical structure of Civil Society.

Hegel's argument in this third moment shifts from a phenomenology of particularity to the presentation of a logical structure. Although the Estates are particular, the fact that each particular in them relates to other particulars that are naturally identical to itself implies a self-reflective structure. Playing on another meaning of *Vermögen,* the philosophical *Zutat* can then make the transition to a new level. The particular member of each Estate recognizes that its particularity is preserved by the guarantee of its property *(Vermögen)* that is provided by the Administration of Justice. The phenomenological necessity of this recognition is not shown. Its rationality cannot be demonstrated immanently because the gathering of things that are alike in content (para. 201) was seen already to be only external, comparative, and accidental. It is a product of understanding, like the "state of need and of the understanding." Hegel recognizes the difficulty without specifying its methodological importance. He notes that modern and Western societies do not leave distribution among Estates to external legislation or natural caste conditions (para. 206, Remark). He adds that youth objects to this particularization to an Estate as the imposition of an external limit (para. 207, Remark). His rejoinder is logical, and therefore limited. The particular acquires concrete social existence, recognition from others, and duties toward them only through this sociological membership. But this objective logic needs subjective justification as well. This methodological demand for a dual demonstration of subjective as well as objective receptivity explains why Hegel does not return here to the kind of external market necessities presented in the subjective aspect of particularity. Hegel's move to a different categorial level of argument implies that the System of Needs as a whole has to be subjectively and objectively integrated into an increasingly complex logical structure. The first two moments of the System of Needs present a subjective structure to which the objective divisions of *Vermögen* correspond. This objective structure now needs a higher-level subjective correlate without which it would be a presupposition that violates the principle of immanence. The two most frequent accusations against Hegel stem from a lack of clarity on this methodological point. Either Hegel is said to have imposed his ontological logic into the field of social relations, or he is accused of presupposing the given social relations of his times which he then proceeds to justify philosophically. Both accusations contain a kernal of truth; neither need be the result of a systematic reading.

The methodological problem introduced in the System of Needs can be formulated formally or substantively. Formally, the phenomenological process of the growth and refinement of needs has to be integrated into the logical structure. Materially, the arbitrary concreteness of the Estates must acquire a rational and reflexive institutional form. Hegel described a series of apparently historical developments within the System of Needs. Growth of need and its multiplication correspond to learning and to labor and its refinement. References to fashion and public opinion parallel the quest for equality and the predicted replacement of labor by machines. These phenomena are only quantitative. Their history is accidental. A different kind of historical creation was seen to prevail in the domain of *Sittlichkeit*, of which the System of Needs is a part. The formal "person" defined by Abstract Right becomes concrete "man" in the System of Needs. The formal "subject" of morality gets concreteness when abstract duty is transformed into a right having the force of law. The singular cases to which particular laws are applied are not resolved by an external judge who subsumes them under pregiven universal laws. Such a judge, and such laws, cannot exist in the sphere of particularity where conflict among self-seeking particulars is necessary because of their very particularity (para. 211, Addition). A parallel to the Kantian reflective judgment moving from the particularity to a kind of "exemplary" universality might be expected in this context. Hegel's presentation of the second moment of Civil Society, "The Administration of Justice," can be evaluated in light of this expectation.

The Administration of Justice has to demonstrate how the law, which is involved necessarily in the world of accident and particularity, can nonetheless claim lawful universality. Legal universality becomes merely quantitative when it confronts a concrete case. It becomes accidental, open to chance; the legal decision is necessarily particular. This means that the law cannot say exactly how many years, dollars, or lashes a crime merits. One year, dollar, or lash too many is unjust; yet a decision must be made. Hegel's argument can be understood as a method attempting to demonstrate receptivity. He transforms significantly the problem of legal justification. The subjectivity involved in the execution of law is not that of the judge. The focus is the subjectivity of the citizens. The law must be known universally if it is to be binding. Unversally known does yet not mean true. As long as they are not administered by a closed corporation (like the scientists who rejected Geothe's color theory or the jurists writing in Latin), even imperfect codes are sufficient for this purpose. As universally known, laws are open to public discussion. Their formulation must permit the introduction of new determinations through this interaction. The public, known, and debatable character is enriched further by the observation of legal formalities. These may appear as a means for rulers or lawyers to earn money. They may appear to signify that the word of others is not trusted. Such skepticism neglects the key point. This legal structure replaces particular judgment by a certitude, fixity, and objectivity that are formulated as explicitly rational and open to reflective questioning. The process is similar to the earlier, more abstract elimination of the natural particularity of need. The result is different. Crime is no longer a personal offense. Crime is seen to threaten society as a whole. On the other hand, society is now stronger because it does not depend so much on particular subjectivity. It is less threatened by the particular injury. This explains the leniency of criminal law in more developed societies. Hegel does not explain the necessity that grounds this historical change in the law. His phenomenological presentation of it is closer to Kant's "culture" than to the laws of the market that he invoked to explain the subjective transformation of need. The discussion of the concrete rendering of justice makes still more explicit the methodological concern with receptivity.

The Court is the locus of concrete justice. It unites the subjective experience of law as demanding a decision and the objective social existence of the public lawful forms. The action of the Court actualizes the universality of justice in the particular case. Revenge is subjective and forbidden. Society as universal is the wounded party. Each particular member of society has the right and duty to appear before the Court (as plaintiff or juror). Each has the right and duty to know the law before which all are equal. Right must be demonstrable rationally according to formal legal forms. Although an individual may lose his case because of these formalities, they are necessary because their presence reaffirms the law as socially valid for all. The methodological implication is clear when Hegel adds that each individual may use all formal means available even if this prolongs the affair, since the goal is the subjective recognition of right by *every* particular. This subjective orientaion explains the need for public proceedings and records. The procedural formalism insures that the citizenry is convinced reflectively that the Court actually preserves the law.

A final step from the side of the particular completes the dual demonstration of receptivity. The matters brought to Court must have an explicitly universal form even though they deal with particular persons and conditions. The role of the jury is crucial to the methodological demonstration. The jury identifies the facts. The facts are singular, accidental, the product of hearsay or subjective description of experience. The function of the jury is not to decide with scientific necessity, just as the nature of the legal code was not to be scientifically true. Its deliberations give certainty *(Gewissheit)* not absolute truth. That this is all that is needed confirms the reading of Hegel's argument or methodology. Because they are the peers of the accused and the public, decisions of the jury inspire confidence in the procedure. Their actions give the particularity of the facts a universal validity analogous to the publicly known code, and superior to the relative and quantitative universality of opinion in the "education" of the System of Needs. With the help of the jury, the Court preserves right as subjectively recognized and objectively valid. Through the Court as process, the law is known; the law is common to all parties; it is applied fairly because publicly; and the facts are related to a universal lawfulness whose validity, established by the jury, is analogous to the communal sense in the Kantian reflective judgment.

The justice guaranteed in the subjective and objective functioning of the Court preserves a system of particularity whose concrete form in the *Vermögen* of the Estates was at first only a presupposition. The final movement of Hegel's argument must integrate this externality. If Hegel were writing a systematic ontology, his third moment would present the concretely universal reflective truth of the first two moments. The third moment would have a unitary form that could, in turn, be transformed into the moment of immediacy from which the next level of the demonstration begins. Instead, Hegel's third moment in Civil Society is explicitly dual. It treats "The Police and the Corporations." This duality complements the subjective and objective concerns in the Administration of Justice. It points again to the independence of methodology on the originary philosophy. Hegel's introductory paragraph makes the point explicit:

> The subsistence and welfare of each individual is only a possibility in the System of Needs. Its actuality is conditioned by caprice and natural particularity, as well as by the objective system of needs. The Administration of Justice destroys the violation of property and personality. But the law [*Recht*] which is actual in the sphere of particularity implies both that the accidentality in the way of the one or the other goal is eliminated, that the undisturbed safety of person and property has been brought into being; and it implies that the assurance of the subsistance and the welfare of the individual—the particular welfare—is treated as a right and is actualized. (para. 230, emphasis omitted)

The first part of this description reiterates the accomplishment of the Administration of Justice. The passage beginning "But the law..." refers to the task of the Police and the Corporations.[15] This last step eliminates fully the comparative external necessity imposed upon calculating actors in an abstract market where they relate only by formal contract. Civil Society loses its abstract particularity when the material content of needs and the labor of their satisfaction is taken into account. The Police stand for the pole of universality in a Civil Society where particularity is the law. The Corporations make certain that each individual is cared for by a particular institution that integrates him into the universal structure of Civil Society. These two institutions complete a web that excludes accident and chance by giving the unexpected its logical place without at the same time denying its particularity. The success of the demonstration is again dependent on a *Zutat* that is not explained. The reasons why Hegel does not stop with this demonstration are partly explained by his need to justify that intervention. Although the argument fails ultimately, that Hegel pursues it so rigorously—and the way in which he violates other rigor—confirms the suggested reading of his theory of Civil Society as the methodological moment of his systematic project.

The external regulation of Civil Society by the Police is made necessary by the inevitable effect that self-seeking particular actions must have on other particulars. There need not be any explicit intention to interfere; particularity must affect other particulars in its necessary pursuit of its own individual particularity. External control is possible, but limited. The principle of particularity means that such control can be only comparative, it has no immanent measure. This is why the Police are said to interfere "pedantically" in the affairs of daily life (para. 234). Although this makes the Police an object of hatred, the lack of measure has a positive implication. Particular actions are no longer the limited affair of particular actors. Particular actions become a public concern when they affect the acquisition and exchange of the means to satisfy, facilitate, or increase public needs. The business of one person becomes a public interest when it affects the good of all. The lack of measure means that the Police can be flexible; they can take account of changed conditions. The Police are charged with supervising the public interest; they are the "public authority" (*öffentliche Macht*) placed above the conflicting particulars. Hegel gives the Police wide powers. They may intervene to regulate the price of necessities or the quality of goods sold to the "universal purchaser" (the public), which has a right not to be defrauded by self-seeking particularity. The public authority is concerned also with larger branches of industry that depend on conditions abroad for supplies or sales. Street lights, bridges, taxation, and health care also fall into this domain. Hegel admits that this violates the principle of private particular choice. It is justified here because the universality of public ends takes precedence over particularity. Hegel suggests that there is no reason to worry about abuse here since the development of Civil Society, which is the concern of the public authority, is based on the increased skills, division of labor, and kinds of capital to which the analysis of the System of Needs pointed. As long as its immanent principle of particularity is not violated, Civil Society can defend itself against abuse.

The intervention of the Police is both called for and limited by the particularist structure of Civil Society. The lack of a move to give it independent political legitimacy points to the methodological status of Hegel's argument. Intervention is necessary because Civil Society has ripped the individual from the Family which protected, educated, and incorporated him in the Estate from which he will draw his livelihood. The individual becomes the "son of Civil Society," which has claims on him just as he has rights against it. This permits Civil Society (in the form of the public authority) to intervene even against the desires of parents when the education or training of the child is at stake. Civil Society must provide not only the possibility but the necessity of the incorporation of the particular individual. Hegel justifies forced school attendance and even immunization shots. The extravagance or imprudence of the head of the family must be countered by the intervention of the public authority. Civil Society is acting here for its own good; it is reacting to what now appears to it as a threat built into the particularism of the System of Needs. The preservation of the system of particularity demands the intervention of the public authority. The justification of this intervention, which is not the political action of the rational state and which cannot appeal to an external agency that would put into question the particularist foundation of Civil Society, points to the moment at which the demonstration of methodological receptivity passes over toward the problem of particularity.

The progress and development guaranteed by the System of Needs contains the seed of its own destruction. The increased division of labor produces a new class whose limited specialization and machinelike labor make its members incapable of enjoying the subjective freedom that labor teaches. This is the Rabble (*Pöbel*). It is not defined so much by its material poverty as by the loss of the feeling for right, justice, and the honor of existing through one's own activity and labor which constitute the particular member of Civil Society. The result is an inner revolt against wealth, power, and social institutions generally. The revolt becomes a fear of work; the lack of honor, a growing dependence; the failed sense of right, a passivity. Moral charity based on love or sympathy is only a contingent remedy for this situation. But intervention by the public authority would transform it into a political state separate from the Civil Society. The burden might be combated by creating private institutions such as monasteries or foundations that could aid and train the Rabble while still making sufficient profit to remain independent of the contingencies of charity. Although it would no longer be accidental, the work done in such institutions gives no honor and no self-respect. Were truly fitting work to be created, the still greater mass of goods that it would produce only worsens the problem, since overproduction was the source of the original unemployment and degradation. This overproduction drives Civil Society to seek colonial markets for its goods, and eventually for the overflow of its population. Such colonization is at first accidental. It can become the systematic attempt by a mature Civil Society to plant itself in a new land. This returns Civil Society to its familial basis and its dependence on the soil. But this self-reproduction only puts off the day of reckoning. Hegel notes (para. 248, Addition) that the new colony will be more profitable to the mother land when it is given its independence, just as the freed slave works better to the advantage of the master. The cycle begins anew; the problem of the Rabble remains and spreads.

Hegel's solution to the problem of the Rabble leaves aside the general concerns of the public authority. The particular Corporations are introduced in order to solve this difficulty from the side of particularity. Hegel's discussion is often inconsistent, although its systematic goal is clear. The Corporations are necessary only for the "business class" whose different types of labor divide it into particular occupations, skills, and interests. Belonging to a Corporation brings its members a comparative equality that becomes self-conscious when each realizes that the self-interest of the corporation is the source of his own particular identity. Equal particularity becomes the foundation of an abstract universality. This permits the assertion (para. 252) that the Corporation does for its members what Civil Society does for its "sons." It does not, however, explain the integration of the Rabble, which was defined by the fact that it had no particular form of labor, honor, or subjective freedom. At best, the corporate structure gives rational justification to the arbitrariness encountered in the first discussion of *Vermögen,* since membership in the Corporation serves as the individual's "capital." Yet Hegel wants to do more. He claims that the conception of corporate honor means that each corporation cares for its own, avoiding the stain of contingent charity. The same notion of honor is said to forbid amassing measureless luxury which is sought only by those who need to insure their dignity and rank by such external signs of identity. By prohibiting the extremes of wealth, Hegel thinks, the corporate structure works against the creation of the impoverished Rabble. The difficulty is that he himself had insisted that it is not poverty that defines the Rabble.

The conclusion to Hegel's account of Civil Society indicates his doubts about the validity of his solution. "Sanctity of marriage and honor of the Corporation are the two moments around which the disorganization of Civil Society turns" (para. 244, Remark). The Addition to this paragraph suggests that the state must intervene actively to prevent the Corporations from becoming merely the representatives of private interests. Such an intervention cannot be justified immanently. The source of Hegel's difficulty is the failure to distinguish the methodological from the ontological analysis. The demonstration of the necessary production of the Rabble is treated as ontologically real, the Rabble is taken to be a real threat, and the state intervention as a real counterthreat. Hegel is treating Civil Society as part of his quest for Reason in history. This conflates *Sittlichkeit* with one of its moments. The result is that when Hegel turns to the State as a separate and higher moment, that apparent étatist solution to the threat of the Rabble turns out to be only the moment of immediacy. Defenseless, this State is thrust into the process of international politics and finally, unable to elaborate a rational politics that would permit it to maintain itself, it is dissolved into the flow of World History. The methodological demonstration of the receptivity of Civil Society to the categories of rationality is replaced by the dissolution of its particularity into the ontological universality of World History.

Had Hegel given the political and the philosophical their proper place, the implications of his methodological analysis would have become clear. The task of Civil Society is its own reflective self-preservation. The particularity of its institutions is both its means and its end. Hegel treats this identity as implying the ontological structure of formal universality. He does not point out that the same structure could be interpreted, with Kant, as *teleological.* Had he drawn this implication, he would have approached differently the two central problems unresolved in his account of Civil Society. Two externalities vitiated the logic of particularity: the *Vermögen* whose division could not be explained immanently, and the *Rabble,* whose lack of property and proprieties leaves it outside of the forms of subjective freedom developed in the System of Needs and articulated in the Administration of Justice. These two structures violate the logic of particularity whose consistent development demonstrates the methodological receptivity. The implication of the teleological approach drawn from Kant suggests that they be reconceptualized. Hegel's *Vermögen* is not Marx's capitalist class structures; Hegel's *Pöbel* is not Marx's proletariat. They are particulars within particularist Civil Society. Their reflective representation from the side of the political forms the methodological complement to the demonstration of the logic of Civil Society. Neither side of method can stand alone; each refers necessarily to its complement; both depend upon, but cannot stand in the place of, their philosophical or political origin.

THE LOGIC OF HISTORY

Marx's explicit remarks on method are scattered throughout his evolution. He never wrote the methodological treatise of which he spoke both in his youth and again in maturity. His approval of Engels's simplifications in the *Anti-Dühring* was the source of misunderstanding that multiplied with the posthumous publication of Engels's *Dialectics of Nature.* The codified system of *diamat* is assumed by orthodoxy to explain the methodological conditions of receptivity. A more "Hegelian" orientation has been opposed to this interpretation since Lukács's *History and Class Consciousness* (1923). With the aid of an ontological theory of constitution, Sartre developed this approach into an explicit method in the *Critique of Dialectical*

Reason, whose promised second volume was never completed. Both types of reconstruction reduce the specificity of method to ontological presuppositions. The apparently more concrete attempts to derive a method by detailed analysis of what Marx actually did, for example, in writing *Capital,* become the kind of epistemological "philosophy of ______" that is inadequate to the originary structure. A different approach to a Marxian epistemology is suggested by Jürgen Habermas's *Knowledge and Human Interest.* Developing Marx's tendency to make history integral to the system, Habermas argues that epistemology is only possible in the form of social theory. Although he sometimes comes close to presenting a constitutive philosophy, Habermas's reconstruction of Marx's place within the framework of German Idealism avoids the difficulty. Habermas's analysis serves as a guide to the reconstruction of a Marxian method for the demonstration of the receptivity of the world to the categories of his philosophy.

The repeated use of the category "critique" indicates Marx's methodological orientation. His early philosophical concern showed that Marx's critique is above all characterized as immanent. Its task is to demonstrate the alienated or repressed potential in the object of the critique. This method is distinct from a hermeneutic approach that results only in a social-theoretical relativism. Hermeneutics begins from the interdependence of knower and known. Its manner of uncovering the preconditions of knowledge demonstrates the conditions of the possibility, but not the necessity, of that relation. The critique makes a stronger claim. Marx's passage beyond the "invertive method" of Feuerbach permitted the demonstration of receptivity on the side of the object. Habermas's suggestion that epistemology must have the form of social thoery is implied by this structure. Not only is the knowing subject affected by the world it seeks to understand. The relation between the two poles has to be shown to be necessary from both sides. Habermas proposes to reconstruct this demonstration by a return to the claims of Kant and Hegel, which Marx synthesizes uniquely. The movement begins from the dualism that the Kantian critique apparently presupposes and justifies. Hegel's phenomenological attempt to articulate a hermeneutical unity that avoids the dualism is vitiated by logical presuppositions that it cannot justify. Marx does not simply reject his predecessors; he builds his argument by playing them off against one another.

Hegel's *Phenomenology* makes three important points against the Kantian critique. Kant takes a specific form of mathematical and physical knowledge as the given whose conditions of possibility must be reconstructed. Hegel's phenomenological descriptions of the multiple forms of knowing challenge this presupposition. Kant's reconstruction of only the natural sciences and the experience of nature attributes a fixed and permanent structure to the concept of knowledge and to its object. There is no reason to think that every object can be known only in this way. Nor should all knowing be reduced to one type. Second, Kant's subject, the "I think" that must accompany all my representations, is put into question by Hegel's presentation of the *Bildungsprozess* through which the subject becomes adequate to experience. The subject externalizes itself in knowing. Its interaction with the world transforms both the world and itself. The externalization and the learning through the remembering reconstruction (*Errinerung*) of the experience described a processual relation different from Kant's always present and selfsame "I think" which tends to become an external standard of normativity. Finally, the criticism of the Kantian object and subject puts into question Kant's distinction between theoretical and practical reason. Hegel's notion of determinant negation is presented by Habermas as both a logical and a practical intervention. Its implication is the interweaving of the practical and the theoretical that occurs in the process of active externalization and remembering. The notion of determinant negation represents the critical break with an established mode of life. The preservation *(Aufhebung)* of an earlier attitude, like the traditional family or the classical idea of virtue, within the newly acquired form of life becomes comprehensible as part of the species' process of development. This interaction of theory and practice in a historical development also implies the elimination of the distinction between transcendental conditions and empirical givens. These premises begin the articulation of an epistemology that is simultaneously social theory.

Although Hegel scores against Kant, criticism of his own position in turn justifies relatively the standpoint of the Kantian dualism. The *Phenomenology* is only apparently (or at best, in its first part) rooted in an individual *Bildungsprozess.* Its actual subject is the species whose developmental education is reconstructed historically in the second part, and is presented through the forms of Absolute Spirit as art, religion, and philosophy as the third part. If the process is to end really in Absolute Knowledge, it must reflect the educational development not only of the species but also of Nature. This unity of Nature and Spirit would have to come about in one and the same process. If Nature remains other and inert, the knowing subject can not achieve self-identity in relating to it. Yet if Nature were actually transformed in this manner, epistemology would be lost, and with it the goals of the critique. The sciences would be reduced to mere empirical understanding or genetic description. The historical process would be merely incidental to a pregiven logic. The *Bildungsprozess* of the *Phenomenology* becomes prescientific and incidental to the real theoretical development that is the ontological *Logic.* The science of Spirit would be subordinated (as it is in the *Encyclopaedia*). Marx enters here, making implicit use of Hegel's critique of Kant without accepting the "identity-philosophy" that the phenomenological Hegel presupposes if his project is truly to end in Absolute Knowledge.

The criterion of immanence explains why Marx takes issue with Hegel's definition of Nature as fully externalized Spirit.[16] If it were fully external, Nature would have its essence in an other. This would mean that Nature must be *aufgehoben* since this externality means that it exists only as a dependent illusion *(Schein).* Feuerbach had already suggested this criticism of Hegel. His naturalist remedy did not satisfy Marx because its structure was only the inverse identical of the Hegelian idealism. Privileging matter instead of Spirit remains within a monist identity-philosophy; this kind of radical materialism is itself still an idealism. Against Feuerbach, Marx insists on the interaction with nature that is *constitutive* of further new objects. The constituted products remain objects while carrying also the imprint of human activity. This implies a new philosophical stance.

> On the one hand, Marx understands the objective activity as transcendental effort. To it corresponds the construction of a world in which reality appears under the conditions of the objectivity of possible objects. On

> the other hand, Marx sees that transcendental effort is founded in real labor processes. The subject of the constitution of the world is not a transcendental consciousness in general, but the concrete human species that reproduces its life under natural conditions.[17]

In the place of a Kantian epistemology based on normative constitution by a transcendental Ego, Marx presents a theory of *real* constitution by a collective material subject who is imbricated in and constituted by this same productive process. (The problem whether this constitution is the work of the individual or the species will return.) The assertion in *Capital* that labor is the general condition of human existence, independent of its specific form in a given society, is normative. Marx claims that there is a necessary and permanent material interaction (*Stoffwechsel*) between man and nature mediated by labor. The synthesis between subject and object achieved by the imaginative schematism in Kant's first *Critique* is made concrete. The achievement which Kant could describe only as an "art hidden in the depths of the human soul" is presented by Marx as founded in social labor. Labor does precisely what Kant's theory needed. It unifies an empirical manifold and makes it mine. It defines the conditions of the possibility of there being a world for me. Indeed, it defines the conditions of the possibility of objectivity in general. Labor accounts for the genesis of the given world of formed objects. From the side of the subject, labor is that which permits valid knowledge of these objects. Labor can thus be said to unite epistemology and ontology. The implication is that labor is not only a real process in nature. Labor can be understood as a methodological mediation making possible the understanding of a world humans have constituted. "When we understand man under the category of a toolmaking animal, we mean thereby at once a schema of action *and* of world understanding."(39). This is why Marx asserts in *The German Ideology* that we become human only when we *re*-produce our means of subsistence by labor.

Marx's stress on labor can be interpreted as accepting the Hegelian criticism of Kant's separation of theoretical and practical reason without abandoning methodology to an ontological philosophy of constitution. Marx's approach is at once empirical and transcendental; his subject is self-creating and historical; his object grows and develops. The argument is not an ontological assertion about an ahistorical "human nature," as in post-Husserlian or Heideggerian interpretations of the logic of labor material synthesis which treat it as an a priori giving sense to invariant structures of possible social life-worlds. Social labor is a historically specific category of mediation between subjective and objective nature. "It designates the *mechanism* of the historical development of the species. Not only is the worked-on nature changed by the labor process; also, through the products of labor, the nature of the needs of the laboring subjects themselves are transformed"(41). This methodological argument explains famous assertions in the *1844 Manuscripts*—that the five senses are the product of all past history and that industry is the "open book" of essential human powers. Habermas extrapolates from this structure to the argument that economics, not logic, is the key to the theoretical reconstruction of our historical world. Real economic processes explain the problems usually posed by epistemology. With this, Habermas can assert that epistemology must take the form of a social theory.[18] This is the first step; problems remain.

Marx's critique of Hegel's concept of Nature should have prevented the illusion that the synthesis through labor can actually reach completion. It should have warned against confusion of method and ontological constitution. The passages in the *1844 Manuscripts* describing communism as a "completed naturalism=humanism and humanism=naturalism" are dangerously misleading. They imply that when Nature is fully humanized by laboring synthesis it will become the fully transparent rational product of self-conscious human activity. Elsewhere, Marx abandons this assertion of an ontological identity-philosophy. Nature remains resistant; it is an independent Other from which we learn by using its own laws; it is external and cannot be eliminated, no matter how powerful technologies become. This more consistent position preseves the Kantian dualism:

> "Nature in itself" is nonetheless an abstractum that we must conceptualize; but we only encounter nature in the horizon of the world historical *Bildungsprozess* of the species. The Kantian "thing-in-itself" reappears under the rubric of a nature that precedes human history. It has

> the epistemologically important function of maintaining nature as contingent. It defends the unavoidable facticity of nature in spite of its historical embeddedness in the universal mediating context of the laboring subjects against the idealistic attempt to dissolve it in the mere self-externality of the Spirit.(47)

This "Kantian" preservation of the particularity of Nature does not exclude the "Hegelian" contribution. The forms through which Nature is understood are not the pregiven, a priori Kantian categories of the understanding. Categories of objective activity perform the synthetic function. Their locus is not formal transcendental consciousness but the functional realm of instrumental economic action. To the Kantian, eternal and unchanging categories are opposed to sensible and historically variant ones. Marx replaces that normative but external application by the real immanent epistemological explanation of knowledge. Habermas draws his first conclusions:

> What is Kantian about Marx's conception of knowledge is the invariant relation of the species to its natural environment, which is established by the behavioral system of instrumental action....The conditions of instrumental action arose contingently in the natural evolution of the human species. At the same time, however, they bind our knowlege of nature with transcendental necessity to the interest of possible technical control over natural processes. The objectivity of the possible objects of experience is constituted within a conceptual-perceptual scheme rooted in deep-seated structures of human action; this scheme is equally binding on all subjects that keep alive through labor. The objectivity of the possible objects of experience is thus grounded in the identity of a natural substratum, namely that of the bodily organization of man, which is oriented toward action, and not in an original unity of appreciation which, according to Kant, guarantees with transcendental necessity the identity of an ahistorical consciousness in general. (50)

This is how each generation recreates anew, and as new, the form in which the unity of subject and object is presented. This historical specificity is not compatible with the classical transcendental project. Habermas draws modern conclusions from the results of Hegel's critique of Kant. The first step is to specify the nature and limits of what he calls instrumental action, and the positivist sciences built upon it. That analysis, which is developed through Habermas's reading of Peirce in particular, lies beyond the present concern. The methodological place of labor suggests a real genesis that accounts for the possibility and the validity of our knowledge of the historical world. The growth of the species comes from the continual interaction of laboring genetic production and the normative reflection of it by a subject whose labor continually transforms it. The unity of these two moments presents what Habermas calls a "quasi-transcendental" argument. Its transcendental features come from the invariant constitutive ontology; the *quasi* is due to the material, historical, and potentially accidental or incomplete relation to natural givenness. Habermas's term suggests a philosophical uncertainty that can be avoided here by treating the account as methodological. The next step in his reconstruction points implicity in the same direction.

The integraton of theoretical and practical reason entailed in the notion of material synthesis through labor suggests a return to Fichte's formulation of the priority of the act of self-consciousness. The Kantian transcendental unity of apperception was grounded deductively through a process of abstraction. The resulting difficulties permitted the constitutive misreading of Kant's systematic intent. As an ultimate normative foundation upon which no further reflection was possible, the "I think" could also be conflated with the (singular or plural) noumena. The result is an idealist formulation (as in Schelling). A different interpretation is suggested by the priority of practical reason, which leads to Fichte's self-positing active subject. Habermas draws implications from this latter parallel.

> At any stage, the social subject confronted by its environment relates to past processes of production and reproduction as a whole by returning to itself, just as the ego confronted with its nonego [in Fichte] relates to the deed of action in which the absolute ego produces itself as ego by positing a nonego in opposition to itself. Only in its process of production does the species *posit* itself *as* a social subject. (55)

The identity of consciousness, Kant's transcendental ego as foundation, is no longer an ontological and external norm. It is itself the result of the labor process. Habermas stresses that for Marx the process is historical, binding the Fichtean absolute "to the limits drawn by Kant's transcendental philosophy and Darwin's evolutionism"(57). The reference to Darwin reaffirms the irreducible Otherness of Nature stressed by the Kantian dualism and dissolved by Hegel's ontology. It implies that the imbrication of natural history and human history, of Nature and Freedom, is the result of laboring reproduction whose necessity is grounded in the very physical nature of hominoids. The quasi-transcendental argument is now placed in the service of methodology. Laboring reproduction is instrumental action. Its subject is the species in its animal givenness. This natural process has produced a self-conscious and potentially free humanity whose acts need no longer follow only the pattern of instrumental action. Human action must obey the dictates of physical nature; but self-reflexion permits the development of a "culture" that, as in Kant, can posit goals and make instrumental use of the lawfulness it discovers in the natural world. The institutions of social interaction produced by a self-conscious humanity are a further part of its social history. This historical social interaction must be integrated into the epistemological social theory.

Marx's path from philosophy to political economy explains how reduction to instrumental economic labor is avoided without transforming the method into an ontology whose universal validity makes it useless. Habermas warns against two symmetrical dangers built into this movement. Instrumental action cannot be treated as the model of all human praxis. Nor can natural and social science be identified. In the first case, the result is a constitutive ontology. The second error is the product of an ontological methodology. Marx can be shown to have succumbed, at least for a moment, to both temptations. He tends toward a positivist scientism of a constitutive type in 1844, when he expects that natural science will subsume eventually the science of man and that the science of man will subsume natural science, so that there will be "one science." The same temptation appears later, in his pleased citation of his Russian reviewer in the preface to the second edition of *Capital.* On the other hand, the ontologized methodology appears in *The German Ideology* and in the later *Grundrisse,* when Marx is tempted to conceive of the history of the species as a history of technology. In Habermas's concise formulation of this interpretation: "First the capacities of the executing organs, then those of the sense organs, the energy production of the human organism, and finally the capacities of the controlling organ, the brain"(65-66). The necessity and inveitability of the next stage of human history—better, of human evolution—is then said to be ordained with natural scientific certainty on this basis. Yet these transformations of methodology into positive science or ontology are not Marx's last word.

The evolutionary naturalism that results from ignoring the difference of social and natural science loses the gains of Hegel's critique of Kant. The subject becomes an incidental factor as technological evolution prepares the future. The interchange with nature continues. Nature is transformed and appropriated to an ever greater degree. The laboring process that mediates this transformation changes only formally. The subject is simply a function in a natural process. Its particularity is indifferent. The reflexive dimension of the *Bildungsprozess* falls away. Liberation is then said to be the result of a linear process of Nature, not a radical necessity for the active subject which must exercise its autonomy. Negative political implications follow from this transformation. One might oppose to it another well-known Marxist phrase that defines history in a nonscientific manner: "All history is the history of class struggle." The generalization of the material synthesis through labor makes History a unidimensional production of the species. It neglects the institutional framework that emerges when natural production becomes conscious re-production of the species. When the ontologization of material synthesis is avoided, the inverse question emerges. How could this fabulous material growth take place without a corresponding change at the level of consciousness? The institutional framework and social relations of power must be taken into account if the picture is to be complete. This is where class struggle enters the theoretical reconstruction of History. Recalling that Nature is not wholly external to a pure consciousness, Habermas defines his basic categories:

> While *instrumental action* corresponds to the force of external nature, and the state of the productive forces determines the measure of the technical control over the powers of nature, *communicative action* stands in correspondence to the repression of our own nature: the institutional framework determines the measure of a repression through the natural [*naturwüchsig*] power of social dependence and political domination. (71)

Communicative action is not governed by the laws of instrumental laboring production. It is the dimension in which the identity of the subject is formed. An institutional framework that furthers the communicative growth of self-consciousness must correspond to the growth in productive forces and the potential emancipation they imply. This dimension, which Habermas calls communicative action, is the correlate of what Marx designates as class struggle.

Habermas's philosophical reconstruction shows how class struggle can be integrated into the necessary synthesis by labor. An institutional synthesis is set parallel to the productive process. Its possibility is implicit in Marx's view of society as determined by both the forces and by the relations of production. Marx's argument runs into difficulty when the class actors are specified "scientifically," in terms of their "objective" relation to the means of production and the logic of instrumental action. This excludes particular subjectivity. Asymmetrical class relations are conceived only as economic forms of material scarcity. Institutional change is replaced by the laboring conquest of external scarcity. Reflection is treated as if it existed actually, in the form of a real logic of production. The particular dimensions of life praxis, class struggle, historical and natural opacity are lost. This instrumental logic creates only a quantitative identity. It brings an end to the process of self-reflexion as well as a (totalitarian) End of History. The temptation to thematize class struggle along these positivist lines is always present. The ground for this continual temptation is only implicit in Habermas's reconstruction of Marx. The source of the difficulty is that the attempt to understand the necessity of social transformation through the ontology of the constitutive subject lends itself to the productivist image of instrumental action. A partial correction and caution are obtained when the institutional relations thematized by class struggle are added to the account. This proposal by Habermas avoids the productivist determinism, but it does not succeed in demonstrating the methodological necessity that holds the productive and institutional analysis together.

Habermas suggests a radical interpretation recalling Kant's Copernican inversion. The history of production can be reconstructed within the framework of "the appearing consciousness of classes"(83). This turn away from the logical presentation of method to its phenomenological complement was implicit in Habermas's manner of reconstructing Marx by playing off Kant (and Fichte) against Hegel. Its necessity at this juncture of the analysis is justified by the return of a "Kantian" difficulty. The history of the species is to be analyzed in the dimensions of labor and interaction, production and institutional class struggle. The presence of class struggle implies that the species is not a single unified subject. The parallel to Kant developed by an ontology of material constitution breaks down at this point. Hegel's phenomenological criticism must be applied again. This criticism begins from the fact of an essential division of class society. The only possible unity in such a society is the process of the formulation of the political question. Politics as a question seeks a universal adequate to represent the sense of the divided whole. The first aspect of the Marxian theory as methodology presents the structure of the divided unity. This explains why Marx could expect that the social world was ripe for the revolutionary appeal. The development of the laboring, interactive class subject is paralleled by a humanization of the external natural and social world. This aspect of the method needs completion by an account of the particularity that permits the full political articulation while avoiding the constitutive and ontological temptations. It is not sufficient to speak of class struggle and class societies in general. Revolutionary receptivity points only to the possibility of change; its actualization must be able to claim rational necessity. The proletariat as the agent of revolution is too general, and too ontological, a solution to this particular problem. Treatment of the question as methodological and as political is a necessary preliminary.

CHAPTER 6

The Phenomenology of Particularity

POLITICS AND METHOD

The interdependence and independence of modern philosophy and politics are mirrored in the internal structure of the methodology appropriate to each of them. The method is neither philosophy nor politics. This independence permits it to serve two masters without being tyrannized by either. A loss of independence can come only from internal weakness. The methodological account of the necessary conditions of receptivity loses its logical articulation if it is divorced from the philosophical premises it articulates. As method, however, its function is genetic. It provides the *Zutat* that avoids the unmediated passage to the political as the completion of the explanation of the necessary receptivity to the categories of philosophy. The foundation of this genetic intervention is the structure of the originary philosophy. The second moment of method is founded by the same originary structure. It is inversely isomorphic to the first. The structure of particularity that completes the system by demonstrating the place of politics loses its phenomenological character if it is treated apart from the political conditions from which it is the mediation. The phenomeological moment of the method plays a *normative* role. The contemplative *Zusehen* in which it culminates indicates that the political is a particular structure that cannot be extended arbitrarily. The method appropriate to modern politics is particular and limited. These polarities indicate that the two moments of method stand in an originary relation to one another. This structure explains how method can remain the independent servant of the philosophy and of the politics that it articulates and mediates.

The orginary relation of the two moments of method explains why problems relevant to one aspect appear as limits—and as the source of error and distortion—in the presentation of the complementary methodological moment. The problem of particularity was encountered in the account of the receptivity. Demonstration that representation was both possible and necessary to insure completeness of the logical structure was not sufficient. The other side of the relation was neglected. The source of the difficulty is the failure to specify what can and cannot be represented. The logical *Zutat* is external and arbitrary without the specification of the type of particularity that induces the reflective judgment that makes representation necessary. Kant cannot assert arbitrarily that any or every object is beautiful. He cannot discover teleological structures at will. Genius or the Happy Chance encountered in nature are no solution. Hegel's difficulties were caused by the arbitrary particularity from which he began. Despite his insistence that Civil Society is defined by the principle of particularity, Hegel can admit this principal only formally within his account. Concrete particularity is only integrated (*aufgehoben*) into the systematic whole which becomes actual world history to which particularity is sacrificed. The achievement of the presentation of Civil Society is sacrificed; Hegel can be accused of idealism or condemned for defending the status quo. The distortion in Marx's account of receptivity is inversely isomorphic to that of Hegel. Labor as material synthesis is a concrete particular interaction through which at every moment the real world can be understood and transformed. No historical *Zutat* is necessary to guide the development which depends, in an unspecified manner, on the particular will that is able to actualize finally the always present potentiality. The logic of history is substituted for the necessary learning process in revolutionary class struggle. The result is a supposed materialism that is in fact an ontological theory of constitution. In the best of cases, Kant, Hegel, and Marx do recognize the need to account for the kind of particularity that articulates the systematic completeness whose lack explains their errors. In the worst of cases, lack of an independent methodological moment of particularity hides the systematic nature of their work. This concealment explains a variety of common (mis-) interpretations, and particularly the failure to identify the systematic need for an independent method.

The originary structure present in the independent method as a whole is not identical with the originary philosophy itself. The independence of method is the result of its being doubly dependent. Its normative legitimation comes from the philosophical system; its genetic completeness depends on the political structure. The logical moment of methodological receptivity articulates the philosophical foundation. The phenomenological moment of particularity presents the necessity of political completion as its practical result. This co-presence protects the originality of the methodological account. Without the pull from both directions, the moment of receptivity is transformed into a general ontology that becomes an empty tautology. Such a generalized ontology can only justify itself by recourse to an external agency. This was why Hegel introduced a presupposed particularity by means of a philosophical *Zutat*. His unjustified introduction of the state on these grounds denies the independence of the political. Marx's difficulty had similar methodological foundations. The class struggle was postulated within a logical framework attributed to historical progress. The political conclusion postulated a unitary species subject—the proletariat as the "nothing that can become everything"—that replaced the essentially divided class society whose articulation would have demanded a political argument. Kant's position is unique. His system preserves the independence of the political. This was not his explicit intent. Politics has no place within the system of philosophy sketched in the introduction to the *Critique of Judgment.* Kant's attention was directed toward the political by the French Revolution. One of his attempts to understand the legitimacy of revolution suggests why the political calls for the articulation of an independent methodological moment. In *Religion within the Limits of Reason Alone,* Kant argues that even if it were possible to know morally and scientifically that a revolution is possible and necessary, such a politics is nonetheless to be rejected. Its results would be fixed and permanent. They could be changed only by another revolution. The kind of scientific and/or moral certainty that justifies this revolution is the predicative subsumption of a particular under a pregiven universally valid law. The result is a "contract made to cut off all further enlightenment."[1] A theory of the political cannot dissolve the particularity to whose role Kant's demonstration of receptivity pointed. Such a political theory will permit the articulation of the methodological moment that was lacking when the three *Critiques* were treated as constituting an inclusive system.

The complementarity of the two moments of method warns against a political parallel to the ontological error that distorts the first moment. The presentation of particularity is not identical to, nor does it replace, a theory of politics. The difficulty arises when method is treated as the tool for finding solutions. Hegel and Marx were confronted with a presupposed particularity that cannot be grounded adequately. They introduced politics to found, or to eliminate, this externality. Instead of the methodological articulation of a problem, both sought its elimination. This presuposes what needs to be demonstrated. Why is *this* particularity a problem? The eradication of particularity demands an account of its receptivity to the proposed solution. A politics that ignores this methodological question falls back to the theoretical position of a constitutive ontology. Politics is replaced by (incorrect) theory. Instead, independent method, posing problems, has to be permitted its autonomy. Only then can politics and theory be related without the one being reduced to the other.

The strengths and weaknesses of the equation of method with politics are presented brilliantly by Schiller's attempt in the *Letters on the Aesthetic Education of Man* to account for the empirical moral concern that Kant presupposed in the *Founda-*

tions of the Metaphysics of Morals. Schiller's reflections can serve here because his combination of systematic rigor and poetic vigor drew implications that the more cautious or less passionate neglect. Kant's equation of Will and Reason is the source of the problem confronted by Schiller. He suggests that man is doubly determined. He is a physical being who nonetheless has a rational understanding. His particular empirical will is the result of the variable interaction between these two determinations. The will is weakened when one or the other aspect dominates. The asymmetry limits the possibility of growth and learning. Aesthetic politics is the method that will restore the balance. Its harmonious result will guarantee socially the growth of a free republican polity. The advantage of Schiller's approach is its identification of the particular will as both the agency and the result of politics. The ontological Reason (or Will) whose universal and presupposed validity subsumes particularity is avoided. The weakness of Schiller's account is its presupposition that the material world will be receptive to the action of the mediating "play drive" that makes politics possible. Hegel correctly attacks the ontology implicit in both these proposals (from which he nonetheless borrowed).[2] The politics of play is neither a real possibility (as Schiller admits) nor effective as a Kantian transcendental Idea (as he suggests). Schiller is unable to explain how the single subjective harmony becomes a plurality that expresses publicly what Kant called a "communal sense." He lacks the notion of a reflective judgment. His politics has no independent method. Schiller's concern with particularity leads him to presuppose a receptivity that he cannot justify. His politics becomes ultimately an ontology.

The theoretical need for an independent methodology must be grounded also in the structure of the political. This aspect of method is commonly called the "theory-practice" problem. The originary philosophy needs a theory of the political to insure its systematic completeness. The methodological mediation is not a step along the path to a political sphere yet to be defined at the end of the road. The political is not constituted by a progressive development from the simple to the complex; it is not the product of an inductive demonstration. The need for methodological independence was demonstrated (in Chapter 4) by the constitutive ontological temptation which moved without mediation from theory to a politics. Because it is defined by theory, the resulting politics cannot be the completion that they system requires. Such a politics cannot provide an independent methodological moment of particularity. A methodology based only on philosophy is insufficient. Its articulation of particularity is conflated with the political just as its account of receptivity is reduced to the presentation of an ontology. In isolation, each moment itself appears to incarnate the orginary domain upon which it is founded. The account of receptivity seemed to demand completion by the particularity that must be represented. But theory alone cannot articulate that particularity. Not every object presents the "lawfulness without law" that is fundamental to Kant's demonstration. When philosophy tries to provide specification it becomes arbitrary and accidental because it depends on the pregiven world that is external and accidental for it. The particularity of the Corporations and the Rabble were facts that Hegel could not integrate into philosophy as he could for example, the indeterminacy in the Administration of Justice. Economistic Marxism, or labor as material synthesis, does not show which particular issues challenge radically the permanently contradictory capitalist class economy. The theory-practice problem is the abstract formulation of the originary relation of the two moments of methodology. The abstraction needs content. Its content cannot be arbitrary. Theory alone cannot provide it. This is where the political affects the methodological presentation.

The foundational relation between politics and the methodlogical account of particularity is the inverse of the relation between philosophy and the methodology it grounds. The substantive formulation—"the political"—points to the originary coequality of philosophy and politics. This interdependence explained the necessity of an independent methodology. The articulation of particularity is phenomenological. The theoretical formulation of originary philosophy showed that the phenomenological method needs the aid of a logical *Zutat*. This theoretical argument was illustrated in the articulation of methodological receptivity. A distortion enters the presentation of particularity when the method is treated as the attempt to give content to a presupposed definition of the political. The Marxist is tempted to appeal to the logic of economic determinism. The Hegelian may look to History as the "Court of the Last Judgment," or he may thematize the assumed rationality of the present. The Kantian may absolutize the formal deliverances of the moral law to compensate for the uncertainty in the phenomena of human finitude. The problem in each case is not the invocation of a logical *Zutat*. The logic applied, not the "application," was incorrect. Instead of preserving particularity, each *Zutat* attempted to eliminate it; instead of presenting a problem, each sought a solution. This error is avoided when the political determination of the second moment of method is stressed. The articulation of particularity is not a formal theoretical imperative derived only from the originary structure of the independent method.[3] The method is also dependent. That is what differentiates it from the political as well as from the philosophical. The methodology of particularity makes clear this specificity which the presentation of receptivity left implicit.

The difference between the theoretical foundation of the method of receptivity and the political grounds that determine the articulation of particularity suggests a change in the mode of presentation. The definition of the political by the originary philosophy provided only general boundary determinations. Its content cannot be specified without the aid of a methodology. This method, however, depends on the very same political results that it must assure. The circularity cannot be avoided by the derivation of method from theory alone. Political and methodological distortions occurred when method was presented as an independent originary structure. The only other option is to presuppose a definition of the political that provides it with content, or to remain at the formal level defined by the orginary structure. Marx and Hegel tend toward the former option, Kant toward the latter. Presentation of the political moment of method in this order will clarify the place of methodological relation of theory to practice. The theory-practice problem can only be posed within the framework defined by modernity.[4] The same modernity that poses the problem also resolves it. There are no external Truths or Goods. The modern formulation of the theory-practice is the (reflective) practice-theory debate. Marx's political historical analyses are the clearest formulation of this aspect of the issue. Hegel's account of the spheres of Abstract Right and Morality in which individual action is overdetermined by *Sittlichkeit* moves closer to the theory-practice formulation. Kant's recognition of the independent place of the political suggests that the apparently classical formulation (in his reply to Garve) needs to be nuanced. The implication of these reversed pairings for the history of ideas can be left aside here.

The theory-practice problem appears at this juncture because of the failure to distinguish between method, theory, and the political. Methodological independence is founded on the dependence of each of its aspects respectively on the theoretical and the political. The conditions of receptivity can be misinterpreted as presenting the theoretical foundation for practical action on the part of particulars designated by the structure of the political. This would not be wholly unfaithful to each of the theorists. This structure would present a Marxism uniting either a logic of economic determinism or a theory of labor as material synthesis with the action of a proletarian subject. It would present a Hegelianism whose theory of the political state determines the structure of Abstract Right and Morality in which individuals live their particular existence. It would leave a Kant whose third *Critique* did not reveal anything that the third Antinomy in the first *Critique* had not already shown, and who, despite his support for the French Revolution, could only expect gradual change from the Idea of the Good Will. The poles that these portraits unite are external to each other. Their justification is external to each of them. They cannot be taken as solutions to the modern theory-practice problem, however true they may be to the actual intentions of each philosopher. The dependence of method suggests that the solution to the problem is found outside its boundaries. The relation of practice to theory is explained when politics is able to show *which* particulars are to be involved in the process of representation, while philosophy demonstrates *how* such representation is possible and necessary. The problem emerged only when method acquired a false independence. Its resolution by the reintegration of the three aspects of the modern political-philosophical structure will become apparent when the Kantian self-limiting theory is able nonetheless to present the richest and most self-reflective articulation of the political. That demonstration will justify the proposed path "from Marx to Kant" of which this methodological chapter is the (dependent) first demonstration.

THE PHENOMENOLOGY OF POLITICS

Marx's three major historical-political essays follow the French proletariat from its defeats in 1848, through its passive presence during Bonaparte's coup in 1851, to the radical upsurge of the Paris Comune in 1871. He presents a phenomenological path through which the alienated and exploited proletariat comes to realize Reason's demands. The phenomenological intention is expressed clearly in the introduction to *Class Struggles in France.* It is "not the victory of February, but only...a series of defeats" that will bring the necessary transformation. The events following the February rising are interpreted as progress by applying the notion of determinant negation. The proletariat "won the terrain for the fight for its revolutionary emancipation itself!" This "terrain" can be interpreted as objective or as subjective. The defeats teach the proletariat what logical Marxian theory had said since "On the Jewish Question." Political action by itself can give only illusory emancipation. The necessary material complement was absent, continues Marx, due to the new "general prosperity" on the Continent. "A new revolution is only possible in consequence of a new crisis. It is, however, just as certain as this." This certainty was misplaced. The next crisis that faced the proletariat after 1848 was not primarily economic but political. Economic stalemate made possible the political coup d'état of Louis-Napoleon Bonaparte. Revolutionary possibility is clearly not the same as its real necessity. The economic foundation is not alone sufficient. Marx turns his attention to the transformations of the political stage. He demonstrates that, and why, these political forms will be unable to maintain the capitalist economic structures. The economic remains present but in the background after 1851. The result of the series of economic and political negations appears two decades later, in *The Civil War in France.* The Paris Commune is described as "the political form at last discovered according to which to work out the economic emancipation of labor." Thus, at the end of its phenomenological development, proletarian politics has absorbed the economic infrastructure that was the omnipresent silent partner in the earlier phases. The "political form" is the key to "economic emancipation."

A phenomenological method is accompanied always by the logical complement that insures that the *Zusehen* will focus on the proper objective "terrain." This phenomenological logic is not always univocally articulated in Marx's description. Remarks about the necessary "new crises" are accompanied sometimes by the linear expectation that historical development will guide the actors automatically. The linear logic is never presented in crude formulations familiar from propagandistic texts like *The Communist Manifesto.* Even when the reductionist approach to ideology is found, its context suggests a cautious reading.

> And as in private life one differentiates between what a man thinks and says of himself and what he really is and does, so in the histoical struggles one must distinguish still more the phrases and fancies of parties from their real organism and their real interests, their conception of themselves from their reality. (*Eighteenth Brumaire*)

Applications of this principle abound. *Class Struggles in France* portrays a petite bourgeoisie unable to admit how similar its position is to that of the proletariat. To hide this unpleasant material reality from itself, it adopts the symbolic name, "the Mountain," taken from its triumphant period during the French Revolution. Those revolutionaries of 1789 are described later, in the *Eighteenth Brumaire*, as themselves needing the disguise of Roman history as they "performed the task of their time." This reference to a task suggests that Marx's theory knows the historical logic that these Brutuses, Grachii, and Publicolas hid from themselves. Yet the need for heroism suggests that the logical pattern from which knowledge of the task would be derived does not work automatically. *Class Struggles in France* portrays the difficulties to which this self-deception leads:

> In France, the petite bourgeoisie does what normally the industrial bourgeoisie would have to do; the worker does

> what normally would be the task of the petite bourgeoisie; and the task of the worker, who solves that? No one.

Marx's solution combined political and economic logic. Only when "the proletariat is pushed to the head of the people that dominates the world market, to the head of England," will the possible revolution necessarily enter the agenda. The dominant place of the political is reinforced by a similar assertion concerning the peasantry. Marx's economic theory shows the necessary demise of the mode of production to which the peasantry is central. He does not use that economic argument in *Class Struggles in France.* Peasant action is explained as the result of a political process encapsulated in the famous phrase, "Revolutions are the locomotives of history." A similar political analysis of the peasantry is found in the *Eighteenth Brumaire.* Reduction to the economic infrastructure is not the basis of Marx's phenomenology.

The logic that dominates Marx's political histories is not economic but political. This confirms the expectation that the phenomenology of particularity gets its methodological specificity from the political. The account of the economic or material logic of receptivity does not guide Marx's phenomenology of particularity. The *Zutat* needed here is explicitly political; it is independent of the methodological argument retraced here. The presence of this political logic in Marx's phenomenological trilogy explains why Marx should not be taxed with economist reductionism. The distinction of method from theory and from politics permits a more nuanced account. The specificity of Marx's approach is seen in the movement of the three historical-political works. *Class Struggles in France* describes how

> In rapid succession the revolution threw all the old opposition parties to the top of the new state, so that they had to deny and revoke their old phrases not only in deeds but in words, and might finally be flung all together, combined in a repulsive mixture, on the dung heap of history by the people.

The revocation in words as in deeds is typical of what the *Eighteenth Brumaire* depicts brilliantly as the "incurable disease of parliamentary cretinism." This malady "holds those infected by it fast in an imaginary world and robs them of all sense, all memory, all understanding of the rude external world." Bonaparte's coup d' état is the result of a process during which the Parliament shows itself impotent before submitting finally to an individual will that expresses "the heteronomy of a nation in contrast to its autonomy." After Parliament has gone through all the possible phases and phenomenological *Gestalten,* the untrammeled executive power of the emperor presents the final unmasking of bourgeois rule. Marx insists that

> the parody of the empire was necessary to free the mass of the French nation from the weight of tradition and to work in pure form the opposition between the state power and society. With the progressive undermining of small-holding property, the state structure erected upon it collapses. The centralization of the state that modern society requires arises only on the ruins of the military-bureaucratic governmental machinery that was forged in opposition to feudalism.

The economic undermining that Marx mentions here becomes important only in the political context. The final act is made possible by a political necessity predicted by Marx nearly twenty years before it occurred. Bonaparte used the symbolism of the first Napoléon to win support from the atomized peasantry. This worked as long as his success endured. Internal difficulties finally led him to risk external adventure, the only escape. Bonaparte's failure in war made revolution possible. The acquired political experience of the French political system made it necessary. The Paris Commune had learned the impossibility of using the existing state machinery for its own ends. It replaced the state by the "great social measure of the Commune," which is "its own working existence." The Commune is not the result of either economic or historical logical necessity. Its novelty remains to be defined.[5]

The absence of the proletariat from the historical stage is explained by the methodological function of the political logic. The method has to explain the formation of this particular subject as revolutionary. The economic and historical demonstration of receptivity by the laboring subject needs to be supplemented. The proletariat as a political class that is uniquely revolutionary can neither be presupposed nor determined externally. Its formation begins with the rising in February 1848. The proletariat was too weak to dominate objectively the situation. It was manipulated in temporary political alliances that were broken by provocations culminating in the June rising of 1848. This failure is literally demoralizing. Seeking private solutions, it

> throws itself into doctrinaire experiments, exchange banks, and workers associations, hence into a movement in which it renounces the revolutionizing of the old world by means of the latter's own great, combined resources, and seeks, rather, to achieve its salvation behind society's back, in private fashion, within its limited conditions of existence, and hence necessarily suffers shipwreck.

Reference to the "great, combined resources" could indicate a residue of economic logic behind the argument. The suggestion that the turn away from politics is responsible for the "necessary shipwreck" is more important. Marx's analysis of the petit bourgeois "Mountain" highlights the same error. This class bases its political aspirations on (correctly perceived) private interest. Such universalization of the particular was seen to be one of the theoretical forms of ideology. Its political complement is analyzed in Marx's account of the stalemate that permitted Bonaparte's coup d'état. "Parliamentary cretinism" is the result of each group treating itself as a universal end-in-itself. Factionalization and paralysis follow necessarily from this egoistic blindness to the place and nature of politics. The nightmare of a "socialist" threat to its social power leads the bourgeoisie to the conclusion: "Rather an end with terror than a terror without end!" Neither economic necessity nor the reality of a proletarian threat explains this self-delusion. Its logic is political.

The appearance of an economic logic in the ambiguous social behavior of the bourgeoisie clarifies the methodological orientation underlying Marx's account. Marx takes account of the transformations introduced by modern society. The divisions between the Legitimist and the Orleanist bourgeoisie once expressed a real division between fortune based on landed wealth and parvenu industrial and banking capital. The "parliamentary cretins" do not realize that these two factions have long since fused. "They do their real business as the *party of Order,* that is, under a *social,* not under a *political title;* as representatives of the bourgeois world order, not as knights of errant princesses; as the bourgeois class against other classes, not as royalists against republicans." Marx appears to treat politics here by means of a reductionist critique of ideology. His explanation of the support Bonaparte received from the bourse and from the nonparliamentary bourgeoisie follows the same pattern. It "sacrificed its general class interests, that is, its political interests, to the narrowest and most sordid private interest." This denial of politics turns against the economistic bourgeoisie. True class interests, its "general class interests," are in fact political interests. Marx draws the consequences in terms of the political logic:

> Thus...the bourgeoisie confesses that its own interests dictate that it should be delivered from the danger of its *own rule;* that, in order to restore transquility in the country, its bourgeois Parliament must, first of all, be given its quietus; that in order to preserve its social power intact, its political power must be broken; that the individual bourgeois can continue to exploit other classes and to enjoy undisturbed property, family, religion, and order only on condition that their class be condemned along with the other classes to a like political nullity; that in order to save its purse, it must forfeit the crown, and the sword that is to safeguard it must at the same time be hung over its own head as a sword of Damocles.

Economic, private interests are illusory guides in politics. When they are presented as universalizable, their ideological nakedness is revealed. The coming of the empire is explained only apparently by a retrospective functionalist economic logic of the "party of Order." The advent of the empire has nothing in common with the revolutionary economic transformation by which capitalism broke the web of feudal political institutions.

Support for the empire comes from three strata whose place and role are determined by the logic of politics. Bonaparte's legal election in 1848 depended on the peasant vote. The economic existence of the peasantry is condemned in the long run by the development of the capitalist society. Its political role is determined by its past political function. Politics has made the peasantry a "class" that is not an economic class capable of positive action. Peasant conditions have not been changed by the capitalist economy. Each household is identical to the others, like potatoes in a sack. Each is at the same time separated from the others by poor means of communication and material poverty. There is no division of labor, application of science, or development of particularity because the peasant has no more intercourse with nature than with his fellow men. This makes the peasantry politically dependent. "Their representative at the same time must appear as their master, as an authority over them, as an unlimited governmental power that protects them against the other classes and sends them rain and sunshine from above."[6] The political logic that constituted the sack of potatoes into a "class" explains the criteria governing its choice of a political master. The Nephew incarnates mythically the power that had created the peasantry. Napoléon's wars had given it a sense of mission and honor. Identification with the nation made it a kind of particular that could claim universal, political validity. The Napoleonic myth is not destroyed by the new nineteenth-century reality that replaces subordination to the feudal lord by debt to the village usurer. The myth is not economic; it is political. The centralizing state and its bureaucracy incarnate the institution of which the peasantry dreams. Conversely, this state and its agents atomize and particularize, homogenize and differentiate society until it becomes the mirror image of the peasant structure. The circle is completed with this step.

The other two groups that support Bonaparte are the political creation of his own empire. Both preexisted the empire as social factors, but their political role emerges only with it. The lumpen proletariat is described as displaced *gens sans feu et sans aveu* who resemble the Hegelian Rabble.[7] Because it has no social insertion, the lumpen can be bought by a combination of garlic sausage, uniformed pomp, and the chance to bully others. With this purchase completed, the lumpen tends to fuse with the other mainstay of the empire—the bureaucrat. Both social groups have a political existence only because of the expanding state. This explains their support for the empire. Fusion with the lumpen stresses the element of brutality and force involved in the operation of the bureaucracy. Marx does not apply the reductionist critique of the separation of politics from civil society that he used in the 1840s. The bureaucratic state machinery does not resort only to force. "All revolutions have perfected this machine instead of smashing it," observes Marx two decades before the Paris Commune undertook this very destruction. The machine is perfected by the development of bourgeois institutions for the political articulation of society. The division of labor permits increased control by atomizing society in the image of the peasantry. Marx does not develop the critique of this bureaucratic domination. Nor does he propose another mode that would permit adequate representation of the society in the political sphere. This self-limitation can be understood as a limitation imposed by the framework of methodology. Marx's expectations of eventual collapse of the empire are based on political rather than economic argument. Reassertion by the bourgeoisie is politically impossible. Their economic egotism gave the empire the political power to manipulate their social pretensions. Marx's predictions are based on the effects of increased taxation necessary to maintain the lumpen and the bureaucracy. The vulgar force employed by the lumpen-bureaucracy to gain state revenue will undermine the political legitimacy of the state. Military adventure will be necessary to preserve the adhesion of the peasantry. Marx's predictions go no further. That is not the task of method.

The limits of methodology explain the absence of the proletariat from the portrait intended to explain how it becomes the particular agent that brings the revolution to fruition. Marx reintroduces it in the final section of the *Eighteenth Brumaire*. Vanquished in the June revolt, "it haunts the subsequent acts of the drama like a ghost." The reduction of politics to economic interest is not the only cause of the political delusions of the bourgeoisie. It makes a second error because it cannot admit this reduction to itself. The proletariat is a social threat to its domination. This menace is only potential as long as the proletariat is divided. Its division is built into its economic position of subordination to different capitalist masters. Each of these masters, and their political mouthpieces, translates the social threat into a political program. The paradoxical result contributes to the political unification of the proletariat. This same logic sets the factions within the bourgeoisie against each other. Each raises the reproach of "socialism" against the proposals of the others. The result completes the phenomenological specificity of the revolutionary proletariat.

> This [reproach of "socialism"] was not merely a figure of speech, fashion, or party tactics. The bourgeoisie had a true insight into the fact that all the weapons which it had forged against feudalism turned their points against itself, that all the means of education which it had produced rebelled against its own civilization, that all the gods which it had created had fallen away from it. It understood that all the so-called bourgeois liberties and organs of progress attacked and menaced its *class rule* at its social foundation and its political summit simultaneously, and had therefore become "socialistic."

A further passage makes the phenomenological orientation more specific. "As long as the rule of the bourgeois class had not been organized completely, as long as it had not acquired its pure political expression, the antagonism of the other classes, likewise, could not appear in its pure form." The political logic explains why the phenomenology does not describe developments in the consciousness of an already existing class. The presupposition of such a preexisting class would violate the immanence of the modern. The phenomenology is not a philosophical presentation of the development of *Geist.* It is not a constitutive logico-phenomenological *Zutat* justified by the methodological account of labor as material synthesis. Marx has been describing the process through which modern bourgeois society creates the political conditions that puts its own foundations into question. Nothing is constituted in this immanent process. The political developments are the methodological means by which the proletariat becomes revolutionary. When the political forms have been completely experienced, with Marx's description of the Paris Commune, the "economic emancipation of labor" is prepared by the "pure political expression" of bourgeois rule.

The limitation on what methodology can propose explains why these historical writings are not a theory of why to make a revolution, or a political statement of how to accomplish this task. There are elements of the why and the how present in Marx's historical trilogy. Their context gives them a different role. A final illustration of the methodological phenomenology in Marx's contrast of bourgeois with proletarian revolutions at the beginning of the *Eighteenth Brumaire* suggests this difference. The bourgeoisie "storm swiftly from success to success; their dramatic effects outdo each other; men and things seem set in sparkling brilliance; ecstasy is the everyday spirit." Proletarian revolutions are more phenomenological. They

> criticize themselves constantly, interrupt themselves continually in their own course, come back to the apparently accomplished in order to begin it afresh... recoil ever and anon from the indefinite prodigiousness of their own aims, until a situation has been created that makes all turning back impossible, and the conditions themselves cry out: *Hic rhodus, hic salta!*

This description is not methodological. Its presupposition of an agent of revolution cannot be justified. Method has to explain why the proletariat (or any other particular) is called to act. Theory explains that revolution is possible and necessary. Method articulates this theory historically. Marx's "*Hic rhodus, hic salta!*" recalls Hegel. But the theoretical methodology cannot be equated with the Cunning of Reason; the political methodology is not the action of the World Historical Individual. When the method is extended beyond its limits, it becomes a means to a politics whose nature it distorts. Marx is not immune to this distortion. Another reading is possible when the phenomenological account remains limited to the tasks of the method. A Marxian theory of the political that is compatible with the methodological insights of the phenomenological reconstruction in Marx's historical trilogy will demonstrate this conclusion.

THE PHENOMENOLOGY OF WILL

Because it is only "a part of the system," the *Philosophy of Right* is based on a presupposition defined first as the "concept of right" (para. 2). This concept is redefined as the will, whose nature is to be free (para. 4). This step could articulate the philosophical concept as a particular. This methodological move was not realized fully or adequately in Hegel's introductory argument. The introduction to the *Philosophy of Right* was seen ultimately to redefine the free will in terms of a logical *Sittlichkeit* that was unable to justify itself. The result was an essentialist or normative theory of constitution. The lack of methodological mediation dissolved the system into the reality of world history. Another interpretation can be proposed when the systematic character of the *Philosophy of Right* is stressed. This approach is suggested by a remark at the beginning of Hegel's 1823 lectures on the *Philosophy of Right*.[8] Like all sciences, a philosophy of right has three parts: (*a*) the concept of the idea of free will, called "practical spirit"; (*b*) the development of this concept, which is the "world of right" as morality (*die Moral*), the state, and its history; and (*c*) knowledge of right, in the form of the history of knowledge of right, morality, and the state. Hegel adds that for philosophy, the third rubric is not its history but rather the *Logic* which presents the immanent history of thinking about truth. Hegel is not referring to the notion that the *Logic* is "the presentation of God as He exists in his external Being before the creation of nature and a finite Spirit."[9] That premise of his "objective idealism" resulted in the unmediated normative theory of constitution. Hegel's insistence that the *Philosophy of Right* is only a part of the system suggests a different interpretation.

The "knowledge of right" is a representation that articulates reflectively the first two moments of the science. Although Hegel does not use these terms, the methodological place of his argument is clear. The paragraph (para. 3) that made the transition from the definition of the concept of right to its formulation as the particular free will contained Hegel's critique of the historical school of law. Hegel did not specify the structure of the history to which he appealed in rejecting the unmediated empiricism for which he criticized the historical school. "A particular law," he wrote in a previously cited passage, "may be shown to be wholly grounded in and consistent with the circumstances and with existing legally established institutions, and yet it may be wrong and irrational in its essential character, like a number of provisions in Roman private law" (para. 3). Althought there are moments when Hegel does treat history as simply the flow of time,[10] a quantitative history could not make so strong a theoretical claim. The methodological remark from 1823 suggests a way to avoid the constitutive suggestion that the concept of the will gets its particular content from the presupposed logic of *Sittlichkeit*. The logic of *Sittlichkeit* presents the methodological demonstration of receptivity. It was seen to need to be complemented by a methodological account of particularity. In the parallel case of Marx's theory of labor as material synthesis, this complement was provided by what Habermas called a history of the "appearing consciousness of classes." Such a history corresponds to what Hegel calls for in the third moment of his description of the science of right. Although the *Philosophy of History* might be read in this light, the inconsistencies already seen in it suggest attempting an immanent approach to the *Philosophy of Right*.[11]

The *Philosophy of Right* articulates the concept of right as two coequal spheres—Abstract Right and Morality—through which the free will passes phenomenologically before the structure of *Sittlichkeit* is elaborated explicitly. The process by which the implicitly *sittliche* world becomes explictly self-conscious in the state, which is then engulfed in World History, was interpreted as the methodological moment of receptivity. The relation of *Sittlichkeit* to Abstract Right and Morality presents a structure of particularity that can be shown to resolve the inconsistencies in the account of Civil Society. This will clarify the relation of *Sittlichkeit* to the modern political state, and thus to World History and its Reason, because the same *Sittlichkeit* cannot play at once the role of the political in determining the method of particularity and that of the philosophical in articulating the method of receptivity. The implicit *Sittlichkeit* illustrated by Aristotle's quantitative notion of virtue exists historically prior to the full development of the forms of Abstract Right and Morality. These logically more simple structures are the particularization of the unmediated universal *Sittlichkeit* which the system provided as the presuppostion of the *Philosophy of Right*. The real historical process can play a methodological role because of the manner in which the system was itself absorbed into the course of world history. The destruction of the immediately universal antique *Sittlichkeit* by the advent of individual subjectivity is explained by the developmental process in the spheres of Abstract Right and Morality. The triadic structure of *Sittlichkeit* is composed of moments that are historically coexistent (with the exception of World History, which is inconsistent with the rest of the argument). The triadic organization *within* Abstract Right and Morality, on the other hand, describes a process of development to increasingly complex stages. These two spheres are historically simultaneous and are also coexistent with the given historical form of *Sittlichkeit*. Since their internal organization is historical, changes in the structure of *Sittlichkeit* can be understood by the analysis of development in these logically more abstract forms. Hegel's leap to the political in the presentation of receptivity was governed by the appearance of an irreducible particularity. The articulation of Abstract Right and Morality as the locus of the political aspect of the methodology suggests an orientation that avoids this politicization of an essentially theoretical problem. The concept of the political that emerges differs from Hegel's own conclusions. The validity of this proposed reconstruction of "Hegelian" theory of the political depends first of all on the demonstration of a methodological articulation of particularity. Such a method depends upon a political premise, which can then be reconstructed in chapter 7.

The phenomenological movement begins from the self-identified will which must incorporate itself in the external world. The grounds for this development are immanent to the structure of the will. The procedure parallels the *Phenomenology*, where "consciousness" is both consciousness of an object and self-consciousness. The phenomenological stages are articulated by the interplay between the truth of the object and the truth of self-consciousness. The procedure is similar in the first two spheres of the *Philosophy of Right*. Abstract Right traces the institutional forms assumed by the will. The escape from formal self-identity demands that the world in which the will incorporates itself be truly external to it. This externality means that there is no pregiven logic to direct the will necessarily toward any specific path. Hegel does not say what sort of *Zutat* will be invoked as a guide. His description can be summarized quickly. The principle of Abstract Right is the sanctity of individual personality. Its structures are institutions that permit the Person to affirm its particular personality. These positive institutions have a negative function. Because the abstract principle of personality has no particular content, personality can be affirmed only at the expense of other Persons. Person seeks to avoid losing itself in external Otherness. In the process of affirming itself, it inevitably harms other particulars who exist alongside it. None of the particular Persons striving for self-realization can achieve more than temporary success in this abstract and undeclared war of all with all. The logical *Zutat* is invoked at this point. Person is wholly particular only when the negative, destructive manner of its behavior is recognized explicitly. Person becomes fully Person only as criminal! This moment of explicit particularity marks the transition to a new formal sphere, Morality. The structure of Morality is inversely isomorphic to the sphere of Abstract Right. The guiding theme is subjectivity, which was the implicit principle of the criminal's self-assertion. Because the subject is nonetheless part of the world, it cannot deny its responsibility for that world. Good intentions do not suffice. The Good Will must produce good actions. Realization of the Good comes to count more than the moral subject from which the experience began. At its height, morality must accept hypocrisy, which stresses effects on the world over the intentions of the subject, as illustrating its truth in the same way that criminality presented the truth of Abstract Right. The impossibility of truly realizing the principle of the moral Subject parallels the impossible realization of the principle of the juridical Person. The transition that now follows differs importantly from the preceding ones.

The relation of the phenomenological and the logical moments within Abstract Right and Morality makes clear the methodological function of these two sections. The logical *Zutat* in each of them has the familiar structure of an originary theory. The movement begins from the necessity that the will incorporate itself in the external world. This necessity is grounded in the theoretical system. Its first result is the institution of private property as a concrete incarnation of the particular will. Yet the will as personality cannot be simply a thing. The interplay between the need to be free and the need to exist in the external world gives rise to the series of phenomenological *Gestalten.* Private property is taken immediately as something to be used. A second moment frees the will from dependence on this immediacy by showing that property is something that also can be exchanged. Further refinements are developed. Possession need not be merely physical. Use permits the rental as well as the complete sale of property. Exchange includes the sale of one's own labor power and mental products (but not the sale of one's self). The articulation becomes increasingly subtle as Hegel describes the various forms of contractual relations. The necessity of "criminality" is described at the end of this mediation. Simple criminality through inadvertence (torts) results from the immediate coexistence of formally identical Persons seeking self-affirmation. The conscious cheating that succeeds by pretending to believe in the existence of a lawful world while in fact affirming only the private Person is a mediate development. The ultimate form of crime finally denies the validity of the laws of the external world altogether. This denial of the external world and sheer affirmation of self ground logically both crime *and* the new moral sphere. The transition is possible because the *Zutat* was invoked. This *Zutat* is logical and theoretical. It needs to be supplemented by another kind of methodological articulation if Hegel is to explain why "the will" fastens on one or another form of property, or contractual, or criminal relations. Hegel's presentation is a only transcendental reconstruction. It cannot claim completeness at the level of the theoretical system. Hegel admitted explicitly, for example, that new developments refine the Roman legal categories or the antique virtues. He offers no reason why his own phenomenological reconstruction of Abstract Right and Morality should remain fixed, as if History had come to an end. Methodological articulation of the problem of particularity must be invoked in order to clarify this difficulty, whose source is not theoretical but political.

The difference between method and theory is illustrated by a comparison of the transition from Abstract Right to Morality with the transition that leads from both of them to *Sittlichkeit.* The theoretical relation between the phenomenological and the logical accounts is seen in the transformation of the necessity of crime into the foundation of the moral consciousness. The movement passes from the abstract universality of Right, through the concrete human interrelations that constitute the contractual forms, to the recognition that personality can only be affirmed at the expense of the abstract universal Right. This self-affirming will is brought to realize that it can achieve its self-given ends only as the moral will. The legal Person becomes the moral Subject. Realization of will in the external world becomes the moral affirmation of inner purity. The new stage is only temporarily successful. Whatever the intentions of the Subject, the presence of the external world is felt in the consequences of its action. Morality learns to recognize and assume consciously its place in the external institutional world. It must care for the Welfare that is furthered or hindered by its intentions. This concern raises the spectre of utilitarian ends justifying the moral means. Casuistry is avoided when the moral Subject recognizes that the Good it seeks cannot be given concrete content. The Good that duty commands is an abstract formal universal inversely identical to the Person whose paradoxical realization was reconstructed in Abstract Right. This is why a form like hypocrisy, which consciously denies the subjective veracity of the Subject while affirming it externally, parallels the form of criminality which rejects the objective validity of the legal institutional order while affirming its own particularity in action. The phenomenolgoical path through these two spheres has come full circle. The self-same will externalizes itself in a series of institutions.. The process affects the external world. The phenomenological actor learns in the process. He passes through a series of moral *Gestalten.* The result involves the moral Subject with the World. At the end of the two cycles, the Subject of the experience has been transformed from an abstract to a concrete particular subject. This new particularity is described in the sphere of *Sittlichkeit.* The System of Needs asserts explicitly that the abstractions of Person and Subject are made concrete only in Civil Society (para. 190, Remark). The justification of that assertion is not provided within the *Sittlichkeit.* This suggests that the demonstration is not theoretical but methodological.

If the *Philosophy of Right* were a phenomenological *theory,* its subject would be a transhistorical, transcendental unity that passes through the moments of Abstract Right to Morality to *Sittlichkeit* as it becomes concretely universal. This is not what

Hegel describes. The subject of Abstract Right and Morality is formal and abstract. *Sittliche* subjectivity is concrete and real. The difference in qualitative and radical *Sittlichkeit* is the presupposition of Abstract Right and Morality. This relation is both historical and methodological. Particularity (or concrete universality) is not the result of the experience of Abstract Right and Morality. The argument needs to be inverted; particularly is the presupposition, not the result. *Sittlichkeit* is a particular totality that preserves itself because it is self-related, autonomous, and free. It knows itself as the positive particularity because it exists as the unity articulated by the spheres of Abstract Right and Morality. The kind of *Zutat* that this presupposed *Sittlichkeit* brings to the spheres of Abstract Right and Morality is not logical but methodological. This is the place of the political, to which the demonstration of the logic of receptivity leaped without mediation. The relation is reciprocal. The institutional and subjective moral choices that the phenomenological actor faces depend on the nature of the particular *Sittlichkeit.* The two abstract spheres articulate the historical specificity of *Sittlichkeit;* they explain its historical character. Hegel's question about the breakdown of the antique unity finds its answer in this relation. His problem with the Rabble needs this methodlogical mediation toward its political solution. Method—not theory!—is the precondition for political practice. Method cannot stand alone; yet it must stand apart. Its articulation justifies Hegel's contempt (in the preface and in the *Philosophy of History*) for those external critics who assume the "proud position." Legitimate criticism is based on the inconsistency between the *sittliche* formation and the methodological articulations that should justify it. When *Sittlichkeit* violates the structures of Abstract Right or Morality, it can be criticized on shared and public immanent grounds. This is the critical method that makes politics necessary.[12]

Methodology shows how the concept of Right (para. 2) assumes its particular form. The philosophical theory that translated the concept as the free will (para. 4) could not provide this demonstration. It presupposed a given historical *Sittlichkeit* which it attempted to reconstruct. This external presupposition entails the implicit assumption of an end to history because the external givenness cannot be affected by the actions and institutions described. It leaves the philosopher incapable of accounting for the demise of the old *Sitte.* This is why Hegel could not deal with the Rabble without a leap to the political State or to World History.[13] The philosophical theory assumes that the existent form of *Sittlichkeit* is the particularization of the concept of free will. The political methodology inverts that relation. The method must explain how the political acquires a particular form. *Sittlichkeit* is particularized by the institutions of Abstract Right and Morality. This is not a constitution-theoretical argument. *Sittlichkeit* precedes historically and methodologically (para. 32) these two abstract spheres that are its reconstruction and its articulation. The methodological precedence explains the *Zutat* that structures these two spheres. The historical precedence explains how change in the *sittliche* institutions can be understood rationally. The transformation cannot be introduced by any external agency because its effects would be ungrounded and accidental. The formality of Abstract Right and Morality precludes their being the source of the change. Their function as methodological simply reformulates the problem. Real existing *Sittlichkeit* is historical *(geschichtlich).* The advent of a particular transformation of the *Sittliche* has to be distinguished from incidental difficulties like the impossibility of determining exactly the distinctions among the kinds of *Vermögen* or the number of lashes to be meted out to the criminal. Whether a particular is incidental or actual can be determined by its methodological articulation. Only actual particulars call for political judgment.

The dependence of methodological particularity on a conception of the political has guided this reconstruction. Whether the Rabble is a particular that poses a threat to the given historical *Sittlichkeit* depends on the historically specific institutions of Abstract Right and Morality. Private property and the morality of possessive individualism make the Rabble a threat. This danger cannot be eliminated by an external instance like the political state. An idealistic attempt to transform directly the structures of Abstract Right and/or of Morality appeals also to an external intervention. The problem must be resolved immanently. The reciprocal dependence of the articulation and what is articulated makes possible valid criticism without resource to the "proud position." This reciprocity that articulates particularity calls for the reflective judgmental form. The Rabble is not to be eliminated physically. Its nature is transformed when it emerges as that particular that demands representation. This suggests an interpretation of the Rabble closer to Marx's theory of the proletariat.[14] The interdependence of the two moments of method reappears. The structure of *Sittlichkeit* had to guarantee receptivity. The particularity that is represented cannot destroy those conditions of receptivity. Hegel's political treatment of the Rabble can be criticized for doing precisely this. Another approach is possible. The abstract fixity of the methodological moments that articulate particularity is only apparent. Abstract Right and Morality have an immanent history. The "debate" suggested by the Administration of Justice, the public power of the Police, and the moral role of the Corporations is a *sittliche* precondition of this historicity. The public debate is a kind of political method. The effect of politics on this presentation of particularity preserves the interdependence and independence between the two moments of method. Their copresence avoids the reproach that such a "debate" is mere chatter, not the real practice that the world supposedly needs. The reduction of method to one of the other aspects would close off the possibility of rational practice.

A politics that eliminates the particularity of the Rabble makes the same error as political action claiming to incarnate a real proletariat under whose necessary sway all particularity is subsumed. A politics that ignores the conditions of receptivity within Civil Society will fail for the same reasons that condemn political action that treats these conditions as if they were causal laws. Politics preserves the unity-in-difference that explains both receptivity and particularity. This maintains the possibility of criticism. Like method, politics is not the presentation of solutions but the articulation of questions. The methodological mediation needed by originary theory implies an originary relation between its two moments. The same relation has to be articulated politically. The relation of method and politics, or politics and method, replaces the ill-formulated question of theory's relation to praxis. This position is not explicit or fully elaborated by Hegel. His criticism of the forms taken by the ruses of the "proud position" that rationalizes an ungrounded criticism suggests that it is at least not inconsistent with his basic arguments. The double interaction within method and between method and politics presents a completeness that the first phase of his theoretical method could not justify. This completeness is reflected in the theory of the political.

METHOD AND PRACTICE

Kant's continuing attempts to explain rationally the French Revolution illustrate the need for a methodological account of particularity. His support for the revolution continued long after his contemporaries had lost their early enthusiasm. Kant's argumentation is uncertain and often changing. The theoretical problem is familiar. A reflection in his posthumous papers formulates the classical difficulty. "In order to institute a Republic from a *pactum sociale,* a Republic must already exist. Hence the Republic cannot be instituted save by *violence* [*Gewalt*], *not* through *agreement.*"[15] Violence cannot be justified philosophically. Kant addresses the issue in the essay "Theory and Practice."[16] He suggests and then drops the proposal that an "Ideal of Reason" binds the legislator to edict laws of freedom. He admits the possibility of flagrantly unjust conditions. "For if the law is such that the whole people could not possible agree to it (for example, if it stated that a certain class of *subjects* must be privileged as a hereditary *ruling class*), it is unjust." Despite this admission and his constant stress on the role of the public agreement, Kant argues that the prohibition against resistance, rebellion, and even incitement to violence is "the greatest and most punishable crime in a commonwealth, for it destroys its very foundations. This prohibition is *absolute.*" Kant admits that the people can "pass general and public judgments" on decrees of the sovereign. Yet, they can "never...offer any verbal or active resistance." Finally, Kant addresses the reader directly. "While I trust that no one will accuse me of flattering monarchs too much by declaring them inviolable, I likewise hope that I shall be spared the reproach of claiming to much for the people if I maintain that the people too have inalienable rights against the head of the state, even if these cannot be rights of coercion." The reader expects a fuller explanation of the nature and place of these "inalienable rights."

Alongside Kant's condemnation of the practice of revolution stands his surprising justification of it when it succeeds. "Theory and Practice" points to the victories of revolutionaries in Switzerland, the Netherlands, and in England. Had these revolutions been defeated, notes Kant, the rebels would have had no grounds for appeal against their condemnation. Kant's support for their success has to be explained.[17] The difficulty is based on a methodological misunderstanding of the relation of theory to practice. Kant can point to rational principles in terms of which to judge a society. These principles can be applied to the success of the rebels. The relation of the a priori principles to the a posteriori results of action appears to be causal. The principles adopted by the revolt seem to explain its success. The difficulty is that this picture is premodern. It sets theory apart from the object on which it is to act. The theory is treated as a universal; the object as the particular. Theory becomes a tool applied to the social world. Conditions of receptivity are ignored. The particular object to which theory is applied is chosen arbitrarily. The success could be accidental. Its results may be temporary. Obviously, the problem needs to be reformulated. Justification of revolutionary practice must articulate the methodological mediation between the political result and the present practice. The causal relation is no more sufficient than the a posteriori acceptance of an event whose necessity could not be explained theoretically. The "maxim" that justifies the rebel must be presented by the political methodology.

Kant never explained what he meant by the "doctrinal" philosophy promised in the preface to the *Critique of Judgment.* Within the *Critique* itself, Kant did not explain how to identify those objects that in fact manifest "purposeless purposefulness" or "lawfulness without law." These objects are the particulars that make necessary a reflective judgment. The structure of the refletive judgment suggests an interpreation of what Kant might have meant by *doctrine.* The critical philsophy explains the conditions of the possibility of the subsumption of a given particular under an a priori universal law. The doctrinal complement would proceed from the particular to the universal. This does not replace the theory of judgment presented in the third *Critique*. Doctrine would belong to the methodological elaboration of the theory presented by the systematic unity of the three *Critiques*. It designates those particulars that call for the reflective judgment that assures systematic completeness. It attempts to discover the condition for the conditioned, the goal for the will, the culture permitting man to be a goal-positing being. The need for this second aspect of method was seen in the discussion of the structure of receptivity. It returns now in the context of the political. The rationality of revolution can be argued only on the basis of an account of the particularity which makes it necessary. Doctrine permits this discovery. Politics preserves the particularity that the method articulates.

Several of Kant's arguments can be unified on the basis of this methodological position. A note (n. 5) in the first introduction to the *Critique of Judgment* explains that reflective judgment does from the side of particularity what the schematism of the first two *Critiques* did from the side of the concept or universal. This suggestion is amplified when Kant turns to "Beauty as Symbol of Morality" (para. 59). He remarks that the symbolic is to the concepts of Reason what the schematism is to the concepts of the understanding. The schematism in the *Critique of Pure Reason* made actual what the understanding showed to be possible. The "concepts of Reason" are the moral categories of practical Reason. Their schematization would explain the actual motivation of empirical men to act morally. This would ground the presupposition of a moral good will in the *Foundations of the Metaphysics of Morals*. Its "revolutionary" political implication is seen in a passage from Kant's last published writing, the *Conflict of the Faculties*, which refers to the French Revolution.

> All this, along with the *passion* or *enthusiasm* with which men embrace the cause of goodness (although the former cannot be entirely applauded, since all passion as such is blameworthy), gives historical support for the following assertion, which is of considerable anthropological significance: true enthusiasm is always directed toward the *ideal*, particularly towards that which is purely moral (such as the concept of right), and it cannot be coupled with selfish interests.[18]

The rejection of the passions, the "anthropolitical" suggestion, and the reference to the ideal are not articulated explicitly. Their unity can be found in the *Critique of Judgment.* The modality of the experience of the sublime awakens in the subject a sense of his moral humanity (para. 29). The account of the beautiful is based on the "exemplary" character that incarnates a rational ideal in the phenomenal world (paras. 17, 18). The result of these two moments is a concept of morality that is not the a priori subsumption of particularity under pregiven laws of Reason. The faculty of judgment as schematic articulates the structure of particularity.

The methodological reading of the *Critique of Judgment* needs to be justified within the framework of the Kantian system. The methodological function of the schematism was described in a passage from the "Architectonic of Pure Reason" in the *Critique of Pure Reason.* "The idea requires for its realization a *schema,* that is, an essential manifold and order of its parts, both of which must be determined a priori from the principle defined by its end" (A 833; B 861).[19] This is not part of the theoretical demonstration of the Transcendental Analytic, which could appeal only to an "art concealed in the depth of the human soul" (A 141; B 180-181). Kant's concern is the domain of application of his theory as method. He distinguishes a contingent empirical schematizing that gives a "technical unity" from an a priori schema that results in an "architechtonic unity." The *Critique of Pure Reason* is concerned only with the latter. The technical unity reappears in the *Critique of Judgment* when Kant distinguishes the teleological from the mechanical unity of nature. Aside from the discussion of receptivity articulated there, a further aspect of the Architectonic points now to the place of particularity. "Historical knowledge is *cognition ex datis;* rational knowledge is *cognition ex principiis*" (A 836; B 846). Kant distinguishes two types of rational knowledge. The constructive knowledge of mathematics differs from the conceptual knowledge of philosophy. The difference between these forms of knowing is that "the one [i.e., philosophy] is derived from concepts, whereas in the other we arrive at a priori judgments only through the construction of concepts" (A 844; B 872). This distinction affects the way that each is learned. Philosophy can become a historical datum in the form of a system. But what is learned in this case is no longer philosophy. This leads Kant to the conclusion that mathematics is the only rational knowledge that can be learned from principles that are themselves lawful. "Philosophy can never be learned save only in historical fashion; as regards what concerns reason, we can at most learn to philosophize" (A 837; B 865). Learning to philosophize and explaining the source of moral practice are structurally identical problems. Their solution is sufficiently important not to be left to chance. A specific kind of historical structure, comparable to the mathematical learning in its result if not its form, must be demonstrated. The notion of "culture" was one aspect of this process (paras. 83, 84; and chap. 5, sec. B above).

Kant's postcritical writings are marked by repeated conjecture about the structure of history and the problem of revolution. The passionate passage concerning the French Revolution was found in the section of the *Conflict of the Faculties* entitled "A Renewed Attempt to Answer the Question: 'Is the Human Race Continually Improving?'" Another set of speculations around this theme is offered in *Religion within the Limits of Reason Alone.* Kant asks how to understand the "Victory of the Good Principle over the Evil One, and the Founding of a Kingdom of God in Earth." The Prussian censorship may have been correct in finding a political threat in the parallel between this account and secular theory. Kant makes use of the methodological distinction between a philosophical and a historical presentation. There can be no history of pure religion. As rational, pure religion is always self-identical. It is like philosophy. The history of religion can only be a history of belief. Kant's definition of this history is methodologically specific and theoretically modern. He excludes Judaism from the historical development of Christianity because of his insistence that growth be immanent. Judaism is described as a religion of statutory law enforced by a worldly state. Moral reflection and judgment are said not to be relevant to its functioning. The commandments of Judaism impose only external obedience. They have no relation to conscience. The Christian religion is said to be structured by the interaction between the demands of conscience and the legal framework imposed by belief. The type of Christian church community that Kant then describes institutes a public interchange that resembles the political Republic. Individual conscience and communal sense reinforce one another reciprocally. Although Kant does not enter into the details, a polemical passage indicates the radical thrust of his argument.

> I admit that I cannot agree with the expression used by quite intelligent men: that a certain people...is not ripe for freedom...Because from such a presupposition freedom will never emerge; for man cannot ripen to freedom before he is placed in free conditions. One must be free in order to use one's forces in a goal-oriented manner.[20]

The parallels to secular political theory that this passage conveys are apparent also in the titles to Kant's sections He begins from a consideration of the "ethical state of nature" from which he moves to a "common ethical organization." The next section redefines this organization as "the concept of a people of God under ethical laws," which is further concretized as the communial and social institution of the Church. The sequence breaks down with the fifth section, "The Constitution of any Church always begins from some Historical Revelation or Belief." This invocation of an external intervention violates the modern historical immanence. Kant's *Religion* tries to do too much. The implication of its failure here is that an adquate method must demonstrate also the limits in its structure of particularity.

A historical argument will not solve the methodological problem of a doctrinal philosophy. The doctrinal account of particularity articulates a problem that is posed historically. Method must explain the source of moral motivation, the necessity of learning to philosophize. Kant's "Theory and Practice" presents the problem clearly. The essay begins from a reply to Garve's criticism of the abstract rigorism of Kant's ethics. Garve believed that finite humans would be awed by moral demands that seemed beyond their capacities. His own proposals claimed to be realistic while also agreeing with the ultimate goals postulated by Kant. Kant's reply is measured. Its implications are drawn gradually. He first restates two points that Garve had garbled. Ethical duty commands behavior that makes men worthy of being happy. This does not imply the renunciation of human happiness in favor of abstract duties. The argument concerns only the motive for behavior. Second, duty is not based on a particular end that is sought. Duty occasions a new end, which Kant calls the striving toward the highest good on earth. Garve's first error is psychological. Kant agrees that we need an incentive to act. But if this motivation is empirical or phenomenal, it is only contingent. The necessary incentive can only be duty itself and the esteem it inspires. Since happiness is empirical and changing, an ethics based on it cannot command universally. Garve's good intentions lead necessarily to an ethics that becomes the rationalization of empirical choices based on contingent passions. Particular content that should be presented by method is instead asserted predicatively of a theoretical proposition. Garve wants to motivate by assuring people that they will be able to be truly ethical. Kant replies that duty can never be known to be fulfilled in the phenomenal world. Concern with fulfillment, like concern for happiness, can never assure the universal certainty on which an ethics must be founded. Kant does not draw the implication from his theoretical rigor. The ethics on which he insists cannot be "applied" to a neutral, tabular *Historie.* The more radical notion of *Geschichtlichkeit* has to be introduced methodologically in order to guarantee the success of the project.

The example that illustrates Kant's argument points to implications that go beyond the abstraction of moral theory and tabular *Historie.* A trustee who has become poor wonders whether he can help himself with the money left in trust. Duty, not mere physical happiness, should of course be his guide. Kant considers some possible empirical motivations for the impoverished trustee's action. They tend to point him in the same direction as the pure concept of duty. Spending the money suddenly would make the neighbors suspicious; the heirs might soon return and reward the trustee for his honesty; and the like. Kant concludes that ethical value is not judged in terms of an external code that evaluates content. The trustee may perform the same action for moral or pragmatic reasons. Garve wants to assure himself that people will act to increase the individual and collective happiness of society. His practical, pragmatic, political concern is vitiated by a methodological error. Practical choice arises only in a *particular* case. A reflective judgment is necessary to avoid subsuming this particular under a priori moral laws. Garve's attempt to guarantee that moral imperatives can be realized errs doubly. He universalizes the particular empirical instance without showing that, and why, it is valid for all men. The resulting structure recalls Kant's rejection of a scientifically necessary revolution in the earlier citation from *Religion*. The realized moral society at which Garve aims would bring history to an end. With the end of history comes the end of moral choice. Kant's moral apriorism has the methodological effect of preserving the possibility of practical particularity; his insistence on universality preserves paradoxically the place of particularity. Kant does not draw this conclusion explicitly in the criticism of Garve, which is only the premise for his more explicit discussion of political practice in the next section of the essay.

"Theory and Practice" moves from this description of individual morality to the application of political morality and then to the practice of international politics. The relation among the sections is not explicit. The formalism of Kant's positive reply to Garve in the first section is supplemented by the polemic "Against Hobbes" in the second part. Kant's moral arguments were based on a predicative judgment that subsumes the particularity which is the key to the political practice. His awareness of the difficulty implicit in this form of judgment is suggested in a footnote query into the "external circumstances within which an object appropriate to these incentives can alone be produced as an end in itself."[21] Instead of developing this question, the second section begins from another formal imperative. Kant distinguishes the original social contract from other particular and private contracts. The original contract is based on an ought. Entry into legal societal relations is a duty. Kant's justification expresses the familiar classical circle. The duty that founds the original contract creates the formal condition for all other duties. Creation of a legal civil society implies the institution of a public sphere where each gets his due while being guaranteed his security against all others. The original public social contract is the foundation of all particular private contracts. It is what makes possible an intersubjectively communicable and binding notion of duty. It is the basis of a common sense and a common culture. The revolutionary theorist confronts the same problem as the political moralist. How can the duty to enter the original contract be founded *before* the original contract itself has been inaugurated? How is the Republic to be instituted without violence? The ascending organizational complexity of Kant's essay suggests that the answer to the question of the political contract will be found at the level of international politics.[22] That argument presents the foundation of a theory of the political. Its methodological articulation can be read from the considerations of political morality "Against Hobbes."

The moral duty to enter the original contract is based on the systematic theoretical argument that made the political a necessary complement of the originary philosophy. A duty is actually an imperative only when a lawful social sphere exists. Imperatives must be realizable if they are to be binding. This means that there can be no duties outside lawful society. This is one reason why the *Metaphysics of Morals* presents first a Theory of Justice (*Rechtslehre*) before turning to the more phenomenological account of virtue (*Tugendlehre*). These classical claims are not original to Kant. Kant's manner of expressing them in the modern problem of the relation of theory (or method) to practice is new.[23] The *Critique of Judgment* provided the methodological turning point. The assertion of a duty that founds the concept of duty itself is only paradoxical because the order of cause and effect seems to be violated. But just such a "violation" was what typified the organism and the beautiful. It has a political complement, to which Kant refers explicitly in an already cited passage from the *Critique of Judgement.*

> Thus one has quite correctly used the term *Organization* in the case of a recently undertaken total transformation [*Umbildung*] of a great people to a state in order to describe the structure of the magistrates, etc., and in fact the entire body of the state. For each member in such a whole must of course not be a mere means but also an end and insofar as it works together toward the possibility of a whole, it is in turn determined in its position by the idea of the whole. (para. 65)

The moral duty to enter the original contract is based on a reflective judgment that asserts a social correlate to the structure of organic nature. The first ground for this conceptualization is the political structure that the methodology articulates. Method cannot be justified only by recourse to politics. The justification of the transformation of the theory-practice problem into a methodological argument is provided by the demonstration that specific particulars—like the beautiful, the sublime, or the organic—demand a process of reflective judgment. These are the particulars that pose the *problem* of the political.

The postulation of a moral duty to enter an original contract that is rational and free contradicts Kant's inability to ground a theory of revolution. His rejection was based on the impossibility of explaining that original contract without recourse to violence. Despite the assertion of the contractual duty to enter lawful society, Kant still does not justify revolution. He repeats the traditional objections. Rebellion implies that social sovereignty is divided, which is contradiction in terms. The assertion that the people should judge the administration of a constitution makes the people judge and party to their own cause. Legislation based on creating happiness is of course ruled out because different segments of the population will define their interests differently. Another criticism of the utilitarian argument goes a step further:

> such errors arise in part from the usual fallacy of allowing the principle of happiness to influence the judgment, wherever the principle of right is involved; and partly because these writers have assumed that the idea of an original contract (a basic postulate of reason) is something which must have taken place *in reality*...Such writers thus believe that the people retains the right to abrogate the original contract at its own discretion if, in the opinion of the people, the contract has been severely violated.[24]

This objection applies the reflective judgment which does not assert the predicative reality of its claim. Its assertions are not presented in scientific form. The original contract is a representation. Treating it as if it were real separates it from the practice it purports to command. The appearance of a division between the rational contractual theory and particular moral practice has its roots in this error. When the reflective judgment and the theory of representation are taken into account, the problem is transformed. The methodological task becomes the explanation of those objects that can call for this sort of judgment. The political formulation of the same problem explains the unity of the particular "what" with the "how" that makes the representation necessary and possible.

Revolution is only equated with the particularity of violence from the standpoint of the predicative judgment of science. Kant suggested in *Religion* that a justified scientific revolution eliminates the political. The implication is that revolution is not a politics! Politics makes this kind of violent revolution unnecessary. Political method is the mise-en-scène of particularity guided by the analysis of the conditions of receptivity. The political "practice" with which Kant deals takes place at the level of international relations. He identifies two "actors." Nature and natural necessity bring about human intervention as the results of war turn attention to the need for peace. This phenomenological process must be guided by a logic. The reflective judgment cannot offer logical necessity because it cannot take the results of its judgments as real. This is the place for the active contribution of the philosopher suggested by Kant's ninth "Cosmopolitan History" thesis. The author of "Perpetual Peace" is this originary philosopher. His theoretical mise-en-scène will be shown in chapter 7 to articulate that theory as the methodology that proposes concrete political structures to assure the completion of the philosophical project. Kant's French Revolution is rational because it is the foundation of an originary movement to which there is no determinant end. The French Revolution is in this sense the political complement to the originary philosophy. A Kantian interpretation of its phases would treat each of them as the methodological representation of a form of particularity. Success or failure depends on the ability to articulate this particularity without fixing it predicatively as a reality. Kant's continual support of the revolution after his contemporaries abandoned its "excesses" can be explained from this point of view.[25] The methodological particularity that he never articulated explicitly can be reconstructed when Kant's politics is elaborated as the "doctrine" to which he intended to turn after completing the critical system. The mysterious schematism that accompanied the system from its beginning will show itself, finally, to be the origin of the structure as a whole. Learning to philosophize, the source of moral concern, and the practical role of theory depend on this approach to the political.

CHAPTER 7

The Modern Republic

POLITICS AND PHILOSOPHY

Modern politics demands philosophical completion just as originary philosophy demanded a political correlate. The political complement that guaranteed philosophical completeness was made necessary by the move beyond traditional transcendental to originary modern philosophy. Politics articulates an object or "world" that demands philosophical thematization. The political functions as the genetic complement to normative philosophy. Politics expresses the necessary involvement of philosophy with the world. This interdependence of philosophy and politics maintains the structure of immanence. The political relation is determined by the structure of objective *Geschichtlichkeit*. The "real" content of this *Geschichtlichkeit* remains open to continual debate. This interrogative debate explains why philosophy and the political emerge simultaneously and imply one another mutually. The immanence of change that this debate entails means that political and theoretical representation cannot aim at the tabular goal of the adequation of thought to thing. The object to be represented is right or justice (*Recht*). Its content is transformed by its public articulation. Specification of the political depends on the translation of concept to institution. Philosophy showed the possibility and necessity of the political engagement. Politics has to demonstrate how engaged philosophy structures institutionally its world. Philosophy is necessary to the legitimation of this systematic political project. A politics has to be able to show why its version of the Good Life is better than the one represented by immediate popular sovereignty, enlightened despotism, or other contemporary experiences. As the normative complement to the genetic political project, philosophy completes the modern political structure. Systematic symmetry is necessary from both sides of the project.

The philosophical complement to modern politics must not be confused with methodology. Treatment of politics as actually intervening in a "world" separate from it parallels the constitutive philosophical temptation. Forms of this error were anticipated in chapter 4. The grounds of the mistake were explained in the presentation of the relation of methodological particularity to the political in chapter 6. The general ground of the illusion is the separation of politics from its object. The result of such a separation parallels the premodern transcendental philosophy that could elaborate only conditions of possibility, which it either treated as if they implied necessity (the *Zusehen*) or which it overcame through a real intervention (the *Zutat*).[1] The illusion that the transition to the political demands a real mediation operated by method on an external world parallels the reduction of politics to method in the political correlate to the constitutive philosophical error. The source of the misunderstanding is not only the usual ascending linear progression from beginnings to conclusions by which theory is presented. The relation between the two aspect of method is itself originary. This explains why method itself gives rise to the constitutive temptation, just as did the originary philosophy. But method cannot found the political. The presentation of receptivity entails implicitly the problem of particularity. However, the explicit articulation of this difficulty was not possible from the methodological moment founded by philosophy. Its solution required the development of a specific methodological place for the political. The originary philosophy had suggested this structure without being able to give it necessary content. The particulars whose structure is determined by politics demand philosophical justification of their nonarbitrary, rational, and reflectively *geschichtliche* character. The political foundation of method correlates to its philosophical ground. Their relation is originary, as is the methodological structure they jointly found. The symmetry is once again the basis of systematic completeness.

Modern politics faces an apparently insurmountable difficulty. Its immanence means that there is no pregiven normative standard that measures the Good Life, just as there is no genetic procedure providing a priori legitimation of decisions. A universally valid methodology founded by philosophy is also useless because it cannot designate its domain of application. This structural problem explains the temptation to substitute the social, the historical, or the personal in order to determine the modern form of the domain defined classicaly as the political. None of these options can solve the problem, although each has been tried. Orientation toward the person was constitutive of the modern state formation. Kant's citation of Frederick's "argue as much as you want...but obey" is typical of political liberalism. Replacement of political by moral judgment is another variant of this structure. Economic liberalism substitues personal interest for personal freedom or morality, but remains still within the same basic pattern. Separation of the two spheres makes mediation impossible. The result is that the personal, which can be known, determines the political. This result contradicts its intention. The personal is a particular whose content cannot be shown to be necessary. It becomes an empty universal form capable of receiving any arbitrary content. This permits it to explain receptivity only at the cost of accepting the arbitrariness of the particular content. The turn to the historical appears to avoid the appearance of an accidental content being treated as if it were necessary theoretically. But this stress on the historical confronts the symmetrical paradox. History appears as a universal structure outside of which no standpoint for judgment can exist. This historical totality implies an immanence that transforms the representation of a historical panorama into an immediate concrete particular in the same way that it transformed the appearance of personal particularity into an empty universal form. In both cases, the public space for political interaction and debate is blocked by a universalizing methodology. Neither the personal nor the historical, alone or in combination, can explain the content of a modern politics. Yet the necessity of such an explanatory foundation is entailed by the originary philosophy, which also suggests the place of method in its articulation. This means that a solution must be possible if the systematic unity is to be maintained. The turn to the social is suggested by this relation.

Concentration on the social as the locus of the modern form of classical politics seems to avoid the methodological difficulties. The social can be conceived as the unity of the personal and the historical. The first step in this direction was taken in Kant's "Cosmopolitan History." The creation of a civil society governed by law is defined as humanity's most important and most difficult task. Similarly, Kant's political concept of the Republic can be interpreted as the assertion of the priority of the social.[2] His politics would be a reaction to social necessity, which it seeks to transform. Social conditions would be treated as if they were constitutive of political institutions or actions. This would mean that Kant's political goals are not defined only by his a priori moral philosophy. Such a constitutive priority of the social is indeed a constant temptation in Kant's historical texts. Its further development would be Hegel's Civil Society, which engenders necessarily the Rabble. The social problem to which politics replies would thus acquire empirical content whose character is shown to be not accidental but necessary. Kant's general concept of "unsocial sociability" is thus replaced by Hegel's Rabble, which is the particular that prevents the functioning of social *Sittlichkeit* and calls for an explicit and separate political instance. Marx could then be interpreted as sharing this orientation, at least in his more reductionist arguments. As opposed to Hegel's Civil Society which poses the problem for politics, Marx would suggest this same instance as the source of the solution.

This complementarity of Hegel and Marx points to the inadequecy of replacing the political by the social. The social correlate to the political replaces the structurally necessary originary philosophy. Philosophical legitimation is absent. The transformation of empirical sociality into a philosophical foundation cannot articulate the methodological mediations that permit politics to reflect rationally on itself and its goals. Sociality that substitutes itself for the political calls immediately for its political representation. This immediacy replaces its modern *Geschichtlichkeit* by a spatial tableau. The reflective articulation permitting rational evaluation, public debate, and historical change is ruled out. The resulting elimination of politics coincides with extinction of the personal and the historical in a "sociology" that can explain everything by itself. Sociological method must be founded philosophically; it cannot replace politics.

The method must be founded politically as well. The social cannot replace the political. Social relations do not constitute political institutions. The social structure is originary only when both methodological moments are reflectively copresent. Either the historical or the formal personal interest can function as the first, theoretically determined, moment of receptivity. The choice depends on the originary philosophical structure which determines this first methodological moment. Hegel and Marx were seen to privilege the historical, Kant the personal, in this aspect of their method. The other moment of method is determined by the political. This explains the impossibility of a linear constitutive development from society to the political. It does not mean that a given social formation may not have an originary structure. On the contrary, the presence of an originary social formation explains why the political may be implicit in a society in which it is not explicitly institutionalized. In this case, the reflective formulation of the political will appear in a "crisis" whose unsettling effect makes explicit the political determination of the moment of particularity in the social structure. This explains why modern political tactics seek to articulate the moment of particularity which makes necessary political reflection. The classical theoretical agruments about the Good Life make no sense in the principled immanence of modern political tactics. (These arguments do have their place in the modern, but their place is determined by the theoretical logic of receptivity.) The political centrality of this or that particular is not determined by an act of will or a dictate of morality.

The philosophical aspect of the method of receptivity points only negatively to the place of particularity. The political intervention whose necessity is shown by the originary philosophy (or by the activist philosopher) restores the originary structure of civil society balanced between its theoretical and political poles. Civil society does not itself replace or determine politics, whose motivation and justification is theoretical. The same theoretical structure explains also why politics does not determine or replace civil society. Their relation is defined by the systematic independence and interdependence that makes method an originary structure.[3]

The conceptualization of modern sociality in the form of civil society makes explicit a further dimension of modern politics. Civil society's methodological function means that is not simply an empirical given. Nor is it reduced to the methodological articulation of political particularity. Its other aspect presents the theoretical structures of receptivity. Neither can be treated alone. Marx's phenomenological trilogy described the process by which particular aspects of civil society become capable of being represented. The political analysis cannot stand alone. Marx criticizes such one-sidedness in the preface to the second edition of the *Eighteenth Brumaire*. He points out that Victor Hugo's mockery of Napoléon le petit unintentionally makes Bonapart a political giant because it ignores the material conditions that make possible his coup. Conversely, the material reduction in Proudhon's contemporary account of the same events is judged equally unsatisfactory. A similar position explains Hegel's avoidance of a constitutive relation between the spheres of Abstract Right and Morality and the concrete *Sittlichkeit*. Hegel and Marx need a mediation to demonstrate the necessity of the politics whose conditions of possibility they explain. Its lack is due to their treatment of civil society as a "really real" foundation. The "revolutionary" whom Kant criticized for treating the social contract as something real makes the same error. Its result in each case is the return of the theory-practice problem.

The problem is transformed when civil society is considered as a doubly dependent and originary methodological mediation. There is no longer the need to ask how the possible political action becomes necessary because the political intervention as method explains the moment of particularity within civil soiety. This structure points to a "hermeneutic" limit on political intervention. Not everything is possible. This does ot mean that politics is reduced to a reaction to pregiven problems. Its implications are not the conservatism of the status quo. The relation of particularity and receptivity within civil society changes constantly as political action brings new particulars to explicitness and as philosophical analysis demonstrates new institutional possibilities of reception.[4] Civil society is not a thing. Politics is an art.

The importance of the political in articulating method leaves intact the question of its own nature. The political is not a "black box" that produces correct mediations for reasons that it cannot itself explain. The question of what is to be represented, and how it is to be represented, has a long prehistory.[5] The French Revolution made the problem acute. Among the candidates were the people or nation, public liberty or social equality, as well as the private interest in freedom or wealth. The concept capable of englobing these pairs is *sovereignty*. Sovereignty translates into the idiom of politics the particularity whose independence calls for the debate and judgment that structure public space. Its content demands justification. Hegel's distinction of laws of nature from those of right suggests the kind of argument that is needed here. Laws of nature permit no debate; they put an end to further enlightenment. Laws of right, like the Kantian concept of culture, insist on the human ability to posit goals autonomously. Neither a genetic procedure nor a normative measure can be presupposed as the justification of these goals. The immanence of philosophy to modern politics explains the possibility of a solution. Like the originary philosophy, the political can take only itself as its object. Yet the tautology is only apparent.

The French Revolution is the decisive historical and theoretical moment. As opposed to philosophy, the difficulty for politics is not beginning but the end. Systematic symmetry prevails here as well. The radically self-critical Revolution can stop only when it has transformed the world in its image. Social groups or political principles that represent different conepts of sovereignty articulate the phases of this process. They represent goals in a manner that has a real social effect, like the teleology Kant attributed to the French Revolution. Revolution and its effect mutually imply one another. Mutual implication does not entail identity. None of its effects exhausts the principle of Revolution. Each effect must in its turn be overcome. The stability that emerges finally will have the form of the Revolution itself, posed now explicitly and reflectively. The self-reflective form of the Revolution is the constitutional Republic. It repeats from the side of politics the experience described by the originary philosophy. The republican form cannot by itself determine a politics. It needs method to avoid the political equivalent of the constitutive error. The Constitution is the methodology articulating the philosophical foundation of its politics. The Constitution articulates the conditions of receptivity that ensure functional results. The manner in which it accomplishes this task structures the space in which the particular action of politics can take place. The Constitution must be structured in a manner that makes its self-transformation by the political possible and necessary. This institutional arrangement avoids the "revolutionary" confusion with a real foundation which Kant was the first to denounce. The republican element enters at this point of the argument.

The relation of the political Republic to civil socity poses both theoretical and practical problems. Its practical expression sharpens the theoretical difficulty. Republican liberty is contrasted to democratic equality. Republican freedom may institutionalize the domination of private property. Republican (Jacobin) centralism may suppress autonomous sociality. The generality of the Republic tends to suppress the particularity that expresses the political moment of civil society. The dilemma is summed up in the well-known assertion that the Republic is only a formal legal cloak perpetuating social relations of domination and exploitation. The theoretical ground of all of these practical criticisms is the implicit treatment of civil society as itself the originary philosophical structure whose necessary completion is presented by the republican polity.

The difficulty can be avoided by reintroduction of the philosophical component of method. Originary philosophy depends on the existence of a world that needs philosophy as its completion. This distinguishes the originary from the classical transcendental argument. The inverse relation is present from the side of politics. The philosophy that shows the necessity of the political depended on a structure of receptivity that makes political action nonarbitrary. The philosophy needed by politics complements the politics demanded by philosophy. The one shows conditions of necessity, the other conditions of completeness. Their unity is civil society conceived as the methodological articulation of the modern structural immanence. Its methodological translation enlarges the concept of civil society beyond the "really real" socioeconomic relations that found implicitly liberal capitalist or Marxist critiques of the republican form. The accusations against the Republic are based on a merely sociological presupposition about the nature of civil society. There is no reason to accept such a limited definition as the foundation of a critical political argument. The broader, methodological interpretation yields positive results that are more interesting than the negative results of the sociological presupposition and its reductionist results.

The structure of republican civil society is determined by the priority of the modern over the capitalist social form. Capitalism is only one of the forms that civil society can adopt within the republican framework. The republican Constitution may of course present conditions of receptivity in the institutions of an economic, means-ends rationality. But nothing prohibits other structures based on different interests, values, or groups. There is no immutable dividing line between a republican captitalism and a civil society expressing a "social democratic" or a "welfare state" model. That other models are also possible is seen in Hannah Arendt's repeated return to the model of a councils or self-management form of the modern polity. The criteria of distinction among these possibilities must be immanent to the structure of civil society. They must articulate the moment of philosophy or the moment of politics. The philosophical concern with conditions of receptivity is expressed by Kant's interdiction of "a contract made to shut off further enlightenment." This maxim is sufficiently general to allow for concrete variety. Debate is closed when the reflective judgment that opens the public space is replaced by the subsumptive orientation of science or moral a priorism. The implication of this principle points to the limits of the capitalist economic rationality extended to civil society as a whole.[6]

The correlative political concern with the conditions of particularity is expressed by Kant's admitted puzzlement as to the criteria that determine admissibility to political participation. That issue was not determined by the French Revolution. New forms continue to emerge in contemporary societies. Participation as private individuals, as members of groups defined by private or by social interests, in terms of the place or kind of work or residence are among the subjective possibilities. There is also an objective moment to the question. The objects admitted to the political arena must be determined and delimited. New objects, and perhaps new limits, must be defined and opened to debate. The private, the social or communal, voluntary or involuntary associative structures may be included or excluded. In short, neither the philosophical nor the political aspects of civil society are defined by the capitalist economy as such. The question should be inverted: What political and philosophical structures explain the possibility of capitalism coming to dominate a modern civil society?

Civil society is neither a philosophical nor a political concept. Its function is methodological. It poses problems. Hegel reduced the richness of modern *Sittlichkeit* to a logic of economic particularity whose incompleteness demanded that it be absorbed into a state caught in the systematic flow of World History. Other possibilities were left undeveloped once the historical solution apparently had been found. Marx's attempt to derive political solutions from the structure of civil society presents the symmetrical error. An economic analysis based on a philosophical account of material synthesis by the labor of its proletarian agent is transformed into an immediate political affirmation. The political demonstration of the role and limits of this agent was neglected once the theoretical solution apparently was found. Only with Kant does civil society remain a problem.

Kant articulates the question in terms of the relation of national and international politics. The relation of philosophy to the political is posed from the side of theory in the notion of reflective judgment. The relation of politics to the philosophical is expressed in the practical relations among sovereign (republican) states. The two relations must be brought together. Kant's incorporation of international relations among sovereign states is suggestive. The difference between individuals and states is that the moral law legislates a priori and subsumptively for men, whereas independent states, by defintion, can accept no law superior to themselves. The political moment of particularity emerges necessarily in the relation among states whose republican form assures their independence. This particularity makes necessary the theoretically possible Republic and the reflective judgment and learning that preserve it. The result is a conception of civil society that has both a political and a philosophical moment. The priority of individual liberty corresponds to the philosophical aspect. The place of material equality is the concern of the political articulation. The coexistence of the two moments preserves civil society as the locus of theoretical and practical questioning. The necessary independence and interdependence of originary philosophy and republican politics is maintained by the Kantian political Republic, whose details will be treated below. The move to the level of international politics is the particular expression of the general structure whereby the political moment serves to protect the methodological status of civil society as the locus of questions, not the source of solutions.[7]

Revolution or Politics

Classical direct democracy with no mediating civil society defined the political by the representation in which the assembled citizens articulate the Good Life. The institutions and the individual representation coincide in this premodern structure which excludes particular individuality. This politics had no need for methodological mediation and no place for autonomous civil institutions. The modern problems are more complex. Modern civil society has to articulate the relation between the subjective choice and its institutional form. It cannot assume a real coincidence between the will of the individual and the political institutions in society. It cannot assume a necessary coincidence between what the society really is and what its political institutions represent. Either of these assumptions can be criticized by Marx's theory of ideology. The real identity of the individual and the political negates the autonomy of both poles. On the contrary, the noncoincidence of the representation as institution and its active individual agent is the foundation of the possibility and the necessity of politics. Marx's phenomenological trilogy elaborated its institutional implications. The logical moment of method, suggested in the account of receptivity, provided an explanation of the structure of individual action. The tempation is to unite these two methodological analyses in order to demonstrate systematic necessity and completeness. Their unity would eliminate the political one-sidedness that results in voluntarism or reformism. The unification would be successful if it shows the necessity and possibility of the philosophical in the same way that originary philosophy showed the necessity of the political. Marx's awareness of this critierion can be shown. On that basis, a successful—if unorthodox—Marxian theory of the political can be suggested.

The *Communist Manifesto* explains the possibility and necessity of political action from an analysis of the institutional structure of capitalist civil society. Marx's central argument appears to unite the subjective and objective moments into a unitary whole.

> But with the development of industry not only does the size of the proletariat increase; it is in larger masses forced together, its strength grows, and it becomes more aware of it. The interests, the mode of life of the proletarians become more and more equal because the machinery more and more erases the differences of work and wages, sinking them nearly everywhere to an equally low level.... The workers then begin to form coalitions against the bourgeoisie; they come together to fight for their wages. They themselves form enduring associations in order to prepare themselves for the eventual revolt.... From time to time the workers are victorious, but only temporarily. The actual result of their struggles is not immediate success but the ever greater unification of the workers. (Emphasis omitted)

Capitalism creates conditions that make the proletariat receptive to political unification. It struggles first for wages and material equality. Its eventual victory is not limited to these materially real external gains. Marx represents success in the form of the further unification that arises from reflective learning by the proletarian subjects. This is the result of what the proletarians themselves achieve in their associations. But this process does not yet explain the moment of the "eventual revolt."

Marx's demonstration of the possibility of revolution cannot be proven to be necessary. The two methodological moments united in his description of capitalism are based on a single foundation. The subject of the description is capitalism. It serves both as the theoretical basis of the moment of receptivity and as the political ground of the moment of particularity. This means that the political phenomenology is replaced by an evolutionary technology. The political moment is only asserted in this first depiction of the political possibility of revolution. Marx's attempt to introduce its necessity comes later in the *Manifesto.*

> The Communists are different from the rest of the proletarian parties only in so far as, on the one hand, in the different national struggles of the proletarians they stress the interests of the entire proletariat independently of the nationality, and on the other hand, in that in the different stages of development through which the struggle between bourgeoiseie and proletariat passes, they continuously represent the interests of the entire movement.
>
> Thus, the Communists are practically the most decisive and broadly directed part of the working class parties of all countries; they have the theoretical advantage over the rest of the proletariat of an insight into the conditions, the path, and the general results of the proletarian movement.

This introduction of the political violates the imperative of immance. The "Communists" replace the class struggle and its institutions which had been the previous foundation of the revolution. The one-sided methodology that resulted in reformisim or voluntarism is replaced by a politics based on a linear conception of a World History known by a revolutionary consciousness that can acquire this knowledge because it stands outside of real and immediate history. Why the proletariat themselves should be receptive to the Communists is no more explained than the danger that the omniscient Communist will mislead the proletariat is eliminated. The foundation of this revolutionary political necessity is a logic of World History that recalls the caricatural Hegelian idealism.

The source of Marx's political difficulty is that his revolutionary intervention is based on a theoretical foundation that apparently makes unnecessary the methodological mediation that articulates particularity. Marx returns to the classical model even while presenting an account of the structure of modern civil society. His theorectical premise is put concisely in a well-known remark in the *Poverty of Philosophy,* written two years before the *Manifesto.*

> The economic relation first of all changes the mass of people into workers. The domination of capital has created for this mass a common situation, common interests. Thus this mass is already a class over against capital, but not yet for itself [*für sich*].

This is a conceptual restatement of the nature of the proletariat as the subject-object which solves the "riddle of history." The theoretical assertion suggests a methodological account of the economic structures that assure the logic of receptivity. The task of the revolutionary politician is left without political mediation. He is to bring what was "in itself" to self-consciousness as a "class for itself." This is a restatement of the problem of the lightning of thought. The practical result of this reformulation is adumbrated by the definition of the Communist in the *Manifesto.* The domination of the Party over whatever action the proletariat themselves might undertake is the result. Lukács's theory of "ascribed class consciousness" provides the theoretical justification of this structure.

The difficulty is not only practical. The theorectical argument implies the opposite of what Marx intended. The initiatives of capital—depressing wages, maintaining a reserve army of labor, creating economic crises—are said to force the class from the outside to unify and to elaborate consciously its goals. This external force is substituted for the political moment that articulates immanently the structure of particularity. Goals elaborated in this way cannot bring about a revolutionary rupture. Marx has not joined the phenomenological with the logical method. The class "in itself" was produced by captialism. Its form as self-consciously for itself only makes explicit what captalism has done to it. As with the peasantry in the *Eighteenth Brumaire*,this awareness does not entail the necessary transformation of capitalism. If the Communist is invoked to provide "political class consciousness" (Lenin), his foreknowledge must be justified. The only possible explanation of his knowledge is based implicitly on the linear or tabular theory of History in the *Manifesto.* The only other political option is revolutionary spontaneity. But that spontaneous politics presupposes the validity of the classical direct democratic form that the Marxian analysis of modern civil society refutes.

Marx's political presentation of the Paris Commune did not pretend that it was the product of revolutionary intervention by theoretical Communists. He offered instead a phenomenological analysis of how "the state power assumed more and more the character of the national power of capital over labor, of a public force organized for social enslavement, of an engine of class domination." The bourgeoisie at Versailles forced the hand of the Parisian workers. Their refusal to surrender was not based on theory nor was it an immediate reaction to economic exploition. The form they gave their action is explained by the phenomenological process that completed the polarization. Marx describes "the great social measure of the commune" as "its working existence." The classical political immediacy in the form of direct democracy appears here as the revolutionary overthrow of modern civil society. This antimodernism suggests the need for a careful reading. The Commune produced a variety of social measures typical of "a government of the people and by the people." These actions are explained by the structural evolution that created the institutional form of the particular class actor.

> The working class did not expect miracles from the Commune. They have no ready-made utopias to introduce *par décret du peuple.* They know that in order to work out their emancipation, and along with it that higher form to which present society is irresistibly tending by its own economic agencies, they will have to pass through long struggles, through a series of historical processes,

> transforming circumstances and men. They have no ideals to realize, but only to set free the elements of the new society with which the old collapsing bourgeois society is pregnant.

This reductionist womb-and-birth imagery in the midst of Marx's invocation of a new world-historical stage is revealing. The lack of ready-made utopias to decree need does not mean that politics is to be eliminated as itself merely the purveyor of utopias. Marx's argument here replaces an originary by a theoretical methodology. The "measures" taken by the directly democratic Commune express only an immediate relation to the conditions in which capitalism has placed the class. The communal institutions eliminate representative politics, which are said to decide every few years who will "misrepresent the people." This reductionist revolution occurs when capitalism on its own (or because of the tragic farce of the Nephew's empire) fails. Such a revolution has no "new ideals"; direct democracy is chosen not for its positive virtures but because bourgeois representative democracy has been discredited. Marx forgets his own ideology critique when he asserts that direct democracy solves the problems posed by modern civil society. He appeals for support to the "well-known" fact that "companies, like individuals, in matters of real business generally know how to put the right man in the right place, and, if they once make a mistake, to redress it promptly." But just this lucidity was previously denied to capitalism because of the ideological structure of civil society. Its introduction here to explain the revolutionary ability to make direct political decisions is not justified.[8] The "historical processes, transforming circumstances, and men" need a political articulation. New ideals *are* essential to modern politics.

A further inconsistency in Marx's argument suggests a different reading. The immediate wisdom of the "working existence" of direct communal democracy restates an agrument that Marx had denounced in the *Eighteenth Brumaire* as "petit bourgeois." The proletariat is supposed to be made of better stuff. Marx tends to treat the proletariat as a fully self-aware revolutionary subject when it behaves as his theory says that it should. For example, when it does not take to the streets after the *coup* of December 2, Marx interprets this behavior as the conscious avoidance of the provocations of its enemies. When the proletariat does not behave as the theory says it should, Marx interprets the results of its actions as necessary stages in its political education. This why the defeat of the February Revolution was treated in *Class Struggles in France* as the victorious gaining of a new phenomenological terrain.[9] The foundation of this kind of argument is explained by a logical theory of history that denies the independence of method. Marx is aware of the problem elsewhere. He observes, for example, that the petite bourgeoisie believes in a concept it calls "the people." It wants to assert the rights and interests of this people, come what may. The logical structures that assure that the people will listen receptively are neglected. The petite bourgeoisie believes that the good people will join the cause immediately once the Good Word is spoken. If the lightning does not strike, the petite bourgeoisie blames "sophists" who divide the individible people, or an army too brutalized and blinded to comprehend the Good Word. Political institutions are neglected; political mediation is rejected.

> In any case, the [petit bourgeois] democrat comes out of the most disgraceful defeat just as immaculate as he was innocent when he went into it, with the newly won conviction that he is bound to win, not that he himself and his party have to give up the old standpoint, but on the contrary, that conditions have to ripen to suit him.

This description fits precisely the behavior that Marx had just attributed to the proletariat. The illusions of the petite bourgeoisie were explained methodologically by their refusal to admit the similarity of their position to the proletariat. Finding the same illusionary structure in the proletariat suggests the need for a closer look. Marx's reasoning appears clearly in the description of the petit bourgeois "Mountain" after 1848, a description that is kinder than usual because this stood as the most "progressive" force at the time.

> Only one must not form the narrow-minded notion that the petit bourgeois, on principle, wishes to enforce an egoistic class interest. Rather, it believes that the *special* conditions of its emancipation are the *general* conditions within the frame of which alone modern society can be saved and the class struggle avoided.

Just this universalization of a particular situation was what defined the revolutionary potential of the proletariat in Marx's 1843 "Toward a Critique of Hegel's *Philosophy of Right.*" Marx would reply that the petite bourgeoisie deludes itself, whereas the proletariat is *really* the unity of genetic production with normative validity. Even in this case, however, the proletariat provides a *capitalist* "solution to the riddle of history." Proletarian revolution realizes the dream of the petite bourgeoisie and of the capitalist. This is surely not Marx's intention. The political presuppositions that underlie Marx's reasoning need further clarification.

Revolutionary politics becomes ideological when it seeks to destroy the structure that makes politics possible and necessary. The proletariat is the expression of a problem. The mediations are lost when it is treated as a really existent solution. History as a real linear and constitutive process is then integrated into a civil society conceived as economic. Without methodological mediation, history is treated either as the genetic source or the normative legitimation of revolution. The unity called "revolutionary practice" in the *Theses on Feuerbach* is lost. Its premises are eliminated by its revolutionary realization. To call this the "end of prehistory" is only a verbal transformation. Such an unmediated theoretical solution cannot be refuted externally by example and counter-example. Rather, its inability to remain within the immanence of the modern condemns it as theory and as politics. The systematic structure that was to ground the revolutionary theory is violated. This need not have been the case. Other conclusions can be drawn if concepts like *bourgeois* are not reified and the vivifying effects of *class struggle* not treated in a manner recalling Hegelian glorification of the necessity of war. Civil society is not economic society. Economic reality and its rulers attempt to eliminate the political. Marx himself shows how reality denounces their reductionism in this domain, as it did in the structure of capitalism as ideology. In a portion of the *Eighteenth Brumaire* that seems only to repeat the lessons from the critique of political alienation in "On the Jewish Question," Marx describes how the political structures inaugurated by the bourgeois class become a threat to it. Marx gives no reason why this politics cannot maintain economics in a subordinate role. The "elements of the new society with which the old collapsing bourgeois society itself is pregnant" need not refer only to economics. The "working existence" of the Paris Commune could be reinterpreted from this political persepctive once it is freed from pejorative labels.

Marx does not articulate the political structure of modern civil society because he reduces it to social relations of economic domination. He reproduces in his own analysis what he shows the bourgeoisie attempt but fail to achieve in reality. French history is said to demonstrate that the bourgeoisie prefers to sacrifice "its general class interests, that is, its political interests, to the narrowest and most sordid private interests." The bourgeoisie feel, correctly, that the open presentation of their interests as political would threaten their class rule by creating the public political space that makes necessary public debate. This explains why the bourgeoisie supports one or another monarchist faction before it finally approves the *coup* that brings "an end with terror" in the place of "a terror without end." The bourgeoisie fears the political consequences of its own social success as "socialistic." Marx does not explain what this socialism means. It can be interpreted as an ideological structure that affects the imagination of the bourgeoisie by forcing it to seek a fixed foundation which, if it existed, would put into question the immanently historical and world-changing charcter of the capitalism that Marx described in the *Communist Manifesto.* Socialism in this sense would be that haunting "spector" from which the *Manifesto* begins. This interpretation suggests that socialism is not just an alternate economic model. Marx suggests why the bourgeoisie fears the parliamentary or republican political form and forum:

> If in every stirring of life in society [the bourgeoisie] saw "tranquility" imperiled, how could it want to maintain at the head of society a regime of unrest, its own regime, the parliamentary regime, this regime that, according to the expression of one of its spokesmen, lives in struggle and by struggle? The parliamentary regime lives by discussion; how shall it forbid discussion? Every interest, every social institution is here transformed into general ideas, debated as ideas; how shall any interest, any institution, sustain itself above thought and impose itself as an article of faith? The struggle of the orators on the

> platform evokes the struggle of the scribblers of the debating clubs in the salons and the posthouses; the representatives, who constantly appeal to public opinion, give public opinion the right to speak its real mind in petitions. The parliamentary regime leaves everything to the decision of majorities; how shall the great majorities outside Parliament not want to decide?

This is not that "parliamentary cretinism" whose normative naïveté Marx was seen repeatedly to deride. Nor is a parliamentary "insurrection within the limits of pure reason" like the attempt by the Mountain on June 11, 1849. This politics does not expect a real solution, incarnate in the proletariat and presented in the immediate form of direct democracy and an economic reform.

Marxism has suffered from Marx's inability to articulate the proper place and function of the political. Marx's haughty ridicule of the politics of the petite bourgeoisie applies too often to those whom claim, with some justification, to be following his lead. The parallel political structures of petit bourgeois and proletarian politics stand as a warning. Marx's successful articulation of methodological particularity in his phenomenological trilogy suggests the need to reconstruct the implicit theory of the political which made it possible. From the other side, the "socialistic" implications of parliamentary politics can be explained theoretically by the concept of modern ideology. This suggests that the central problem for a modern politics is the nature of representation. The "bourgeois" form of parliamentarism is condemned for its inability to articulate the particular interests that it seeks to represent. It becomes "parliamentary cretinism" at worst, the meliorist and vain "insurrection within the limits of pure reason" at best. The fault is not that of the political form itself, any more than the republican institutions can be said necessarily to carry only capitalist economic content to its expression. Marx does not draw the conclusions that his own description permits. That does not, however, mean that others are forbidden from pointing to their presence. The theory of proletarian representation remains to be elaborated. Its incipient premises can be found in these aspects of Marx's own agrument. The further element that would be necessary comes from reconsideration of that other shibboleth with which the *Manifesto* concludes: "working men of the world, unite!" A theory of the political would make necessary the elaboration of a Marxian theory of international relations to replace the reductionist hope of a sudden worldwide tranformation. This international theory would, in turn, have national implications—but this takes us ahead of our story.

Philosophy, History, or Politics?

The resigned contemplative conclusion to the preface to the *Philosophy of Right* does not explain the place of the political in a modern system. The practical limits imposed in the preface are Hegel's reaction to Plato's mistaken overstress on state activity to control the new individualism threatening Greek *Sittlichkeit.* The difficulties confronting a modern society cannot be resolved by a utopian leap that simply ignores the particularily and necessity of the threatening novelty. Hegel learned from Plato that simple, immediate political reaction is no wiser than abstract revolution. The particularity that threatened Greek society had to be integrated positively into an enriched institutional world. Hegel proposes to transform the classical *Sittlichkeif* into a civil society whose principle is particularity. But the further analysis of this modern *Sittlichkeit* demonstrates a new threat: the Rabble. Consistency suggests the integration of the Rabble as altered or enriched into a *Sittlichkeit* that can incorporate the new. The negative definition of the Rabble must be translated, just as threatening particularity became the positive "education" developed-through the moments of civil society. The philosopher is not an enlightened despot acting externally on society. The implication of Hegel's *Philosophy of History* can be applied to the *Philosophy of Right,* whose systematic conclusion also integrates its politics into the "Court" of actual world history. The political state provides the principle of rationality that makes history the rational "progress of the consciousness of freedom." The system of particularity articulated in a specific economic and legal structure is only one possible form of modern *Sittlichkeit.* The political state of the *Philosophy of Right* may or may not be adequate to this structure. Hegel's rejection of theories that treat the political contract as simply another instance of private contracts among competitive individuals applies to his own state structures. The political is not identical with the *Sittlichkeit* which accounts for its necessity and of which it is the explicit completion.

The theory of the state presented in the *Philosophy of Right* is not a theory of the political. The institutions of "public authority" which first play the role of the state were developed from the rudimentary appearance of comparative universality and necessity in the System of Needs. This "state of need and of the understanding" *(Not-und Verstandesstaat)* was the institutional recognition of the external lawfulness encountered in the economic marketplace. This abstract economic model is then developed through the Administration of Justice and the concern with welfare translated by the Police and the Corporations. The explicit theory of the state should represent a further conceptual and institutional enrichment of the moments of abstract economic rationality and the social relations of particularity. Hegel resorts to metaphor more than concept in his initial presentation. The lapidary designation of the state as the seat of "rationality" is not helpful. The assertion that it brings to public awareness and debate what had been private and particular group interests is open to the Marxian criticism of "accommodation" with the established relations of domination. The problem is that Hegel's theory of political institutions is too formal; it is dependent on conceptual distinctions that it cannot ground immanently.

To escape these criticisms, Hegel would have to show how the divisions of the social *Vermögen* that he reuses politically are transformed by their new context. There is no reason in principle that Hegel could not at least make that attempt. He had resolved a similar problem in the integration of particularity into modern *Sittlichkeit.* The institutional transformation that made possible the translation of Aristotle's natural character or virtue in order to redress the threatened norms of the old states could have a modern parallel. The political state that replaces the palliative provided by the Corporations and the pedantic Police would introduce a new institutional structure based on a new principle. This phenomenologically new state is then the logical precondition of the self-affirming particularity of the civil society that produces the threat of the Rabble. It is the completion of a civil society that makes it necessary. But such a dependence seems to condemn the state to impotence. The only option is to recognize that the state presents a phenomenologically new principle. This means that the structures of civil society are transformed, just as the new principle of particularity transformed classical *Sittlichkeit.* The phenomenologically new particularity of the state has to be justified by recourse to the political. Unfortunately, this is not Hegel's argument. The state is introduced; the political is not considered as such. Hegel's failure needs systematic explanation.

The distinction of the state from the political is justified by the immanently historical character of Hegel's systematic arguments. The possibility that a new principle of *Sittlichkeit* will transform the state structures is explicit in the concluding passages of the *Philosophy of Right.* Hegel shows how the state's structure of concrete universality becomes only one particular in the progress of World History (paras. 344, 347). He draws no conclusions from this categorial shift, which is described rather than justified. The presupposed concept of the will from which the development began (para. 4) is transformed into World History at its conclusion. A very different conception of historical change was present when the spheres of Abstract Right and Morality were treated as methodology, although Hegel did not explain its conditions of possibility. His phenomenological presentation reconstructed these abstract spheres with the aid of the philosopher's *Zutat.* A logical moment was seen to be necessary for the full rational argument. The two phenomenological moments depend on its presence. Hegel is careful to avoid the constitutive illusion. The two formal moments are not presented as constituting their *sittliche* presupposition. They are its methodological articulation. Abstract Right and Morality must change when *Sittlichkeit* changes. They are dependent, methodological moments. *Sittlichkeit,* in turn, is open to constant change because of its methodological principle of particularity which depends on the political. Changes in the Administration of Justice entail debate and participation; they articulate new relations within the System of Needs. These new forms affect Abstract Right and Morality. Hegel does not ask how these new abstract moments affect their *sittliche* premises because of his concern to avoid the constitutive illusion. The notion of an independent methodological mediation makes possible a different interpretation. Abstract Right is not immediately translated into the System of Needs; Morality is not immediately reflected in the Administration of Justice. The mediated change within *Sittlichkeit* has to be explained immanently. Hegel's account of the place of the Family shows the importance of the problem, although he does not deal directly with it. The individual Family member grows up to become the "son of Civil Society." This change of status justifies the institutional intervention of the "public authority" in the affairs of the Family. Intervention by the state in civil society would have to invoke a similar justification. But Hegel does not develop this argument. *History* is too general a category to satisfy the methodological need. The principle of the "public interest" that justifies interference in family affairs is not articulated as a political structure.

Hegel's failure to thematize the political is due to his ontological orientation which condemns the system to neglect the need for an explicit methodological analysis. Hegel treats the institutional relations of civil society as real. They are considered immediately accessible to the understanding. This attitude is most evident in Hegel's exploitation of economic theory. He expresses his wonder at the lawfulness demonstrated in a mass of accidental occurrences and capricious choices (para 189, Remark and Addition). This philosophical innovation for which he is often credited should not be overstressed. Although the patterns he analyzes in the *Philosophy of Right* are more detailed than those invoked by Kant's "Cosmopolitan History," their conceptual structure is not fundamentally different. In both cases, the methodological mediation is taken for granted. The teleology asserted is predicative, not reflective. This leads the philosopher who wanted contemplatively "to grasp his time in thought" to violate his own recommendations. He tries to leap beyond the particular structure that he himself has shown to distinguish the modern social form. He makes the methodological mistake against which Kant had warned. He treats a reflective judgment as if it were real. Civil Society and the State are moments within a common *Sittlichkeit*. Their logical interrelation is expressed in the formal relations of Abstract Right and Morality. Hegel does not consider the possibility of changes at this abstract level. He freezes the development of further particularity. The result is the sheerly negative definition of the Rabble.

Hegel's rejection of the constitutive argument that derives the state from the more abstract moments explains why he ignores the place of method. The Rabble is a problem only for a *Sittlichkeit* treated as having the immediate institutional reality presented by the economic relations described by Hegel. Treating the *Sittliche* as the methodological mediation between the philosophical (the Will) and the political (World History) makes possible a different interpretation. The relation could be shown to present the kind of reflective structure that permitted Kant to escape a hypostatized natural teleology. Such a structure would explain the necessity of the "debate" that the preface asserted to be fundamental to the character of social law. Limitation of the political by means of the methodological mediation permits an understanding of the role it plays implicitly in a modern system.

The Corporations illustrate Hegel's attempt to escape a real dilemma confronting his times and his system. The rational colonial policy to be introduced by the Police (or the "public authority") is a *Zutat* guided by the philosopher's historical experience. There are no immanent grounds for this policy decision. Hegel's model was the private colonial ventures charted by the royal houses, which were temporarily successful only in the British case. Royal political decisions successfully harnessed particular economic interests for the public good. The theoretical basis of this state political action is not built into the structure of Hegelian civil society. The "public authority" incarnated by the Police is only an abstract external universality. As a structure based on comparison, it is not capable of autonomous rational initiative. The initiative cannot come from the Corporations alone. Hegel's stress on the particularity of their interest leaves only the formal possibility that they intervene in civil society in a manner similar to the way the World Historical Individual served the Cunning of Reason. But such a claim that self-interest of the particulars coincides with and works for the welfare of the whole cannot be justified without methodological articulation.

The demonstration at the level of the System of Needs is still a constitutive argument. The atomized, self-seeking formal individuals from which the presentation began have been replaced by the particular institutional structure of civil society in its *sittliche* concreteness. The political state seeks to preserve the institutions of reciprocity and particularity at the same time that it completes them. The danger is that one or the other task will dominate the state, which then becomes either the immediate instrument of civil society or its actual replacement. The formal model is developed in Marx's unpublished manuscript "Critique of Hegel's Philosophy of the State." Marx's line-by-line criticism intends to show an "accommodation" of Hegel's state structures to the existent civil society.[10] The more frequent interpretation portrays the state as intervening to transform civil society by eliminating the threat of the Rabble. But such a state is separated from the society into which it intervenes. It is no more a sufficient solution than the first proposal. The source of the difficulty is the confusion of state and politics. The identification of these distinct moments makes immanent change impossible or irrational. The result is either a "conservative" Hegel or the philosopher as "secretary" to the World Spirit.

The relation of the state to civil society is defined neither by total independence nor total dependence. Two distinct accounts can be found when the problem is presented as methodological. The phenomenological moment of method presents an elaboration of the "public authority" into the structure defined as the "internal Constitution for itself." This constitutional structure is analyzed in detail under the headings "Monarch," "Executive," and "Legislature." It has no autonomous principle of movement or rationality. Its content comes from civil society through the concrete detail provided by the executive agencies and the action of a legislative that represents the different aspects of civil society. The institutions of this political state are structured and staffed according to the social divisions of the collective *Vermögen* that was rationalized within civil society. But the justification of the state cannot be the task of providing the rationalization of material already offered in civil society. Its principle of movement can come only from the conflictual external relations, of which war is the concretion. The brief account of this moment culminates in the dissolution of the state into World History. This moment of methodological particularity is supplemented by a logical demonstration that proceeds through the double negation of the constitutive poles. The Police and the Corporations legitimated the presupposed division of the social *Vermögen* that was put into question at the end of the System of Needs. The Police must deal with such particulars as the Rabble by giving them universal significance. The Corporations preserve the principle of particularity that makes possible and necessary the regular work of the Police. This duality is self-contradictory: the Police eliminate what the Corporations produce necessarily. Explicit unification of these poles in the form of the state raises the contradiction to a self-fulfilling unity. This is the Hegelian State. The phenomenological and logical accounts are unified as an originary structure. The pole of particularity depends on the principle of the political. The validity of this concept of the political is confirmed by the demonstration of the interdependence of philosophy and the political.

The relation of the state to civil society (including the Family) defines the structure of a given *Sittlichkeit* considered as methodological. The particularity of this historically specific *Sittlichkeit* is articulated first in the forms of Abstract Right and Morality. The abstract character of these two spheres implies their dependence. They cannot be equated with the political (unless the analysis becomes constitutive). Their dependence on the structure of *Sittlichkeit* suggests that their methodological principle is ultimately philosophical. The other expression of particularity within the *Philosophy of Right* appears when the state enters into relation with other sovereign states. Hegel's account is surprisingly brief. The relations and development he portrays tend toward the kind of formal logical portrait against which the *Philosophy of History* had warned. One state principle replaces another according to a principle that cannot be accounted for within the historical process itself. After the famous passages that portray the salutary effects of war in awakening patriotic sentiments and shaking sodden habits, the clockwork wears down. This is unsatisfactory, as was seen in Hegel's philosophical integration of the originary system into the flow of real history. The need for political reflection, to which the methodological mediation points, makes possible a different reading. Its political implication is that the structure of *Sittlichkeit* need not be fixed to the one (capitalist) structure portrayed by Hegel.

The opening of *Sittlichkeit* to the political explains the possibility of change within the formal spheres of Abstract Right and Morality as articulated by the strucutre of a philosophy that calls for the political as its completion. The definition of the political in this reconstruction defines the relation between the state and civil society as necessarily open to transformation. Neither the state nor the civil society have political priority. The positive transformation of the Rabble does not eliminate it by the external intervention of state institutions. The explicit immanence of the Rabble forces the historically specific structure of state/civil society to represent itself through different institutions. The presence of the Rabble within a given *Sittlichkeit* puts into question the philosophical basis of that structure of receptivity. It is a particular that must be represented. The institutional form of its representation can lie within civil society or within the state. Its principle is articulated by the political.

The possibility of and the failure to develop a theory of the political explains the structure of Hegel's philosophy itself. The political is replaced by World History as the logical structure that specifies the particularity of the state at any given moment. The concept of *Sittlichkeit* disappears at the level of World History. Its all-encompassing character rules out the necessity or possibility of a methodological articulation. The philosophy that correlates to this conception of World History reverts to one or another of the constitutive errors. This need not have been the case, for the philosopher or the political thinker. The originary philosopher could be shown to develop a theory of history-in-reason that made necessary a political moment that brings it to explicit completeness. The methodological mediation made necessary by the concept of *Sittlichkeit* can be interpreted in its independence as originary. The further distinction between the political and the institutions of the political state does not violate the intent of the author of the *Philosophy of History*. The *Philosophy of Right* does not repudiate him. The state structure that is portrayed as the "internal Constitution for itself" presents a division among the constitutive powers that articulate the moments of civil society. This division is not treated as a fixed opposition along the lines of a liberalism that sees civil society as needing protection from politics. The state is then seen as processual. It is not external to society. The turn toward external relations and history is not integrated adequately by Hegel. The relations among sovereign states reproduce the fundamental problems of political theory. The source of the first contract that ends the state of war, or articulates premises of peace, needs to be grounded. The logical or phenomenological "will" cannot serve as the particular presupposition of the argument. International relations among states whose modern structure permits attributing them with rational intent articulate the grounds that the theory of the state of nature does not provide. This foundation, in turn, makes necessary the definition of a (republican) internal politics that completes the systematic whole. The Republic preserves the rational state structure necessary to modern international relations. International politics then explains the moments of particularity articulated in the republican internal politics.

This picture is not Hegel's. It presents particular relations that cannot be reduced to the unity of empire. Hegel's politics, like his philosophy, are swept up ultimately into the Imperium of World History with which the *Philosophy of Right* concludes. This is why Hegel treats civil society as posing a real problem to which the state must provide a real solution. It explains the appearance of systematic completeness that left his earnest (left and right) successors no room to philosophize. But their quarrels could concern only the application of the supposedly finished system. The notion of an open or a political system was foreign to them.

System and Politics

The systematic relation of Kant's philosophy and politics is fully elaborated only in one essay: "Perpetual Peace." Kant subtitles his essay "A Philosophical Project." His intention emerges only from a close reading that looks for system beneath an often arbitrary or puzzling formal structure. Kant's conscious goal may not have been systematic; his essay, however, makes sense only in that assumption. A description of the essay will present familiar ingredients and problems. Kant invokes the guarantee of Nature, just as he did in 1784. The relation of morality and politics quickly becomes the one-sided affirmation of the priority of the moral. The suggestion of a "permissive law" that would avoid the subsumption of the particular under a pregiven universal is not pursued. When he avoids the appeal to Nature, Kant explains the creation of a lawful civil society by recourse to the level of international politics. Although the account is more concrete than the one proposed in 1784 or in "Theory and Practice," its practical results and theoretical form leave the reader frustrated. Of the six Preliminary Articles to the Project, three are to be introduced immediately while the others are to be set into force only gradually. Kant does not explain this distinction. Nor does he explain why all six fall nonetheless under the same rubric. He does not justify the absence of an explicit order—the first, fifth, and sixth articles are absolute, the others relative. When Kant later asserts that politics is so simple that "a race of devils" could produce a good constitution "if only it were intelligent," syncretism seems the only description of his project.[11] On the other hand, the formal structure of the text suggests a systematic intent. Preliminary Articles lead to Definitive Articles, which are justified by two Supplements *(Zusätze)* and two Appendixes *(Anhänge).* These reproduce the systematic stages of the Kantian originary philosophy. This suggests the possibility of discovering here the place of the political.

The theoretical difference between the immediately applicable and the gradually introduced Preliminary Articles appears to be merely pragmatic. The relative articles deal with matters about which diplomats could negotiate. Kant insists that "No Independent [State], Large or Small, Shall Come Under the Dominion of Another State by Inheritance, Exchange, Purchase, or Donation." Premodern European history explains this concern. Gradualism is wise, since states acquired in this manner may have accustomed themselves to their old relations. A similar gradualism justifies the demand that "Standing Armies (*miles perpetuus*) Shall in Time Be Totally Abolished." Diplomats could negotiate reductions toward this end. The same logic dictats that "National Debts Shall Not Be Contracted with a View to the External Friction of States."

Caution is necessary because the state may have already such debts, which first must be repaid. These commonsense explanations are put into question by another side to Kant's pragmatism in these articles; Kant is aware of *Realpolitik.* He does not simply condemn the national debt, this "ingenius invention of a commercial [English] people." He admits its domestic usefulness for the stimulation of trade and industry. He does not rule out "periodic and voluntary military exercises" that permit a people to "secure themselves and their country." Nor does he exclude (although it is relegated to a footnote) a ruler inheriting the right to rule a new country. Kant notes only that in this case "the state acquires a ruler" not the ruler a state. More than pragmatism must justify Kant's distinction between the two kinds of Preliminary Articles. Theoretical consideration of their content shows their complexity.

A moral imperative can be found beneath Kant's apparently pragmatic Preliminary Articles. He notes that the state is a moral person. Its incorporation into another state "contradicts the idea of the original contract without which no right over a people can be conceived." Similarly, the categorical imperative, which forbids treating men as means or tools, explains the need to abolish the army. Paying men to be killed or to kill is "hardly compatible with the rights of mankind in our own person." The moral basis for the abolition of the national debt is less apparent. It is said to add the means to make war to "the inclination to do so on the part of rulers." This justifies a preventive alliance against the offending state. The inevitable result of the first debt is thus the potential bankruptcy of all from a "preventive" arms race. The debt of the first state involves the "inflicting upon [the others] a public injury."[12] Their aggressive action is the result of the immoral action of the first state. In short, Kant's moral and pragmatic concerns are not mutually exclusive. The proposed gradualism is not justified only by political expediency. Kant's politics is neither solely pragmatic nor merely moral. Its autonomous role must explain the possibility of both of these incomplete attitudes.

The imemdiately applicable Preliminary Articles make explicit the warning against a facile pragmatism that forgets the moral basis of politics. Kant asserts that "No Treaty of

Peace Shall Be Held Valid in Which There is Tacitly Reserved Matter for a Future War." A tacit reservation transforms the treaty into a truce that will be broken once the combatants regain their energies. A similar logic guides the assertion that "No State Shall by Force Interfere with the Constitution or Government of Another State." When this article is brought into relation with the second, its immediate applicability is obvious. Finally, Kant forbids a warring state "Such Acts of Hostility which Would Make Mutual Confidence in the Subsequent Peace Impossible." These acts include the use of assassins, poisoners, incitation to treason, breach of agreement, and the like. Once again, Kant's concern is that there must be no grounds for the outbreak of hostilities once the peace is concluded. Although Kant does not draw explicitly the theoretical consequence, perpetual peace is therefore both the end sought and the means by which it is achieved. As means, the treaty must not contradict the end. But this moral imperative does not exclude considerations of *Realpolitik*. The first article comments ironically that, "if, in consequence of enlightened concepts of statecraft, the glory of the state is placed in its continual aggrandizement by whatever means," these remarks remain academic.[13] The fifth article points out that civil war is a state of anarchy that permits other states legitimately to enter the fray. Finally, the rejection of dishonorable means admits that war is "only the sad resource in the state of nature (where there is no tribunal which could judge with the force of law)." The results of war are not rendered just or injust by a "so-called judgment of God." Kant's moralism does not blind him to political reality. Morality cannot be separated from the world in which it is to be realized. Its independent validity must not condemn it to abstract formality and externality.

Isomorphic to the moral aspect of the relative articles, the immediately moral Preliminary Articles are justified pragmatically as well. Grounds for future wars "perhaps unknown to the contracting parties" are invalid "even if they should be dug out of dusty documents by acute sleuthing" that discovers the "secret reservation." Kant's warning against the pretended obligation to rid the world of a bad example rules out another pretext for war making and treaty breaking. The strict injunctions of the sixth article apply in the state of nature brought by war. They are necessary to avoid "a war of extermination, in which both parties and right itself might all be simultaneously annihilated," creating "perpetual peace only on the vast graveyard of the human race." Each moral imperative is also a pragmatic necessity whose place Kant stresses. This suggests that the six Preliminary Articles cannot be explained by reference to the critical system or by the difference of morality and politics. Their order and difference in applicability remain to be clarified. The articles do not themselves explain their status within the systematic argument. Nor are the Definitive Articles helpful on this score. Only the supplementary materials added to the text of Kant's treaty provide an indication of his intentions. This unusual means of philosophical exposition suggests that they play a systematic role.

The moral imperative present in each Preliminary Article directs attention to the first appendix, "On the Opposition between Morality and Politics with Respect to Perpetual Peace." It may explain the theoretical framework Kant has adopted. The approach is at first familiar and apparently contradictory. Morality can show the defects of a constitution. It can demand that they be repaired. Repair, however, must come only "as soon as possible" since "it would be absurd to demand that every defect be immediately and impetuously changed" before conditions have matured. Reform can come only within a republican framework, which Kant admits does not yet exist. The only possibility seems to be a revolution, which Kant of course cannot justify. Although he insists that revolutionaries are liable to punishment, Kant stresses that, once revolution has occurred, there is no ground for a return to the old regime. He adds here a footnote concerning "permissive laws of reason" which would explain why morality need not intervene immediately and imperiously. The note concludes with a justification of revolution that points back to the question of pragmatism and morality.

> Thus political prudence, with things as they are at present, will make it a duty to carry out reforms appropriate to the ideal of public right. But where revolutions are brought about *by nature alone,* it will not use them as a good excuse for even greater oppression,

> but will treat them as a *call of nature* to create a lawful constitution based on the principles of freedom, for a thorough reform of this kind is the only one that will last. (Emphasis mine)

The "thorough reform of this kind" will be a political act like "perpetual peace" which is both the end sought and the means for achievement. The notion of a "permissive law" is introduced to counter the actions of "despotic moralists" whose unmediated subsumption of the particular is contrary to political prudence. It is a two-faced law. A future mode of action is declared invalid at the same time that one that preceded the law is accepted. Such laws are said to exist "in the transition from the state of nature to a civil state." Kant is trying to justify a prudent pragmatism. But his own critical philosophy insists that law must be universal, like mathematics. Kant concludes that without a principle like those of mathematics, laws will be valid only "in general," not universally. The implications of this distinction are not drawn. This theoretical appendix does not by itself clarify the Preliminary Articles. The foundation of Kant's pragmatism will not be theoretical; it will be political.

The brief transition to the Definitive Articles does not provide the explanation of the Preliminary Articles or of their relation to the three basic provisions of the treaty. It does offer a negative methodological suggestion that reinforces the systematic orientation. Kant does not use the permissive law to suggest a constitutive development from the provisional to the general. He does not invoke the moral a priori to subsume the pragmatic morality of the Preliminary Articles. His insistence that the state of peace is not identical to the state of nature points to the place of the political. Peace, he asserts in italics, has to be "formally instituted." A footnote then explains "the postulate on which all the following articles are based." This postulate is the familiar assertion that "all men who can at all influence one another must adhere to some kind of civil constitution." Kant offers no justification. The transition to the Definite Articles is not a transcendental or theoretical deduction. That missing originary political deduction can be found only by a systematic reading of the supplementary materials that validate the politics of the "philosophical project." The systematic movement of these four sections reproduces the philosophical stages through which Kant's critical project reached its full elaboration before moving to the "doctrinal" phase. This suggests that the philosopher was aware of the systematic place that the political occupied within the whole. Reproduction of the originary philosophical structure in the supplementary sections supports the claim that the political theory articulated in the Definite Articles stands in a systematic orginary relation to the critical philosophy. The transition from the Preliminary to the Definite Articles is thus justified politically, not philosophically. The politics of the Definite Articles can then ground the pragmatic moralism of the Prelimary assertions.

The beginning of the first supplement repeats briefly the development through the three Kantian *Critiques* before it strikes out on its own. Kant begins from the invocation of "that great artist, nature." He refers immediately to its "mechanical course." Nature produces harmony for humans "against their will" by means of the kind of unsocial sociability described in 1784. To avoid the difficulties in the older position, Kant insists in a footnote that he is talking about ends and goals. He distinguishes the senses in which one can talk of Providence, and suggests that although physical-mechanical causes explain how trees are carried north by the Gulf Stream to barren lands, "we must not overlook the teleological cause." The teleological cause is not the deity. Providence must do for the system what the Postulates of Practical Reason did in the second *Critique:* "compensate for our own lack of justice, provided our intention was genuine" so that we will "not relent in our endeavor after the good." After this allusion to the systematic contribution of the second *Critique,* Kant's account develops concepts from the third. The plan of Providence is seen "in questions of the relation of the forms of things to ends in general." This argument from the particular form of things demands that "we can and must supply [the ends in general] from our own minds." The "analogy to action of human art" means that there is no predicative theoretical guarantee for these assertions. The limits of human reason indicate that the guarantee cannot be casual. Yet, continues Kant, there is a guarantee that "does possess dogmatic validity and has a very real foundation in *practice*. . .which makes it our duty to promote it by using the natural mechanism described above." This summary of the critical path completes Kant's introduction. What at first seem like inconsistencies are in fact a systematic progression. The natural rationality of the first *Critique* is combined with the moral imperative of the second by means of categories from the third. Kant knew full well the differences and limits of each of the domains of objectivity and the kinds of lawfulness proposed by each critical argument. This systematic structure suggests that Kant is proposing a new strategy in the supplementary materials.

The remainder of the first supplement develops a model of progressive human history that is only apparently similar to that of 1784. The difference is signaled by the fact that no attempt to mediate laws of nature with those of freedom is offered. The difficulties of the last of the "cosmopolitan History" theses are avoided. The practical obligations of philosophy are left aside. Nature acts on men "even against their inclination and without this *ought* being based on a concept of duty to which they were bound by moral law." Nature acts "to lead the human race, considered as a class of animals, to their own end." Her laws are mechanical, not organic. Man is an animal, not rational or moral. Kant's formulations are deliberate. He asks "how has she guaranteed (by compulsion but without prejudice to his freedom) that he shall do that which he ought to do under the laws of freedom." The subordination of the moral is clear in the question, "What has nature done with regard to this end which man's own reason makes his duty?" Lest he be misunderstood, Kant continues, "I do not mean that she imposes a duty on us to do it, for this can be done only by free practical reason; rather, I mean that she herself does it, whether we will or not." This primacy of natural necessity over moral duty needs explanation. Mechanical determinism is stressed to such a degree that the systematic reader expects an explanation that will balance the extreme and reintegrate the whole. The mediations of 1784 are ruled out by the explicit rejection of a constitutive orientation. The political context of the argument must clarify what the theoretical cannot explain.

The justification for the appeal to mechanical nature reintroduces the acting subject without reference to the moral law. Kant suggests that "nature comes to the aid of the general will established on reason, which is revered even though impotent in practice." The mode of nature's intervention is explained without recourse to Providence or to the moral a priori. The creation of the Republic is "only a question of a good organization of the state...whereby the powers of each selfish inclination are so arranged in opposition that one moderates or destroys the ruinous effects of the other." Kant's appeal to this familiar eighteenth-century topos is surprising. Its implication is that "the problem of organizing a state, however hard it may seem, can be solved even for a race of devils, if only they are intelligent." This political program rejects morality explicitly. "A problem like this must be capable of solution; it does not require that we know how to attain the moral improvement of men but only that we should know the mechanism of nature in order to use it on men." Kant's goal is the creation of institutions in which "man is forced to be a good citizen even if not a morally good person." Such an amoralism cannot be Kant's last word on the matter. The conception of a politics applied by the "race of devils" supposes the externality of theory to practice. It is based on the kind of misuse of the teleological judgment that the concept of culture in the *Critique of Judgment* (paras. 82-84) tried to avoid. Kant's final remarks in this supplement admit the difficulty. He has shown how "nature guarantees perpetual peace by the mechanism of human passions." Yet, he continues, the demonstration does not give "sufficient certainty that we can predict theoretically" on its basis. It implies only that it is "our duty to work toward this end, which is not just a chimerical one." This is not a reflective teleological argument. The stress on natural necessity points toward the practical moral domain on the same ground that the first *Critique* claimed to destroy reason in order to make room for faith. The first supplement thus reiterates the first stage of the systematical critical unity. It demonstrates the need for a moral moment in the critical system. The politics of the "race of devils" makes sense only within this structural unity.[14]

The politics proposed in the first supplement is only apparently independent from morality. It is only apparently political. Kant's insistence on "a state of peace...in which laws have force" is a moral demand. Its justification is theoretical, not political. Moral injunctions are valid only if they are realizable. Kant must demonstrate that moral freedom can be realized in actuality. The first supplement provided the material element of such a demonstration. The second supplement and first appendix bring a complement from the side of morality itself. The first appendix does not break new moral ground. It reasserts the Kantian moral theory. We cannot say that honesty is the best policy, since practice at times refutes that observation. What must be said, rather, is that honesty is better than any policy. Acting from duty guarantees worthiness of being happy; it is the moral and theoretical presupposition of politics. The empirical opportunism of the "political moralist" is doomed to failure. Only the "moral politician" acting from duty can be accepted. The familiar arguments are more polemical than usual here. Kant lambasts those who "make a great show of understanding *men*...without understanding *man* and what can be made of him." He denounces the three "principles" on which the politician acts—do, then seek excuses; if you act, blame the other; divide and conquer—and finally cries: "Let us put an end to this sophism, if not to the injustices it protects." This cry is followed by Kant's surprising acceptance of revolution as a "call of Nature." The appendix then concludes with the simple affirmation that "true politics can never take a step without rendering homage to morality. Though politics by itself is a difficult art, its unity with morality is no art at all for this union cuts the knot that politics could not untie when they were in conflict." This short circuit which reduces politics to morality is no more adequate than the revolutionary "call of Nature." Kant does not leave the moral argument at this. He adds a further element in this second edition of "Perpetual Peace." The role of the new material is accentuated by its label as a "Secret Article"; its function confirms Kant's systematic intention.

Kant might have moved immediately to a discussion of politics on the basis of a suggestion at the beginning of the moral theory in the first appendix. He had noted that "reason is not yet sufficiently enlightened to survey the entire series of predetermining causes...to be able to foresee with certainty the happy or unhappy effects that follow human actions by the mechanism of nature." The argument could have developed suggestions elaborated in the teleological judgment of the third *Critique.* The systematic intention explains why Kant repeated the immediate defense of the moral politician even when the limits of the subsumptive judgment of morality were clear to him. These same systematic reasons explain the new supplement, which insists that the philosophers must be consulted publicly by the politicians. The role of the philosopher in this Secret Article is not just Kant's ironic criticism of the government that had censored him. The Secret Article should have followed the first appendix.[15] The analysis of morality in the first appendix has the same structure and function as the critical grounding of morality in the *Foundations of the Metaphysics of Morals.* Morality is taken as a given whose conditions of possibility are analyzed. The systematic contribution added by the *Critique of Practical Reason* was the Postulates of Practical Reason. These postulates were seen to guarantee that the moral imperative is realizable. The moral imperative whose conditions of possibility are analyzed makes sense only when these conditions are actual. The role of the philosopher guaranteed by the Secret Article provides a structural foundation complementing the natural necessity. Once they have been introduced together, Kant has a systematic justification for the turn to the approach suggested in the third *Critique.* The public debate that the philosopher's intervention is to guarantee then can be developed in the last of the supplements. That final appendix makes explicit the systematic structure of Kant's supplementary arguments by its title, "On the Harmony that the Transcendental Concept of Public Right Establishes between Morality and Politics." The content of this argument justifies the political interpretation of the structure of reflective judgment and the forms of its justification. The argument is still philosophical, and its conclusions methodological. The political correlate does not become explicit until the Definite Articles are analyzed.

The justification of Kant's "transcendental formula of public law" is a constant theme in his critical method. It is articulated here as a methodological logic of receptivity. "All actions relating to the right of other men are unjust if their maxim is not consistent with publicity." The explicit qualification of this assertion as "transcendental" is new. The argument itself is familiar from the political texts dating to 1784;[16] its theoretical grounds were articulated in the "Deduction of Pure Aesthetic Judgments" of the *Critique of Judgment.* Kant illustrates the application of this principle. From the sphere of civil law he chooses the issue of rebellion. His expected rejection is justified now by the need of its leaders to keep their plans secret. Such a rebellion is not politics because it is not public. An illustration from international relations develops the point. The "transcendental principle" forbids a state from breaking its promise to give aid or from striking preemptively at a threatening neighbor, because to say publicly what it intended to do would permit the other party to counter its intention. Kant leaves the third domain, that of world citizenship, with the remark that "its analogy with international law makes it a very simple matter to state and evaluate its maxims."[17] The implications of the "transcendental" theory are now drawn. Kant provides what can be called a Transcendental Dialectic to accompany the Analytic formula. "We cannot infer conversely that the maxims that bear publicity are therefore just, since no one who has decidedly superior power needs to conceal his plans." This "dialectic" avoids the formalist conclusion that rulers who do not hide their aims are not unjust. From the standpoint of the system, these first two moves develop the logic of a critique; they explain the conditions of the possibility of just political relations. The expectation is that the second phase of the appendix will show the political form of the necessity of that political structure. The result will parallel the methodological unity of a phenomenological and a logical moment. Its articulation indicates the structure that the political moment must assume.

The phenomenological phase of Kant's argument has two parts. It begins from an "affirmative and transcendental principle of public law." The qualification "affirmative" suggests a new moment. Kant does not illustrate the way this proposed principle will work. He asserts that "All maxims that *stand in need* of publicity in order not to fail their end, agree with politics and right combined." The additional phrase indicating agreement with "politics" as well as with "right" provides a hint at its application. The first "transcendental formula" dealt with the logical conditions of right. It did not explain how these conditions came into being, nor how they are preserved. It did not permit a solution to the problem of revolution, which Kant accepted but could not justify. The formula explained only the logical conditions of receptivity. Its foundation is the theoretical system of the *Critiques.* Kant's second transcendental condition must articulate the moment of particularity that the systematic reconstruction makes necessary. The generality of Kant's claim is disconcerting: "The condition of the possibility of international law in general is this: a juridical condition must exist first." The dilemma is familiar. The systematic context now permits an interpretation that preserves the distinction of philosophy and politics. The concern with "politics and right combined" suggests that the theoretical problem of founding morality as the guarantee of the receptivity of the social world to political measures needs a political complement. The dual orientation of this final supplement, which corresponds to the function of the *Critique of Judgment* within the system as a whole, suggests that the form of the political founds the methodological moment of particularity.

The generality of the second transcendental formulation implies that the political moment cannot be defined from within method. The political articulates one of the moments of method; it is not itself constituted by the method. The universality of international law and its juridical condition is a reflective formulation. This logical moment cannot stand alone. It is not like the universality of mathematics which can be "learned" from principles that function as data. Its universality grounds the necessity "to philosophize" that Kant's methodological particularity had to justify. In the systematic context of the supplements' relation to the Definitive Articles, this familiar formulation of the theory-practice problem is a hinge between the methodological and the originary theoretical and political structures. This necessity to philosophize was the definition of the political moment that the originary philosophy made necessary. The correlation is preserved. Politics and philosophy are interdependent. Method is their mediation. The supplementary materials point to the function of the Definitive Articles as articulating the structure of the political whose particular content they explain. The systematic recall in these supplements of the phases of Kant's argument suggests that the political is central to the interpretation of the Definitive Articles for Perpetual Peace.

The disconcertingly general and vague structure of the Definitive Articles confirms negatively the systematic orientation. Several interpretations could be suggested at first. The first article affirms that the civil *(bürgerliche)* constitution in every state must be reublican. The second claims that the law among nations *(Völkerrecht)* must be founded in a federation of free states. Finally, Kant defines a law of world citizenship based on conditions of universal hospitality *(Hospitalität)*. The first temptation is to treat these articles as merely classificatory. They describe the situation of the individual within a single state, among states, and within the most general structure of human being as such. If this appears too general, another reading might develop the parallel to the final section of the *Philosophy of Right.* The difference is that Hegel's third moment is World History as the "Court of the Last Judgment." A different approach might treat these articles as the result of the contractual diplomatic negotiations based on the Preliminary Articles. The interdictions of the immediately applicable articles—forbidding tacit reservations, interference by force, or use of illicit methods—are the presupposition of any contract. The permissive articles—concerning continuation of older, noncontractual traditions such as inheritance, exchange, or donation; the attempt to equate the partner by forbidding either to grow at the expense of another; or the denial of the right to enlarge oneself by borrowing from a third party—are elements to be weighed in the contractual negotiations. The problem is that this interpretation presupposes what it wants to prove. A contractual relation is only binding if legal structures already exist that make it possible. An alternative could follow the pattern from "Cosmopolitan History" which invokes international relations among states to explain the constitution of republican civil society. This constitutive proposal is refuted by Kant's use of natural mechanical causality and categories of moral obligation in the supplementary discussions. An adequate reading will depend on the ability of the systematic framework to interpret the "universal hospitality" of the third article. The first two articles are made dynamic only on the condition that a principle of particularity can be elaborated so that their formality is overcome.

Kant's assertion that the Republic is the only normatively valid state form is familiar. The Republic derives from the idea of the original contract which is the basis of all legislation. It is a universal form excluding all manifestations of privilege save that "to lend obedience to no external laws except those to which I could have given consent." This means that there can be no hereditary titles; a nobleman is not necessarily a noble man.[18] Hierarchy is permitted if it ranks only offices, not the present holder of office. This definition of the Republic is still formal and external to the society whose institutional articulation it permits. Kant's abstract structures must be given a content whose necessity and completeness can be demonstrated.

The Republic requires an active definition that explains how it articulates a methodological content. Kant's political proposals begin from the assertion that "no one can lawfully bind another without at the same time subjecting himself to the law by which he also can be bound." This reassertion of Rousseau's insistence that the law protects against particular injustice because laws are by nature universal recalls also the practical problems of giving content to Rousseauian politics.[19] Kant argues negatively first, comparing the Republic to the immediate social activity of "democracy." Republican institutions provide formal guarantees of our freedom as men, our dependence on common legislation as subjects, and our equality as citizens. The Republic is an administrative institutional structure. Its opposite is not democracy but tyranny. It is a political form defining the exercise of power, not its source or its content. The Republic does not pose the question of sovereignty. The democratic concern with the sovereignty of the people treats a political form as if it were identical to its content. It unites in one hand what the Republic divides. Its identification of the executive and the legislative functions leaves no space for the formation of political judgment. It does not distinguish the properly political from what is only the political moment of method. The democratic immediacy cannot explain the necessity of the particular content of its political action. The formal Republic provides criteria of inclusion and exclusion. Its constitutional and representative structure guarantees that the Republic is open to change, public debate, and communal education. Republican institutions are a political structure that makes necessary the articulation of particular content. The justification of that content depends negatively on the philosophical moment of methodological receptivity. The positive definition of content has no other limit than the republican agreement "with politics and right combined." The Republic can be democratic; democracy need not be republican. The conditions in which the two coincide depend on the political constitution of the Republic.

The representative character of the republican institutions explains the process by which their formal structure acquires necessary content. The "democratic" identification of executive and legislative is rejected. The task of politics is to determine the particularity that makes necessary the reflective communal judgment. Within Kant's republican framework, the executive is the locus of the political. Kant's argument is consistent, although his definition of the two institutions is idiosyncratic. The General Will legislates. The laws it institutes are universal. If the executive only subsumed particular cases under these laws, it would be a bureaucracy. This would make the executive merely the agent of the legislature. The necessity of the particular contents it subsumes could not be justified. Kant proposes instead an independent executive, prescribed by the republican structure, whose political task is defined by the reflective judgment. The executive proposes actions that correlate reflectively to the particular facts. The executive articulates those particular issues and reflective universals that the legislative may consecrate as law. The legislative and the executive complement each other. Each needs the contribution of the other. The republican constitution defines their relation, which can vary. The legislative is the expression of the logical moment of method; the executive is its phenomenological counterpart. This explains another apparent paradox. Kant asserts that the "smaller the personnel of the government...the greater is their representation and the more nearly the constitution approaches the possibility of republicanism." Kant's goal is not to limit the exercise of sovereignty.* His concern is to preserve the place of the political. He insists that "the mode of government...is incomparably more important to the people than the form of sovereignty." The mode of government must be representative. Its goal is not efficient execution for its own sake. Pope's what's best administered is best" is philosophically naïve and practically wrong (as Kant illustrates with Roman examples in which a well-administering emperor is succeeded by a tyrant). A constitution guaranteeing the representative function protects against the abuse that results from reducing the executive to a subsumptive bureaucrat. The ability of the executive to define those particulars with which legislation must deal protects against stagnation or oppression. The separate existence of both branches, and their complementarity, represents the methodological unity of the theoretical and political moments. Neither can replace the other, nor can either function alone. The republican constitution articulates their unity.

Kant has not yet explained what particularity republican politics is to represent. He notes that the representative Republic makes possible "gradual reform," whereas the democratic unification of executive and legislative permits change only through violent revolution. His citation of Frederick the Great for having "at least *said*" that he was the first servant of the state is ironical. He is not paying obeisance any more than he is seeking a theory for revolution. The error of the monarch and the revolutionary is that they take the goal of political action to be the constitution of something empirically real—real happiness for the subject or a real original contract. The "Copernican revolution" eliminated such illusions. The phenomenological doctrine implied by the *Critique of Judgement* proceeds differently. Representation does not argue from an empirical given to its reproduction. The political relation of representation to the represented does not judge whether political action actually or adequately expresses

*For a similar argument more familiar Americans, C. *The Federalist*, number 58. The parallels to the American republican experiment are striking. A further illustration concerns the interpretation of Kantian notion of "hospitality" discussed below. Garry Wills's suggestions of a Scottish influence on the American Founders (in *Inventing America. Jefferson's Declaration of Independence*) take on a move than philological importance in this context. Hutchison's notions of "benevolence" and the "moral sense," and Reid's elaboration of the Scottish premises concerning the theory—practice problem are (if the anachronism be permitted) Kantian. One should not forget that the founders of classical economic theory—Ferguson and Smith—belong to the Scottish Enlightenment, to which Kant is endebted, and in whose light he should be interpreted by future scholars.

empirical things or interests. This premodern, external notion of representation is the basis of the "democratic" confusion. Politics would be redundant if it were only the immediate representation of society and its empirical interests. Useless at best, it would become a hindrance to "further enlightenment" like the "scientific" revolution condemned in Kant's *Religion* (ch. 6, above) The particular that is to be represented by a modern politics must be produced in and by the very political process that represents it. This interdependence reproduces the relation of the political moment of method to the originary politics and philosophy. Theory and practice are related reflectively. The political Republic presents its content in the dual articulations of particularity and receptivity. This content is developed through the specification of a first political moment that inaugurates the modern state structure. That first political moment must explain the origin of a civil society under law without recourse to providential, mechanical, or teleological nature or moral impetus.

Kant insisted that republican institutions would lead to an end to war. The second Definite Article develops this argument beyond the limits of the first. A king can make war without sacrificing "the pleasures of his table, the chase, his country houses, his court functions, and the like." He can "leave the justification that decency demands to the diplomatic corps who are ever ready to provide it." The wars inaugurated by the revolutionary French republic cast doubt on this analysis based only on internal politics. Kant therefore begins his account of the founding of international law from the parallels between interstate and interpersonal relations. A common civil constitution is necessary because the Other is a threat to the sovereign individual or state. This argument had previously explained the transition from the Preliminary to the Definitive Articles. But there is an important distinction between the operation of the two imperatives. The moral law commands the individual absolutely. Since the state is independent and self-legislating, it cannot accept such a law standing above it. It cannot give up the very independence that defines it. The foundation of international law can only be a Federation of Free States, not a unified Empire.[20]

Kant notes the paradox that classical theorists like Grotius, Pufendorf, and Vattel use the concept of a law among nations to justify war. Why not treat the law as preventing war? Granted, no law can coerce a nation. That would contradict its independence and the federal relation. The "homage that each state pays (at least in words) to the concept of law" appears to imply, counterfactually, that the others have a similar disposition. Yet nations do not plead their case before a common court. They war. War does not prove right. The treaty ending a war is by nature temporary, since each state is judge in its own case. The state cannot be forced, as can the individual, to enter a lawful constitution. A Federation of Free States can only be a "league." It is neither a treaty of peace nor the formation of a world state. Despite the homage paid to the concept of law, there appears to be no means of assuring that interstate relations will be lawful. Kant speaks finally only of a "negative surrogate" that might avert tendencies to war. When he asks himself whether his Federation can work, his reply is disappointing: Yes, "if fortune" permits a powerful and enlightened people—the French—to become a Republic! This second article gives no positive content to Kant's Republic. Its suggestion of a Federation or League among sovereign individuals implies negatively the need for a concept of law different from the subsumptive universality of the moral a priori. The positive solution will have to be sought in the final article.[21]

The third Definitive Article does not at first seem to provide the political content that explains the necessary success of Kant's republican politics. Applicable to humans as world citizens, it has apparently the formal and abstract status of the initial philosophical assertions about "man" in general. However, Kant stresses that he is not arguing from philanthropy. The ground of his position is the concept of right. The content of the third article is painted in details that would please the staunchest anticolonialist. The discussion concludes that "universal hospitality" is "a supplement to the unwritten code of the civil and international law, indispensable for the maintenace of the public human rights and hence also of perpetual peace." This is the first mention of an unwritten code, which is not defined further. The similarity to the "exemplary" schematizing role of the beautiful incarnation of the rational ideal *(Critique of Judgment,* paras. 17, 18) is not developed. The details of Kant's criticisms of colonialist depredation suggest an interpretation. He attacks the Barbary pirates and Bedouins for violating a "natural law" that guarantees communication among peoples. This condemnation is followed by lengthy, erudite footnote on the intercourse of China and Europe via Tibet. The concern with communication among peoples is Kant's "unwritten" premise. Its implication is that the unwritten code is the right and duty to further public communication among the nations of the earth. The code is to apply in civil and international law. Its international legal result is the condemnation of colonialist exploitation. The positive implication of this condemnation reaffirms the argument of the second article for a federative League by assuring a relative equality among the participant nations. Its domestic civil-law implications for the first article are not clear. The stress on the role of publicity in the "affirmative and transcendental principle of public law" from the final supplement suggests that this unwritten code will play a central theoretical role. Its political correlate remains undefined. The imperatives of the systematic orientation suggest an interpretation.

The lack of a philosophical justification for the unwritten code points to the place of the political within the Kantian system. The philosophical function of the code is to explain the logical conditions of receptivity that join the independent states into a federative league assuring perpetual peace. The moral worthiness or social desirability of this goal is not sufficient to make necessary its achievement. The lawful relations among independent subjects are neither the result of the subsumption of particularity under an a priori universal nor are they the result of empirical deduction from pregiven facts. Perpetual peace is neither the constitution of a single world empire nor is it the isolated existence of autarchic singular subjects whose content is fixed eternally because no interaction with others is permitted.[22] Perpetual peace articulates explicitly the republican political structure at the level of international relations. Philosophy can explain how the republican logic guarantees the conditions of receptivity that make politics necessary. Philosophy cannot explain the establishment of either the national or the international League of Republics. Kant pointed to the difficulty in his comments on the transition from the Preliminary to the Definitive Articles.

Peace he insisted in italics, is to be instituted politically. This means that entry into the original social contract is explained by the political. The "positive transcendental principle" in the final supplement articulates the transition. It stresses the role of those particulars that "stand in need of publicity in order not to fail to meet their end." This is the political correlate to the theoretical assertion of the place of the philosopher in the Secret Article. The necessity of publicity could not be demonstrated theoretically. The *Critique of Judgment* could deduce its role only in incomplete analyses that presupposed a concept of "culture" as the ability to set goals, or had recourse to an "exemplary" schematizing function of the beautiful. The systematic place of "Perpetual Peace" indicates that the difficulty results from the inability of theory alone to accomplish fully the tasks to which it points. The political must articulate the logic of particularity.

Politics explains the philosophical logic of the unwritten code. Philosophy explains the structure and content of the corresponding politics. The implicitly republican structure defined by the "law of hospitality" demands that the particular states interact explicitly. They must communicate, exchange, learn to think in the place of the other. Isolationism would fix their content like a contract that shuts off further enlightenment. The interaction among autonomous subjects defines those particulars that stand in need of publicity. They are the object that republican politics is to represent. Kant's condemnation of colonialism is neither formal nor moral. It has a positive political implication. Criticism of the negative material effects of exploitation implies the positive demand for increasing the material equality among particular states that will continue to exist, whatever form their particularity may adopt. This material equality is not an empirical goal, like the happiness sought by the rebel, the despot, or Garve. It is not a preexistent material thing within the lawful phenomenal world. Nor is it the abstract formal equality of individuals subsumed under the moral law. The interaction among particular states which must remain autonomous although their content can change means that the content of political equality will change continually. It is the "nonreal thing" that politics seeks to represent. Material equality in this sense is the political form of the modern demand for justice. It is constituted in the same process by which it is articulated.

The parallel between the international League and the national Republic points to the way this particular content is founded politically and philosophically. The structures that Kant calls "executive" articulate the particular content of the material equality that necessitates reflective judgment whose result is given institutional form by the equivalent of what Kant called the "legislative." The stress on the role of publicity suggests that these logical legislative structures will tend to have increasingly democratic, participatory forms. The explanation of the political moment that necessitates entry into the original republican contract is found in this same parallel of the national and the international.

The systematic reading is now complete. The parallel structures of the national and international Republic explain the political moment that makes necessary the entry into the original contract.[23] The three Definitive Articles present a unitary structure articulated by the independence and interdependence of philosophy and politics. Each article can explain the philosophical structure of receptivity for the others. Each can also serve the others by articulating the particulars with which politics is concerned. The national Republic is the condition for the success of the federative League that, in turn, puts into practice the law of hospitality. The federative League and the unwritten code designate the particularity that the national politics must articulate. The federative League, finally, has the particular political form that the international political particularity of its constituent states makes necessary. The changing content of the League, and of the internal politics of its members, affects and is affected by the concrete form in which the quest for material equality is articulated nationally and internationally. These structural interdependencies explain Kant's repeated attempts from 1784 onward to derive the origin of the Republic from the international relations that demand the treaty of perpetual peace.

This same structure permits, finally, an interpretation of the apparent arbitrariness of the Preliminary Articles. The immediately applicable articles define measures that can be taken by the Republic itself. The permissive articles concern problems over which the Republic has no direct control. The first immediately applicable article condemns the "tacit reservation." This guarantees publicity in interstate relations. The next three permissive articles present international framework conditions that must be resolved before further internal measures can be considered by the Republic. Their political solution presupposed the public space guaranteed by the first article. This political determination explains the "pragmatism" that the theoretical approach to the Preliminary Articles could not decipher. The successful interpretation of the order and function of these Preliminary Articles in turn confirms the need to distinguish the theoretical from the political moment of method. The supplementary materials were only theoretical premises for the political argument. The systematic unity and interaction of all the parts of Kant's essay are demonstrated thus by this interpretation. The conclusion points to a new set of problems for our contemporaries.

Peace is to be instituted politically through a process in which material equality is defined as the particular whose representation is articulated by politics. The relationship between politics and the political parallels the relationship between philosophy and the methodological articulation. The politics defined by the republican constitution has a moment of particularity and a moment of receptivity, just as the articulation of philosophy joined a moment of particularity to its explanation of receptivity. Republican politics must preserve the originary form. It faces the double danger typical of this situation. Overstress on the critical phenomenological orientation to actual equality can transform the representative relation into a formal subsumption or into an empirical judgment that treats its object as real. Either form of this error closes off the possibility of "further enlightenment." The symmetrical risk overstresses the formality of the republican institutions in its concern to preserve particular freedom. The formal peace neglects particular content. The result is the reduction of politics to philosophy. Kant's successors confronted an apparently successful capitalist civil society dominated by its economy. Liberalism's legitimation of this order tended to stress the formal logical moment. Marxian productivism presented the critical phenomenological counterpart.

The crisis of the contemporary capitalist civil society suggests a return to Kant. The philosophical moment of logical receptivity is not reduced to the structures of an already constituted civil society. Politics is not the articulation of pregiven and fixed interests. The political moment suggests that the particular issues and agents of politics need to be redefined. A republican politics that preserves the originary relation of these two moments is the modern theoretical and practical structure that confronts contemporary society once the veil of the economic has been lifted. The missing ingredient is the sphere of international relations. That is the topic for another study.

Notes

PREFACE

1. To illustrate and to acknowledge my debts, the priority of the theoretical was clear in my early concern with Husserl, for example in the article "Phenomenology and/or Psychology," in *Review of Existential Psychology and Psychiatry*, vol. 5, no. 3, Fall 1965, pp. 139-265. That phenomenological phase led to my association, until 1978, with the journal *Telos*, when the orientation of the journal seemed to become overly scholastic. Priority of political concern produced *The Marxian Legacy*, which shows that the political inadequacies of Marx's most astute sucessors are rooted in theoretical failings of Marx himself. The major influences on that book were Cornelius Castoriadis, Claude Lefort, and the journal *Socialisme ou Barbarie.*
2. Cf. Dick Howard and Karl E. Klare, eds. *The Unknown Dimension* (New York: Basic Books, 1972), as well as my editions of *The Selected Political Writings of Rosa Luxemberg* (New York: Monthly Review Press, 1971 et. seq.) and Serge Mallet's *Essays on the New Working Class* (St. Louis Telos Press, 1975). See also the collective work of the journal *Telos.*
3. The most important chapter in *The Marxian Legacy* presents the details of this claim. Comparison of that presentation to my earlier introduction

to the *Selected Political Writings* shows the origins of the present systematic approach.

4. Habermas's *Theorie des kommunikativen Handelns* (Frankfurt am Main: Suhrkamp Verlag, 1982) explains the qualification *late* in a suggestive argument. The life-world is structured by the three domain of strategic, communicative, and affective action. The first is the domain of the economy, the second is the affair essentially of a bureaucracy, while the third is managed by the "culture industry." Capitalism enters its late phase when the first two domains are entirely "colonized," and the third is under attack. Full colonization of the affective domain will exhaust the potential of capitalist development. What will follow, however, is not explained. The political dilemma remains. Habermas's most recent work on the concept of modernity—presented in lectures at the Collège de France in February, 1983—moves in a direction parallel to the one suggested here. Its political completion, however, remains to be articulated.
5. It had a Kantian moment as well, as Leonard Krieger points out in his *Essay on the Theory of Enlightened Despotsim* (Chicago: University of Chicago Press, 1975). My debt to Krieger's work is expressed in a review essay in *Telos*, no. 33, Fall 1977, pp. 219-30), and in "The Origins of Revolution," in *Journal of the British Society for Phenomenology*, vol. 14, no. 1, January 1983.
6. The interpretation of the French Revolution suggested here is based particularly on François Furet's *Penser la révolution française* (Paris: Gallimard, 1980). Three works are fundamental for the American Revolution: Bernard Bailyn, *The Ideological Origins of the American Revolution* (Cambridge: Harvard University Press, 1967); Gordon Wood, *The Creation of the American Republic, 1776-1787* (Chapel Hill: University of North Carolina Press, 1969); and Richard Buel, Jr., *Securing the Revolution* (Ithaca: Cornell University Press, 1972). My own study of the American Revolution will be published by Editions Ramsay (Paris), in early 1986. Concerning Prussia, the fundamental source is Reinhard Koselleck's *Preussen zwischen Reform und Revolution* (Stuttgart: Klett-Cotta Verlag, 1967).
7. The expression is not quite accurate. The political is present constantly, although in a manner distorted by the structures of capitalist civil society. This is the point at which to recognize my debt to the thought of Hannah Arendt, who is often criticized for her inability to account for the origin of the political, which seems to present itself suddenly, without previous announcement, to solve her problems. This is most clear in her discussion of the "workers' councils" in *On Revolution*. The argument suggested here explains why, at least in the modern age, the political can be suddenly rediscovered by actors who break the spell of ideological solutions.
8. I have tried to use the systematic framework suggested here to analyze the recent peace movements in an essay, "D'une nouvelle gauche à une autre," *Espirit*, July 1983, pp. 116-24.

Chapter 1. Introduction

1. R. Haym, *Hegel und seine Zeit* (Berlin: Verlag von Rudolpf Gaertner, 1857; reprint Darmstadt: Wissenschaftliche Buchgesellschaft, 1974), pp. 4-5.
2. I do not distinguish between these two categories at the present level of abstraction. The use of one or the other depends simply on grammatical felicity.
3. I will use the term *temptation* frequently and systematically. I do not mean a subjective possibility. The temptation to which I refer is systematic. The systematic originary structure is constantly open to the splitting of one of its poles, which is then treated as a solution. The need for a specific methodology is explained by the immanence of this temptation, whose most vivid expression will be seen in the presentation of Marx's theory of ideology.

Chapter 2. From Transcendental to Originary Philosophy

1. Habermas's *Theory of Communicative Action* tends to restrict itself to the epistemological and the sociological, at least in the author's self-understanding. The implications are, however, broader. The discussion of rationality with which the book begins attempts to show the immanence of this problem to all social theory and to all social systems. The proposed theory of communicative action is a powerful argument whose potential is illustrated in the second volume, when Habermas treats the relation of the social system to the life-world in which it is embedded. Habermas refuses to draw the radical implications of his own advance, limiting himself to reconstructing the tradition of critical theory in the wake of Marx and the Frankfurt tradition. He rejects what he calls the "classical transcendental philosophical" attempt to formulate a "foundationalist" philosophy. This is the major difference between his attempt and the present effort, which was largely completed before the appearance of his book.
2. This general description could be concretized by figures or arguments chosen from modern or contemporary philosophy. Its generality applies beyond the properly philosophical, as is illustrated particularly by Merleau-Ponty's *Phenomenology of Perception* which, without insisting on the principle of modern immanence, demonstrates its functioning. It is not without significance that Merleau-Ponty's attention turned increasingly to the ontological premises of his earlier work in his *Visible*

and the Invisible, as well as in his final lectures on Hegel and Marx, to which reference will be made later.

3. There is no need to stress that my use of the concept *system* is taken from the German Idealist tradition best articulated in Kroner's *Von Kant bis Hegel* (Tübingen: J.C.B. Mohr [Paul Siebeck], 1921, 1924). I am not referring to the systematic philosophies inspired by Peirce, Whitehead, etc.
4. The foundationalist danger is still present here, since the *Geschichtlichkeit* itself can be taken as an (external) essence from which the events of human history emanate. This error is built into the modern structure. It can be avoided when the political and the philosophical are given priority over the historical and epistemological dimensions.
5. See Klaus Hartmann's "On Taking the Transcendental Turn," *Review of Metaphysics*, vol. 20 no. 2 (1966), pp. 223-249.
6. This normative external constitution has its parallel in the French Revolution, whose orientation generally is captured by the genetic approach, as we shall see later.
7. Krieger, *Essay on the Theory of Enlightened Despotism*, pp. 34, 89, 84. Cf. my review essay in *Telos*, Fall 1977, pp. 219-230.
8. "Conflict of the Faculties," in Hans Reiss, ed., *Kant's Political Writings* (Cambridge: Cambridge University Press, 1970), pp. 188, 189. The problem of the "education of the educators," which is usually associated with Marx's *Theses on Feuerbach*, occurs frequently in Kant's political reflections, as will be noted in the course of this interpretation.
9. The formalism of Kant's ethics has been the object of criticism since Hegel's demonstration that its inability to determine its content rationally makes it merely the rationalization of whatever material is brought to it externally. Two political conclusions can be drawn from this criticism. Leonard Krieger's *The German Idea of Freedom* uses it to show how and why "Kant ended in a condition of virtual political paralysis." From this, he conludes ominously: "All that remained was his counsel to accept, after they had succeeded, the revolutions which one must oppose in their origins and their course. And even so were the German liberals to act in the revolutions of 1848 and 1918." *The German Idea of Freedom* (Chicago: University of Chicago Press, 1957), pp. 124, 125.

    The other variant of this criticism is presented by the Frankfurt school Marxist, Max Horkheimer, for example in his essay, "Die Juden in Europa." Because it is an empty, formal process, the Kantian free individual has no central axis or point from which it could revolt. Instead of being a subject in quest of autonomy, it is manipulable from without. Horkheimer develops this thesis further in *The Dialectic of Enlightenment* (with Adorno), and his own *Eclipse of Reason*, expanding it beyond Kant to the entire history of Western thought.
10. A similar passage from the third *Critique* can be cited as another justification for starting this discussion from the political sphere. In "Things as Natural Goals are Organized Beings," Kant asserts: "Thus one has quite correctly used the term organization in the case of a recently undertaken total transformation [*Umbildung*] of a great people

into a state in order to describe the structure of the magistrates etc., and in fact the entire body of the state. For each member in such a whole must of course not be a mere means but also an end, and insofar as it works together toward the possibility of the whole, it is in turn determined in its position and function by the idea of the whole" (para. 65).

The reference is to the French Revolution. Its implications will be drawn when we come to the discussion of Kant's fully developed political theory.

11. Cf. Otto Pöggeler's summary of Hegel interpretations, "Zur Deutung der Phanomenologie des Geistes," in *Hegel Studien* vol. 1, 1961, pp. 255-294.

    The irony is that Hegel's own introduction to the *Philosophy of History* presents the transition to truly philosophical history as the result of precisely this kind of detective work, as will be seen.

12. *Geschichte der Philosophie*, ed. Suhrkamp, Band 2, p. 334 The same point, with the same image of learning to swim, is found in paragraph 10, remark, in the *Encyclopaedia*. A similar image occurs in the first preface of the *Logic*. where Hegel mocks those who act "as if the study of anatomy and physiology are necessary before one can learn to digest and move." Similarly, in paragraph 2 and its remark in the *Encyclopaedia*, Hegel picks up the same image. In neither of these cases is the reference directly to Kant.

13. This does not mean that Hegel is developing a philosophy of consciousness with "constitutive" implications. Merleau-Ponty's last lectures at the Collège de France (printed in *Textures* 74, no. 8/9, and in *Telos*, no. 29, Fall 1976) present a significant reading of the introduction to the *Phenomenlogy* on which I comment in some detail in *The Marxian Legacy*. The following passage from the lectures is relevant here: "one might object; Consciousness is impossible, it is in principle a failure since it is fissured and overhanging. One might object as one is tempted to do with Husserl. Consciousness is consciousness of something, always correlation of noesis-noema—but how can it have its noema if it is not in possession of itself as noesis? If it possesses itself as noesis, then it can take itself for an object (reflexion) and to that degree there is not always a one-way correlation of noesis-noema but a possible reversibility. That is just what Hegel will say. Consciousness is that reversibility, that exchange." (in *Textures*, p. 109, and *Telos*, p. 64.)

14. This might explain why and in what sense we talk of "modern science," as well as indicating abstractly how science is either transformed into inert, value-free technology or made into the normative basis of a "good" society. It would suggest also that when the modern artist appeals to "science," he is not reflecting naïvely the ambiant values of the culture. So called narrative, for example, can claim to be "scientific" either in its recording of the facts or in its method of working with the materials it is given. Only when the two, genesis and normativity, come together do we have a successful modern work.

15. I do not mean to take a position here concerning the systematic status

of those works that Hegel himself did not publish, such as the lectures on the philosophy of history, the history of philosophy, aesthetics, or religion. The fact that Hegel takes up this particular issue in the *Encyclopaedia* and the way he does it, justify the later use that I will make of such materials. I do not use them to try to support an argument, for example, that Hegel was "really" a liberal in the *Philosophy of Right*. Such "proofs," based on student lecture notes or other external evidence, are interesting bedtime reading. The most detailed documents in this regard are found in Ilting's four-volume edition of the student notes of the *Rechtsphilosophie* (Stuttgart: Fromman Verlag, 1972).

16. The implications of this modernism, first asserted by the critic Harold Rosenberg, are developed in "The Polictics of Modernism: From Marx to Kant," in *Philosophy and Social Criticism* vol. 8, no. 4, pp. 361-386. A different reading of its implications is found in Marshall Berman's "All That is Solid Melts into Air," reprinted in I. Howe, comp., *Twenty-five Years of Dissent* (New York: Methuen, 1979).
17. *Anthropological* in the sense of philosophical anthropology, where the question What is Man? becomes the key to answering all of the traditional philosophical questions concerning ontology, epistemology, ethics, etc. The putative primacy of Reason, Sensibility, Spirit, or what-have-you is replaced by the primacy of man. The resulting "philosophical anthropology" can be empirical or rational, normative or genetic, modern or premodern.
18. Jürgen Habermas has returned frequently to this relation in a series of provocative analyses. The account offered in his *Knowledge and Human Interests* presents a Marx whose notion of labor as "material synthesis" draws together the positive implications of Kant, Fichte, and Hegel. I will make use of this account in chapter 5. On the other hand, Habermas's recent *Theory of Communicative Action* seems to drop this approach, perhaps because it is based too much on a theory of constitution by a subject. Habermas's criticism of the neo-Kantian synthesis of Max Weber that was developed first by Lukács, then by the Frankfurt school, is based on their having placed a theory of subjectivity at the center of their descriptions. Habermas's own theory attempts to show how the "decentering" of the subject can accomplish what a theory of constitution cannot. To this degree, his conclusions point in the same direction as the present argument.
19. In the Cotta edition, pp. 703-705. (I have not given page references for citations of Marx that are easy to identify because they are part of short, often-translated essays. Translations are my own, based on the more reliable Cotta edition, edited by Hans-Joachim Lieber and Peter Furth, *Karl Marx: Frühe Schriften* (Stuttgart: Cotta Verlag, 1962).
20. *Transparent* is simply another categorical term for an identity philosophy that seeks to eliminate otherness, difference, particularity, etc. in a quest for an Absolute which would imply the end of history, philosophy, and politics. The term is used frequently in contemporary French theory's adaption of Freud *via* Lacan into a theory of modernity.

The quest for sameness, the fear of otherness, can be part of a reading of Freud's Thanatos.

21. This "best" has had devastating practical consequences when the telos is assumed to be known to the Marxists. The political ground for that assumption is found in the *Communist Manifesto's* definition of the communist as having "the theoretical advantage over the rest of the proletariat of an insight into the conditions, the path, and the general results of the proletarian movement." This difficulty will be discussed below.

CHAPTER 3. ORIGINARY PHILOSOPHY AS POLITICAL PHILOSOPHY

1. The best "modern" example of the failure to resolve this problem is of course the continual search for a beginning by Husserl. The fundamental text for my thinking on this matter is Klaus Hartmann, "On Taking the Transcendental Turn," in *Review of Metaphysics*, vol. 20, no. 2, 1966, pp. 223-249.
2. This movement is traced interestingly from the standpoint of the history of ideas in Meinecke's *Die Entstehung des Historismus, Werke*, vol. 3. Meinecke's notion of "historism" is close to what is meant here by *Geschichtlichkeit.*
3. This notion is suggested by Louis White Beck's introduction to Kant's writings *On History*, with reference to the argument of Renato Composto's *La quarta criticica kantiana* (Palmero, 1954). The suggestion is unconvincing. Kant does not follow the "critique" paradigm in asking for the conditions of the possibility of history because, as will be seen, history has a different structure than the objects of theoretical or practical science. The foundation of the Composto-Beck misreading is explained in chapter 4.

   It should be noted that the theorectical foundation of my critique of the tabular view of history is found in Merleau-Ponty's critique of what he calls the *pensée du survol*. An historical illustration—which does not admit its evident debt to Merleau-Ponty—is found in Michel Foucault's *Les mots et les choses*, from which I have borrowed the word *tableau*. The 19th century "episteme" which succeeds the tabular classical form described in Foucault's work manifests many of the characteristics which are here attributed to the modern.
4. This is supplemented later by the more genetic approach brought by the *Critique of Practical Reason*. I disagree with the interpretation, based on external analysis, that the *Foundations* relates to the second *Critique* as the *Prolegomena* does to the first—in Beck's words, as "a briefer, less 'scholastic' work on the same topics." Beck also suggests that the shorter works are analytic or "regressive," moving from the known,

whereas the *Critiques* are synthetic, moving from principles to experience. This is descriptively true, but philosophically uninteresting. At best it is a psychological explanation of Kant's taking the trouble to write popular works. (Beck's remarks are repeated at several points in his voluminous work. The direct quotes are from his introduction to his translation of the second *Critique* in the Bobbs-Merrill edition).

5. The two most famous illustrations are the doctrines of Genius and the assertion of a natural teleology. Genius is to produce unconsciously and naturally the "purposeless purposefullness" and "lawfulness without law" that characterize the beautiful. If this proposal were taken literally, Kant would be returning to a theory of external constitution. The assumption of a purposefully organized nature is invoked from the other side to insure the completeness that the noumenon and/or the postulates of practical reason represented. This replaces the causality of freedom by a natural cause. The philosopher treats a unity of genesis and validity which can stand only within the originary immanence as if it were real. These two doctrines were the ones that tended to excite Kant's successors, especially the Romantics but also Schelling and Hegel. They will not be discussed further here because they add nothing to the systematic theoretical account.
6. My concern is not to decide whether Hegel is a "progressive" or a "reactionary," or something in between. There is much biographical evidence to show that his political orientation was "liberal" and that his philosophy was not separate from this approach. The major sources of English are S. Avineri, *Hegel's Theory of the Modern State* (Cambridge: Cambridge University Press, 1972), and the debunking by Walter Kaufman in "The Hegel Myth and Its Method," in A. MacIntyre, ed., *Hegel: A Collection of Critical Essays* New York: Anchor Books, 1972). In French, the several books of Jacques D'Hondt can be consulted for biographical details. D'Hondt's *Hegel secret* is a good source for the Fries affair, to which reference will be made in a moment. In German, K.H. Itling's contemporary and introductory material to his four-volume edition of the various student notes from Hegel's lectures on the *Rechtsphilosophie* (Stuttgart: Froman-Holzboog, 1974) should be mentioned. To illustrate the sort of debate that can emerge, it might be noted that the last lectures, interrupted by Hegel's death, stress that a "philosophy of right" is important because of its usefulness to the citizens! Is one to conclude that Hegel was (or had become) a "progressive"? (In D. F. Strauss's lecture notes, band 4, pp. 918, 919.)
7. Marx was obviously haunted by this description of philosophy's task and limits. In the crucial text that points to the role of the proletariat—the "Introduction to a Critique of Hegel's *Philosophy of Right*"—Marx paraphrases Hegel while giving an ironic twist to the Hegelian conclusions. The rose on the cross of the present reappears, as does the necessity to dance in that present. Marx's usage reverses the signs, turning active the contemplative Hegelian implication. For example, he suggests that "one must make these petrified relations dance by singing them their own melody." The Marxian critique aims at setting free what

Hegelian doctrine founds structurally. A similar reversal takes place around the *hic rhodus, hic salta* when Marx describes the nature and course of proletarian revolution in the *Eighteenth Brumaire*, as will be seen later.

8. The resigned conclusion to the preface is echoed in the transition to the thematization of world history. "World History," writes Hegel, "is the world's Court of the Last Judgment." Hegel's sketch of world historical development seems to demonstrate that his own Germany is the rational culmination of world history. The task of philosophy would be accomplished by the real processes of historical development. In fact, Hegel's account is more complicated. The concluding three paragraphs to the *Philosophy of Right* do treat "The Germanic Realm." But their historical referent is not the Protestant Prussian state that supposedly served as Hegel's model. Nor is the referent that situation described in the corresponding paragraphs of the *Encyclopaedia*, where Hegel asserts (para, 522 remark) that without a reformation there can be no revolution of the conditions of unfreedom. Instead, Hegel describes the advent of Catholic Christianity and its growing opposition to the worldly Empire. The result of this opposition to the world loses its capricious, barbarous external charcter while the realm of Truth is no longer portayed as beyond and apart from the present. The implication is the curious threefold reconciliation (para 360) with which the book concludes. The state is present to self-consciousness as the actual and substantive expression of Reason. Religion presents the feeling and representation of this Truth as an ideality. Philosophy (*Wissenschaft*) shows the free conceptual understanding of the unity of this truth in the state, nature, and the ideal world. When this triad is interpreted in parallel with the conclusion to the *Encyclopaedia* where Absolute Spirit takes the forms of Art, Religion, and Philosophy, a further implication emerges. The state stands in the place of art. Given the role of Kant's aesthetic and theory of judgment and the crucial importance of a theory of political representation, one would wish that Hegel had played out this implication. He did not. Representation tends to be treated within his theory of religion. Hence, these remarks remain in the form of a footnote.

9. Hegel does not make this terminological distinction of *Historie* and *Geschichte* here or anywhere else in his writings. The only text on which the distinction might be founded—if it were a question of philology—is the section in the *Philosophy of Religion* that treats the proofs of the existence of God. Hegel does criticize there a *historische* manner of dealing with truths of Spirit—a manner that he says is external and superficial. Yet the same criticism is applied to those who have merely *geschichtliche* learning. (In *Werke*, Band. 17, pp. 386, 387).

   Legitimation of my use of the distinction can be found in the introduction to the *Philosophy of History*. Hegel notes that "in our language history (*Geschichte*) unites the objective as well as the subjective side. It thus means equally the *historiam rerum gesarum* and the *res gestas* itself. It is just as much what has happened [*das Geschehen*] as it is the recounting of history [*Geschichtserzählung*]." The implications of this passage (from *Werke*, Band. 12, p. 83) will be discussed below.

10. *Philosophie der Geschichte, Werke*, Band 12, p. 17. I have made use of this English translation by J. Silbree, as reprinted in Jacob Löwenberg, ed., *Hegel Selections* (New York: Charles Scribner & Sons, 1957), modifying where it seemed necessary. I will indicate references first to the German, then to the English texts. The present English reference is to p. 345.
11. Hegel twice mocks this approach as being typically German. (In *Werke*, Band. 12. pp. 22 and 32; English pp. 315 and 361.)
12. *Werke* Band. 12, p. 65; English, p. 388.
13. Ibid., p. 82; English, p. 418.
14. Ibid., p. 83; English, p. 419.
15. Ibid, p. 66; English, p. 399.
16. Ibid., p. 87; English, p. 422.
17. Ibid., p. 94; English, p. 430. I have replaced the misleading English *National Genius* with either a paraphrase or simply be leaving the German *Volksgeist*.
18. Ibid., p. 87; English, p. 422.
19. Ibid., p. 99; English, p. 435.
20. Ibid., p. 105; English, p. 422.
21. The images are found at ibid., pp. 98 and 100; English, pp. 434, 437.
22. Hegel's description of this structure violates his own logical method by placing the sovereign first. In fact, he violates his method frequently in this section of the *Philosophy of Right*, as Marx demonstrates in great detail in his 1843 essay-notes. (Interestingly, Marx did not pick up on this particular point, for reasons that will be seen in due course. The point is made by Klaus Hartmann, especially in his *Politische Philosophie* [Freiburg/Munchen: Verlag Karl Alber, 1981]. Hartmann notes [pp. 173ff.] that a more careful approach would have brought together sovereignty of the people and that of the state. Elsewhere, however [pp. 241ff.] Hartmann indicates doubt as to the possibility of unifying society and the state in this manner.) The important point here is that the usually more consistent Hegel violates his procedures for reasons whose structural role must be demonstrated.
23. Hegel's own marginal notes are reprinted in the Suhrkamp edition from which I have been citing. Commenting on Paragraph 142, he remarks that what he is talking about here is not a relation of subsumption. This point is not developed further, however. More interesting is the comment to Paragraph 147, which recalls two passages in Herodotus that distinguish the Greeks who have a state and a *Sittlichkeit* from the barbarians with whom they enter into contact. Hydarnes tells the Spartan envoy to remain and be happy, to which the Greek reply is: "Your advice is good and corresponds to your experience. Had you tasted the happiness that we enjoy, you would advise us to give up life and property to preserve it."
24. This point is made in Cornelius Castoriadis's *L'institution imaginaire de la*

société (Paris: Le Seuil, 1975), to which I am indebted for far more than just this pun.

25. On these points, three authors are highly recommended. Polanyi's *The Great Transformation* (Boston: Beacon Press, 1957) explains the radical change that the introduction of capitalism demanded and stresses the artificial nature of this system. Albert Hirschmann's *The Passions and the Interests* (Princeton: Princeton University Press, 1977) suggests that the moral and political thinkers of the seventeenth century gradually discovered that there was one "passion" that was in fact rational and governable: the interest in economic gain. This notion then took on a central role in the conceptualization of human nature and its needs. Louis Dumont's work, most recently *Homo aequalis: Genèse et épanouissement de l'idéologie économique* (Paris: Gallimard, 1977; English edition forthcoming from University of Chicago Press), elaborates this same set of problems from the standpoint of the anthropologist.
26. The difference between the two, in a word, is that the authoritarian state justifies itself by an appeal to Nature whereas the totalitarian state appeals to (historical) Reason. The contemporary neoconservative distinction that suggests that authoritarianism is more benign and reformable than totatilarianism is belied by, for example, the Czech or Polish reform movements. It is a rhetorical distinction valuable only for partisan purposes.
27. There has been a constant temptation to supplement the abstraction of Marx's analysis with positive and even utopian motivational elements. This can be found as early as Engel's suggestion that Marxism will become a functional force answering the felt needs of the masses just as did the early Christian ideology. Gramsci picks up the theme, suggesting that since the masses are not ready for the disquisitions of science Marxism must have a psychological dimension appealing to their emotions. Gramsci's remarks do not jibe with the situation in Germany, expressed by the books loaned by worker libraries, or with the former Marxist Dietzgen's definition of socialism as the "religion of science." They might come closer to the place of "myth" in Sorel's actionism. (These, and too many more such expressions, can be found in Fetscher, *Der Marxismus. Seine Geschichte in Dokumenten* (R. Piper Verlag: München, 1965 Band 1, passim.)

    Missing in all these arguments is the kind of positive approach suggested by Bloch's "ontology of the not-yet," and elaborated across his multifaceted work, which deserves more than the footnote consideration with which I leave it here.

Chapter 4. System Without Method

1. An interesting variant of this option is found in Jurgen Habermas's *Knowledge and Human Interests*. Reconstructing the philosophical debate

between the Kantian and the Hegelian positions, Habermas shows how Marx's notion of "material synthesis" permits a differentiated account of the way a knowable world is constituted for us humans. He points out that there are other kinds of knowledge than the objective scientific type with which Kantian epistemology is concerned. The other object domains—the hermeneutic social structures and the emancipatory escape from distorted self and social understanding—cannot be explained by the Marxian material synthesis through labor. Each is based on a specific kind of cognitive interest. This permits Habermas to have at once a philosophical theory of the genesis of object domains and an epistemological application of this theory to the social and material world. It implies, in his phrase, that epistemology *is* social theory. Habermas's argument is presented with respect to Kant, Hegel, and Marx in chapter 5, section D. Habermas's recent *Theory of Communicative Action* does not return to this constitutive project or even note its differences from the earlier phase. Having based his new approach on a "decentered subject," it is difficult to see how Habermas could now return to the constitutive orientation of the earlier book. On the other hand, Habermas still rejects ontology (or what he calls "classical transcendental" or "foundationalist" philosophy). This rejection was understandable in the constitutive framework of *Knowledge and Human Interests.* It stood there as a "Kantian" antidote to a "Hegelian" or "Marxian" image of spirit or the human laboring species *actually* creating the world. In the new context, this antidote no longer seems necessary. As noted at the outset of chapter 2, I do not see a necessary incompatibility between his approach and the present one.

2. This claim is not entirely accurate. A further historical point must be made to show how the constitutional demand moved gradually from appeal to external justification (of a genetic or a normative type) to the immanence of the modern. The Americans' appeal to the "Rights of Englishmen" had to be transformed such that the Articles of Confederation became the Constitution of 1787. French resistance to the Crown had to abandon its particularistic feudal and customary basis for a natural-law theory of sovereignty to make revolution more than revolt. Prussian codification would have had to go not only beyond Cocceji's codification of existing law, but also beyond Svarez's more rational (and Kantian) Roman law compromise with feudal remnants if the Allgemeines Landgesetz were to become a modern constitution and Prussia a modern state.

   I am working on a historical study of these three cases, whose empirical development has influenced my theoretical arguments. This further historical "turn" is what makes the transcendental question become originary. The three major historical interpretations to which reference should be made are: Wood, *Creation of the American Republic;* Furet, *Penser la révolution française;* Koselleck, *Preussen zwischen Reform und Revolution.*

3. One historical irony may cast light on the structure portrayed here. The radical Jacobins who took happiness as the goal of institutional life were, personally, rigid, legalistic ascetics. They were overthrown by a

stratum that wanted calm so that it could, personally, enjoy its new wealth. The justification of these latter groups was not "happiness" but the appeal to constitutional legality as a norm.

4. I am not claiming that this historical structure "explains" or justifies the politics that I have reconstructed for Kant, Hegel, and Marx. The coincidence to which it points merits further argument, elsewhere.
5. Hannah Arendt's essay, "The Concept of History," in *Between Past and Future* (New York: Viking Press, 1961) points to interesting implications of the manner in which this type of theory of history has come to replace the classical notion of politics. She asserts that, "In Kant, in constrast to Hegel, the motive for the modern escape from politics into history is still quite clear. It is the escape into the 'whole,' and the escape is prompted by the meaninglessness of the particular" (p. 83). This argument can be given theoretical justification in the criticism of any constitutive theory in Kant, Hegel, or Marx. Kant need not, however, be interpreted only in this manner.
6. Yirmihau Yovel's *Kant and the Philosophy of History* (Princeton: Princeton University Press, 1980) is an excellent account of the constitutive theory. The author makes wide-ranging systematic claims about the place of history in the Kantian oeuvre. Although I disagree with his conclusions, his book is a pleasure to read and a storehouse of scholarship.

   Another variant of the constitutive approach are the neo-Kantians of the late nineteenth century. It is curious that the two competing schools—the Marburg group oriented more toward the theory of science and the Heidelberg thinkers turned more toward the social and cultural sciences—both have recourse to a constitutive reading. The reason that the Heidelbergers were tempted in this direction is obvious since the imprint of human action in the social-cultural world and the effect of the world on the hermeneutic structure of subjectivity is essential to a cultural sociology. The explanation in the case of the Marburgers seems to be their concern to bring together Marx and Kant in a peaceful coexistence. On their failure, see my essay "Kant's Political Theory: The Virtue of his Vices," in *Review of Metaphysics*, vol. 34, no. 2, December 1980, pp. 325-350. That essay was written before I had developed the Kant account to the full degree expressed here. *Caveat emptor*!
7. Kant's debt to Rousseau is evident here. On this point, cf. my "Rousseau and the Origin of Revolution" in *Philosophy and Social Criticism* (vol. 6, no.4, pp. 349-370), which does not sufficiently stress the manner in which Kant's theory of representation goes beyond Rousseau. On this, cf. the discussion of Kant's politics in part 3.
8. Citations from Kant use the Akademie Ausgabe, reprinted on *Kant's Werke* (Walter de Gruyter & Co: Berlin, 1968). References are abbreviated AKA, followed by a volume number and the page cited. Here, AKA, 7, p. 331.
9. Citations follow the pattern used previously for *Philosopie der Geschichte.* The reference here is to ibid., p. 34; English, p. 364.
10. Ibid., p. 42; English, p. 372.

11. Ibid., p. 35; English, p. 365.
12. Ibid., p. 44; English, p. 375.
13. Ibid., p. 47; English, p. 378.
14. Both passages are at Ibid., pp. 44-45; English p. 375.
15. Ibid., p. 46; English, p. 377.
16. Ibid., p. 91; English, p. 426-427.
17. Ibid., pp. 481, 482.
18. Ibid., pp. 481, 482.
19. Ibid., p. 49; English p. 380.
20. I will be citing this passage throughout the next few pages. Each citation follows the one before it in the thread of Marx's argument. This permits the commentary to point to the complexity of the issues being addressed.
21. The passage is from the introduction to the *Philosophie der Geschichte*, p. 53; English, p. 354. This notion of a "proud position" recalls Merleau-Ponty's criticism of the *pensée* du survol.
22. This explains why Kierkegaard is counted among the "left" Hegelians. The fact that the more orthodox Hegelians were politically active and innovative in the pre-1848 period is not sufficiently stressed, even by those who want to reconstruct a "liberal" Hegel. They were certainly a more real threat to the regime than were Marx and his "left" Hegelian friends.
23. Cited from the Insel edition (Frankfurt am Main: Insel Verlag, 1966), p. 427. The passage is taken from Schiller's inaugural lecture as Professor of Universal History at Jena.
24. Marx's stress on the anthropology of labor explains the difference of his picture from the in-many-ways similar phenomenological history of civil society in Hegel's *Philosophy of Right*. A different reading that stresses the learning process and its logic is found in Jürgen Habermas's *Zur Rekonstruktion des historischen Materialismus* (Frankfurt am Main: Suhrkamp Verlag, 1976).
25. The passages cited from Engels are taken from his letters to Bloch (September 21, 1890), Schmidt (October 27, 1890), and Starkenburg (January 25, 1895).
26. Jean L. Cohen has argued this position from the point of view of sociological theory in her excellent study, *Class and Civil Society. The Limits of Marxian Critical Theory* (Amherst: University of Massachusetts Press, 1982). cf., also our joint political critique using these arguments, "Why Class?", in Pat Walker, ed., *Between Labor and Capital* (Boston: South End Press, 1978), pp. 67-95.

CHAPTER 5. THE LOGIC OF RECEPTIVITY

1. The most detailed articulation of this methodological difficulty is found in the Husserlian phenomenology. Unfortunately, it has not been

carried into the social and political domains. The exception was Maurice Merleau-Ponty, whose premature death cut short the process of further elaboration. An explicit and concise statement of the problem of the relation of ontology and its method is found in Merleau-Ponty's late essay, "Partout et nulle part" (in *Signes*, Paris: Gallimard, 1960), whose title itself indicates the kind of structural problems confronted by the ontological temptation.

2. The structure parallels the ontologization of method by the philosophers. It can be illustrated from the reflections of modern natural science on the effects of the measuring instrument on the measure, or from social scientific considerations concerning the active and self-reflective participant interaction. Illustrations of the former are found frequently in phenomenological approaches to the philosophy of science and philosophy of technology (for example, the ongoing work of my colleagues Patrick Heelan and Don Ihde). The latter has been developed especially by Alain Touraine and his co-workers: theoretically in Touraine's *La voix et le regard* (Paris: Seuil, 1978), and practically in a series of field studies published in the collections "Sociologie permanente" by Seuil and "Mouvements" by Fayard. The debates of a meeting at Cerisy-la-Salle, *Mouvements sociaux d'aujourd'hui: Acteurs et analystes* (Paris: Les éditions ouvrières, 1982) are a lively introduction to this orientation. More systematic is Jürgen Habermas's *Logik der Sozialwissenschagten* (Frankfurt: Suhrkamp, 1975), and his debate with Gadamer's hermeneutic approach in *Hermeneutik und Ideologiekritik* (Frankfurt: Suhrkamp Verlag, 1971).
3. One of the temptations in this direction is hinted at frequently by Hannah Arendt. The analogy between the way a judgment of beauty or a political judgment are justified is tempting but incomplete. Morality and politics are different, as Arendt's own distinction of civil disobedience (political) and conscientious objection (moral) shows clearly. Arendt's is the first step toward the development of a theory of the political. The first step needs further adumbration in the kind of structures presented here. Arendt herself never completed her projected volume on judgment. The "phenomenological" method applied in her early historical studies is treated in the context here called "receptivity." To this can be added the remark from "Truth and Politics" that "out of acceptance, which can be called trustfulness, arises the faculty of judgment." This points to the concern with particularity.

   Philosophically, the third *Critique* can be used to demonstrate the completeness and necessary receptivity of the manifold lacking in the Transcendental Deduction of the first *Critique*. A brilliant technical demonstration of this point is found in George Schrader, "The Status of Teleological Judgment in the Critical Philosophy," in *Kantstudien*, 45, 1953-54, pp. 204-255.
4. A similar dilemma is present in Hegel and Marx. Hegel tries to solve it as a difficulty for politics instead of remaining within the framework of method. Hegel's first attempt is illustrated in the "dialectic of desire" in the *Phenomenology*. Solution to the endless chain of new needs is found in

the struggle for recognition which concludes in the new figure of a master-slave relation. The instability of the new figure is due to the merely apparent introduction of a structure of intersubjectivity like the Kantian "culture." The relation dissolves into the forms of the Stoic, Skeptic, and Unhappy (Christian) consciousness. Hegel's second attempt takes a different and interestingly political form in the account of Civil Society in the *Philosophy of Right*. His unmediated leap to the political will be analyzed and criticized below. Marx's attempt to resolve this natural dialectic makes the opposite error by reducing method to a constitutive philosophy. This was presented briefly in chapter 4's account of *The German Ideology*.

5. Cited from Reiss, *Kant's Political Writings*, p. 90.
6. AKA, 5. 195. Translation modified from Bernard, *Critique of Judgement* (New York: Hefner Publishing Company, 1951) p. 32.
7. Hegel in fact makes this suggestion in his treatment of the Paralogisms from the first *Critique* (cf. *Geschichte der Philosopie*, Suhrkamp edition, band 20, pp. 354-365.) The three modalities (*Vermögen des Gemüths*) are unified in a subject. Kant's error is to treat this subject as a thing. As such it can only be known in its phenomenal form and falls into the dilemmas of the Dialectic. The subject conceived of as thought is not an unknowable thing-in-itself because thought is by definition self-knowing. The result is that Kant's proposed "unification" becomes the ontological premise that unifies both the laws of freedom and the laws of nature. But method loses its autonomy in this Hegelian reconstruction of Kant.

   Since method also loses its autonomy in Hegel, a different version of his criticism of Kant can be mentioned here. In the *Lectures on Aesthetics (Werke*, Band 13, p. 89), Hegel writes that "One must give Schiller credit for the great service of having broken through the subjectivity and abstract thought of Kant, and for having dared make the attempt to go beyond them in thought to the unity and reconciliation that is grasped as the truth and actualized in art." The importance of representation in the "Kantian" method is implicit in these suggestions. It is developed systematically below.
8. Kant includes the encounter with mathematical immensity as well. Had this not been added, and had this section preceded the analysis of the beautiful, it might have been explained by a parallel to the dual structure of the Analytic in the *Critique of Pure Reason*, which treats the material of intuition in a Transcendental Aesthetic separately from the account of the categories of the understanding dealt with in the Transcendental Analytic proper. The lessons of the third *Critique* are of a different order.
9. This point illustrates the interdependence of the two moments of method to which reference has already been made.
10. This introductory discussion (through para. 9) has echoes in Schiller's *Letters on the Aesthetic Education of Man*. The interplay between the first two moments seems to lead toward the role of the imagination and the "aesthetic determinability" that become the Schillerian substitue for a political theory. Schiller moved too quickly, without methodological

mediation, to the political. Politics becomes for him the contemplative "play" paired with a presupposition (in Letters 26 and 27) about the receptivity of the world, which is simply the ontologization of Kant's third moment here. That Kant is able to go further is seen in the one exception to his exclusion of interest and need from the aesthetic judgment. Kant admits the need for sociality in paragraph 2. His example is that on a desert island, with no hope of rescue, one would not beautify one's life because beauty is a social concern! The implications of this remark will emerge in the fourth moment.

11. The implications of this notion are clearly drawn in Schiller's *Letters*. The balanced, reflective play of the sensible and the rational puts the individual in that state of "aesthetic determinability" that makes learning and political transformation possible. The structure of the *Letters*—twenty-seven letters, grouped in triadic arguments, each of whose "synthesis" becomes the basis for a new movement—is simply the adumbration of this argument. The best account of this structure is found in the introduction and commentaries by Elisabeth M. Wilkinson and L. A. Willoughby to their bilingual edition (Oxford: Clarendon Press, 1967). The weakness of their presentation is its lack of philosophical, as opposed to literary-critical, rigor.

12. The *Encyclopaedia* makes this point explicitly. At the end of its treatment of *Sittlichkeit*, before proceeding to Absolute Spirit, Hegel adds a long Remark on the relation of the state and religion. He had just traced briefly World History's progression of *Volksgeister*, suggesting that his concern is similar to the present one. Hegel attributes Plato's inability to go beyond a substantialist state that replaces subjective freedom by the truths possessed by the philosopher-king to the fact that true religion had not entered the Greek world. Somewhat earlier in this Remark, Hegel had made the point more polemically with regard to his own times: "to think that one could make a revolution without first making a Reformation" is one of the "stupidities of modern times." (para.552, Remark)

13. Here, as throughout this discussion, I shall not undertake the comparison with Marx that obviously suggests itself, whether it consists in mere hints—comparing the replacement of labor by machines with Marx's vision in the *Grundrisse* for example—or whether Marxian retrospect could show the "ideological" naïveté stigmatized, for example, in Lukács's *Der junge Hegel*, which stands as a negative model of this sort of criticism.

    It should be noted here, however, that the Addition to paragraph 197, which discusses the theoretical and practical education, points to the lack of such an education as definitional of the "barbarian" who produces something other than he intends because he does not control his own action. This is an anticipation of one of the characteristics of the *Pöbel* of which Hegel is so afraid. The significant point here is that this "barbarian" has no control of his *own* action, not of matter on which he is to work. One can be a barbarian in the most refined or egalitarian society.

14. These three Estates reappear at the political level of the state, and are the object of detailed criticism by Marx. It is interesting that Hegel devotes only on quite general paragraph (para. 205) to the "universal Estate" whose role in the state becomes more important than the others. One wonders also why the "business class" is broken down into three parts (which play no important role in the discussion of the state) while the agricultural estate is not. This is the more curious since Hegel does see (in para. 203, Addition) that one can run agricultural enterprises in a reflecting manner, "like a factory." In this context, one might also note that he adds to paragraph 204 the comment that the natural conditions of the life of this Estate not only make it nonreflective; because it depends on the "gifts of nature" it tends to feel dependent, to let events take their course, and to lean toward subservience (*Unterwürfigkeit*)!
15. What Hegel in fact means to designate by these two terms is not important here. *Police* may refer to the early modern notion of a *Polizeistaat* and *Polizeiwissenschaften*, whose last great theorist was Kant's predecessor, Ch. Wolff. The term also existed in French, to designate a "civilized" society with well-regulated behavioral codes. *Corporations* may have been in part modeled on the medieval guilds; or, as Knox points out, there may be an anticipation of Mussolini's corporations here (translator's note to para. 229, p. 360). I shall let Hegel's meaning emerge from his arguments, which are methodological, not historical.
16. *Encyclopaedia*, paragraphs 381, 384. It should be noted that the situation criticized here is, mutatis mutandis, identical to the reductionism in Marx's own use of the infrastructure/superstructure model. Nature as fully external spirit is treated like the superstructure in relation to the base.
17. Jürgen Habermas, *Erkenntnis und Interesse*, p. 38. References in this section will be indicated in the text.
18. Kant's common and communal sense could be introduced at this juncture. The difference between the aims of Marx and Kant is that Marx has no notion of the reflective judgment. He tends to make uncritical use of the theory of constitution, violating the specific and limited place of methodological argument.

CHAPTER 6. THE PHENOMENOLOGY OF PARTICULARITY

1. The passage from *Religion within the Limits of Reason Alone* is found at *AKA*, 6n, p. 122. The present citation is of course from "What Is Enlightenment?"
2. Schiller, in the fifteenth Letter, speaks of the play drive as both receptive and active. The material it receives is said to be already formed, a "living form." The notion returns in the twenty-fifth letter. Justification is offered in the twenty-sixth letter by reference to a "gift of nature."

This is inadequate. The aesthetic anthropology in a conjectural poetic mode that concludes the final twenty-seventh letter is no more convincing. A presupposed concept of politics, transformed into method, becomes an unjustified ontology.

Hegel's praise for Schiller is typified by a passage in the *Lectures on Aesthetics:* "One must give Schiller credit for the great service of having broken through the subjectivity and abstract thought of Kant, and for having dared make the attempt to go beyond them in thought to the unity and reconciliation which is grasped as the truth and actualized in art" (*Vorlesungen über die Aesthetik*, 1, p. 79, in *Werke*, Band 13, Suhrkamp edition, Similar passages are found elsewhere. For example, section 55 of the *Encyclopaedia* praises Schiller's presentation of the concrete unity of thought and the representation of the senses.

Hegel's criticisms, and the influence of Schiller on his development, are presented in George Kelly's *Hegel's Retreat from Eleusis* (Princeton: Princeton University Press, 1978). Kelly's proposal is that "Hegel drew on Schiller not only for the misquoted strophe at the end of the *Phenomenology*, but for some of his crucial portraits of *Geist*. And, beyond this, he assimilated certain cultural and political problems raised by Schiller, and made them his own" (p. 59). The result is that "the *Phenomenlogy*...is at once a vast and genial reduplication of Schiller's theme and a bitter, yet affirmative, surpassing of Schiller's aesthetic prescriptions for the healing of divided humanity. Thus the citation of Schiller at its very conclusion may not be mere happenstance: it may clothe a profound irony."

3. The elimination of particularity in the examples cited means that the method itself was only apparently treated as originary. Politics and philosophy were left as external to each other. This violation of the imperative of modernity is due to the traditional notion that a classical polity is a noncontradictory harmonious unit. Yet modernty is defined by its contradictions, not their elimination.

   A contemporary form of the same error illustrates this methodological independence. Opposition to the ever-growing contemporary state may take the form of social movements that stress the necessity of a participartory democracy that integrates the entire citizenry. The difficulty that these antipolitical movements tend to ignore is that the universalization of particularity destroys particularity! One aspect of politics must be the protection of particularity (whose nature has to be specified, in the form of constitutional guarantees of the rights of minorities. Such guarantees insure that the kinds of issues that are treated in the political sphere remain open to public debate. A constitutional politics founds a political method that insures the preservation of the particular against a massification of the "movement" and against the external universality of a bureaucratic state. This issue forms one important line of the research project of Ulrich Rödel, "Die Rekonstrucktion nicht-staatszentrierter Demokratie-traditionen" (Max-Planck-Institut 'fur Sozialwissenschaften, 1983).

4. Classical theory is concerned with the technique by which a pregiven

eternal, and external Truth is to be discovered or applied. In its moral variant, the classical assumption is that to know the (eternal and external) Good is to do the good. Nuances, anticipations, fruitful distortions of the basic structure can be read from Aristotle, across the Casuists, through the Reformation...to the modern. The structure remains premodern.

5. Whether this "working existence" is the completion, the negation, or the transcendence of the political will be discussed in chapter 7.
6. Marx's scornful descriptions of the peasantry recall those of Hegel. (The same is true of his depictions of the other two supports of Bonaparte's regime.) The difference between the two accounts is due partially to Hegel's optimism grounded on the developments in England as opposed to Marx's negativism. One further passage will give the full flavor of Marx's account. He speaks of Bonaparte as the "symbol" of the peasantry: "clumsily cunning, knavishly naïve, doltishly sublime, a calculated superstition, a pathetic burlesque, a cleverly stupid anachronism, a world historical piece of buffoonery, and an undecipherable hieroglyphic for the understanding of the civilized—this symbol bore the unmistakable features of the class that represents barbarism within civilization."

   It is hard to see how the peasantry can have any other future than the industrialization of agriculture, which transforms the group into an appendage to the proletarian movement in whose name Marx is speaking in this polemic. In this case, the linear historical logic is introduced for strategic political as opposed to analytic argumentative purposes. Marx's suggestion, in the *Eighteenth Brumaire*, that the peasantry will join with the proletariat "when they come in contact with the relations of production" neglects the other aspect of methodology—the demonstration of receptivity to political possibility. The "material synthesis" is not the basis of his assertion. He is suggesting only that realization of their common subordination will bring together the two groups. Alone, this is not a sufficient systematic argument.
7. Marx speaks of a lumpen who "in all big towns form a mass strictly differentiated from the industrial proletariat, a recruiting ground for theives and criminals of all kinds, living on the crumbs of society, people without a definite trade, vagabonds, *gens sans feu et sans aveu*, with differences according to the degree of civilization of the nation to which they belong, but never renouncing their lazzaroni character" (*Class Struggles in France*). The comparison with the lazzaroni is also found in Hegel (para. 244, Addition), as is the stress on the comparative national differences (para. 244).

   Marx's description in the *Eighteenth Brumaire* is less structural and more of a polemic. It is applied explicitly to the members of Bonaparte's Society of December 10th. "Alongside decayed roues with dubious means of subsistence and of dubious origin, alongside ruined and adventurous offshoots of the bourgeoisie, were vagabonds, discharged soldiers, discharged jailbirds, escaped galley slaves, swindlers, mountebanks, lazzaroni, organ grinders, ragpickers, knife grinders, tinkers, beggars, in short, the whole indefinite, disintegrated mass, thrown hither and thither, which the French term *la bohéme...*"

8. As transcribed by Hotho, and reprinted in the Ilting edition, Band 3, p. 89. As already mentioned, use of Ilting is not intended to prove points by appeal to isolated statements from the lectures. The principle illustrated here is present throughout the Hegelian corpus. These passages have the advantage of referring directly to the material under consideration. This consistency with the rest of the work explains why the reference to *die Moral* in (*b*) need not be taken literally. The "world of right" can refer to what is described as *Sittlichkeit.*
9. "Allgemeiner Begriff der Logik," in *Wissenschaft der Logik* (Hemburg: Felix Meiner Verlag, 1963) p. 31.
10. This was the case for the example of the monasteries, referred to in chapter 4. Another illustration is found in the remarks to para. 64 which contain a discussion of the laws of copyright and which justify the theft of Greek and Egyptian art from Turkey. The explanation of these assertions is that the sphere of property does concern a quantitative and external factor that is not identified with the will of its owner; property can be exchanged against other property.
11. The parallel of Hegel and Marx on this methodological point clarifies a further ground of Marx's "economism." Marx's *Capital* was originally to have contained four volumes articulated in a manner similar to Hegel's systematic program. The first three volumes were to treat the immediate process of production, the mediations that account for the circulation of the produced commodities, and the process of capital as a whole. The fourth volume was to have been a reconstruction of the manner in which economic theory has presented itself historically in the form of "Theories of Surplus Value." Marx's work was left incomplete, and his editors were unsophisticated philosophically. Aside from the confrmation of the need for an independent method, there is not much to be drawn from this parallel as concerns the economic theory itself. As concerns Marx's politics, the fact that his "phenomenology" of French working class history is not presented as the methodological articulation that his economic theory needs leads to the conclusion that—despite the place of class struggle at various moments of the economic descriptions of *Capital*—Marx's politics of class struggle was ultimately economistic.
12. A passage already cited from the *Philosophie der Geschichte* suggests the plausibility of this approach. "Much, therefore, in particular aspects of the phenomenon might be criticized. This subjective fault finding which only keeps in view the individual and its deficiency without taking note of Reason pervading the whole is easy. Since it asserts a good intention [*Absicht*] with regard to the good [*Wohl*] of the whole, and seems to result from a kindly heart, it feels authorized to give itself airs and assume great consequence. It is easier to discover deficiency in individuals, in States and in Providence, than to see positive actual import and value. For in this merely negative fault-finding, a proud

position is taken [*man steht vornehm . . . über der Sache*]—one which overlooks the object without having entered into it—without having comprehended its positive aspects" (op.cit., pp. 53-53; English, p. 384). The categorical pair *die Absicht* and *das Wohl* forms one of the moral *Gestalten* treated by Hegel in the discussion of Morality in *The Philosophy of Right*. The criticism of the "proud position" suggests the need for a methodology. Hegel does not go further in this direction. The Marxian notion of "immanent critique" that might be suggested here also lacks methodological refinement.

13. The solution to political problems by recourse to a theory of history was criticized earlier. With regard to the specific problem at issue, attention should be called to Jürgen Habermas's essay "Hegels Begriff der Französchen Revolution," in *Theorie und Praxis* (Luchterhand Verlag: Neuwied, 1963) which argues that Hegel's acceptance of the Revolution was based on his refusal of revolution. Making revolution a principle of World History excludes the political action of actually trying to make a revolution in one's own particular circumstances.
14. Marx's incomplete manuscript from 1843 is a "Critique of Hegel's Philosophy of the State." He does not take up the issue of the Rabble. Nor does he criticize Hegel's defense of private property at the outset of Abstract Right. His later criticisms of private property are based on its consequences, not its premises. Lack of reflection on the methological mediation explains why Marx's proletariat could be interpreted as the real goal and agent of politics. The Rabble here calls for a politics—it does not replace the political. The same should hold for the proletariat.
15. Cited by Vorländer, in Sandkühler and de la Vega *Marxismus und Ethik*, (Frankfurt am Main: Suhrkamp Verlag, 1970) p. 285.
16. I will refer to this essay "Concerning the Common Expression: It's Fine in Theory But It Won't Work in Practice" as "Theory and Practice." The citations that follow are from Reiss, ed., *Kant's Political Writings*, pp. 79, 81, 85, and 84.
17. It is of course not explained by the simple rejection of theory's ability to affect the world. Nor can he appeal to the mysteriously rational ways of nature invoked in 1784. Worst of all would be to read Kant as anticipating Hegel. Lewis White Beck, Kant's faithful exegete, does just that in a passage that bears citation: "Kant's enthusiasm for the French Revolution is based upon his teleological conception of history, which is a forerunner of Hegel's definition of history as the progress of the consciousness of freedom. That the final purpose of the world is moral, not eudaemonistic, makes if possible for Kant to have a moral enthusiasm for the Revolution which his formalistic moral system does not justify. Had Kant's approval of the Revolution been eudaemonistic, the inconsistency would have been greater. But some inconsistency remains because Kantian ethics is not adequate to resolve the painful problems of conflicting duties" (in Beck, 1978, p. 187). The "painful problems of conflicting duties" are said to be analysed in detail in the discussion of Morality in *Philosophy of Right*. My disagreement with Beck needs no polemical supplement.

18. Cited from Reiss, *Kant's Politcal Writings*, p. 183.
19. Kemp Smith's translation of *wesentlich* as "constituent" is especially misleading given my arguments against a constitutive approach to Kant's theory. His *Commentary on Kant's "Critique of Pure Reason"* (New York: Humanities Press, 1962) suggests that the present section is chiefly of interest for the light it casts on Kant's personality (p. 579). I cannot imagine what that remark means!
20. *AKA*, 6, p. 122 (*Religion within the Limits of Reason Alone*).
21. "Theory and Practice," in Reiss, *Kant's Political Writings* p. 65n.
22. The third section will not be treated in this chapter. The concerns with international politics are thematized explicitly in Kant's "Perpetual Peace." That essay contains the kernal of Kant's theory of the political, which is treated in the next chapter. The presence of similar arguments within "Theory and Practice" can be taken as another confirmation of the political orientation of the demonstration of methodological particularity.
23. The social nature of duty, the structure of the *Metaphysics of Morals*, and the modernity of the thoery-practice problems are of course controversial assertions for Kantians or philosophers. My thinking was influenced by Dieter Henrich's introduction to *Uber Theorie und Praxis* (Frankfurt am Main: Şuhrkamp Verlag, 1967), which is weak on the role of the detailed debates concerning the French Revolution. The classical statement is the debate between Burke's *Reflections on the French Revolution* and Paine's *Rights of Man*. The issues raised there have to remain for now in the background.
24. "Theory and Practice," in Reiss *Kant's Political Writings*, pp. 82-83. Another illustration of the same error is more specific. In the *Conflict of the Faculties*, Kant points to the case of a certain Postellus of Venice in the Sixteenth century: "Thus, if not the abstraction of humanity but a real man is assumed, ,this man must be of some sex. If this creation of God is assumed to be a male (a son), who has the weakness of men and takes their guilt upon himself, then the weaknesses and excesses of the other sex which are of course specifically different from those of the male must be considered. The result is that one will have no trouble in assuming that the female sex will also have its own particular representative (that is, a divine daughter) to absolve it—this is what Postellus thought he had found in the Person of a holy virgin in Venice" (*AKA*, 7, p. 39n). A similar error is made by Garve when he takes a reflective for a predicative judgment.

    A contemporary illustration of the same point is found in Freud's development. After coming to realize that the origin of his patients' difficulties was not a real but a phantasized event, the late Freud nonetheless reverted to the myth of a real origin in "sociological" studies like *Totem and Tabou*.
25. This conclusion based on an interpretation of Kant's systematic orientation is not without historical support. François Furet's *Penser la révolution française* suggests a similar reading over a longer term: "The history of the French nineteenth century in its entirety can be

considered as the history of a struggle between the revolution and the restoration across episodes dated 1815, 1830, 1848, 1851, 1870, the Commune, the 16th of May, 1877. Only the victory of the republicans over the monarchists at the beginning of the Third Republican marks the definitive victory of the revolution in the depths of the country; the lay teacher of Jules Ferry, that missionary of the values of 1789, is the symbol more than the instrument of that long victorious battle" (pp. 16-17).

A reading of the revolution as originary is suggested by Furet's interpretation of the Toquevillean long-term structural explanation accompanied by the change of genetic modes of action based on the salons, clubs, freemasonry, and the like are analysed by Cochin. I developed this view in two papers leading toward this manuscript: "The Politics of Modernism: From Marx to Kant" (in *Philosophy and Social Criticism*, vol. 8, no. 4, Winter 1981, pp. 361-386); and "The Origins of Revolution" (in *Journal of the British Society for Phenomenology*, vol. 14, no. 1, January 1983, pp. 3-16). Claude Nicolet's recent *Idée républicaine en France* (Paris: Gallimard, 1982) makes similar points by analysing the practice of the republicans through 1924.

CHAPTER 7. THE MODERN REPUBLIC

1. Symmetry would demand not only a chapter parallel to the discussion of the constitutive error. Symmetry would call also for a parallel to the presentation of the transformation of transcendental philosophy in chapter 2. Such a chapter would treat the modern orientation within the development of classical political theory that appears only after and on the basis of the demonstration of the structure of the modern political sphere. The development of natural-law theory could be an illustration. Moving from the high point in Rousseau, the tensions and immanent antinomical structures of the traditional could be traced back, for example, by contrasting H. S. Maine's utilitarian *Ancient Law* with Leo Strauss's denunciation of the "modern" perversion of the normative classical tradition. The tradition from a tabular spatial view of nature to its temporalization as *geschichtlich* could be illustrated in this manner. The fuction of such a chapter would parallel chapter 2. The reader schooled in political theory could work backwards to the philosophical beginning just as the philosophically oriented reader begins from the reconstruction of the transcendental demand as originary.

   I have not followed the symmetries here. It did not seem wise to confuse matters by introducing new originary theorists of the political such as Rousseau, or practicing politicians such as Sièyes. Had I remained with Kant, Hegel, and Marx, a parallel to the constitutive error could be demonstrated at best with regard to their epigone. The beginning of a different conclusion is sketched in my article, "Rousseau and the Origin of Revolution", in *Philosophy and Social Criticism*, vol. 6, no. 4, pp. 349-370, which was part of an earlier version of the present study. Other hints at its structure are found in various articles published while this essay was taking its final form, to which allusion has been made along the way. My proposed comparison of the American, French, and Prussian routes to modern politics will take up the task independently.

2. This sociological reading of Kant is frequent among the "Kantian Marxists" reprinted in Sandku[3]hler and de la Vega, *Marxisms und Ethik*. It is not incompatible with the other orientation, suggested by Hannah Arendt (c.p. Ch. 4 n.5) that Kant flees the political by recourse to a philosophy of history. Neither assertion captures Kant's uniqueness.

3. A brief concretization may be useful here. A political action attempts to articulate a particular grievance. Its effect may surprise the participants who thought they were making only immediate demands. The explanation of this overflow is not to be sought in "outside agitator" myths. The issue raised by this politics turns out to be one of those particulars that determines the precarious (originary) balance of the system at the given moment. Different particulars determine this balance at different moments. (There are also moments when the originary structure is not present. Social formations that permit no civil society to emerge make modern forms of political action impossible). A strike from wage demands, for work-rule changes, against governmental policy abroad, may or may not spill over into the political arena. If and when it does, this can be explained by the theoretical account of receptivity which depends, ultimately, on the demonstration of which particulars call for the reflective judgment. This is where theory enters political strategy. The reflective character of the theory means that this calculation is not bureaucratic-technocratic. It depends on the "republican" structure within which the political actors organize themselves. The theoretical and practical successes of the New Left—beginning from the civil rights movement in the United States and extending at least through May 1968 in France and, perhaps, through December 13, 1981 in Poland—can be understood in this context. The failures that followed the first successes, and that ended for a few in a logic of terrorism, are explained by the inability to understand the place of "republican" judgment in the analysis of the structures of receptivity. The story has of course a longer history, from which only the superiority of Rosa Luxemburg's account of the "mass strike" over Lenin's theory of the party need be mentioned here. On this, cf. my discussion in *The Marxian Legacy*, chapter 3.

4. A brief contemporary illustration may help again. Political action that seeks commercial advantages against others leads to transformation of basic industrial relations (cartels, government support of research, cooptation of trade unions). The result influences the role previously played by key social or industrial groups. Philosophical analysis

demonstrates that the changed educational qualifications or job structures present different conditions for the reception of political intervention. The two analyses must accompany one another. The caricatural error that otherwise emerges is present in classical liberalism and Marxism. A structure of receptivity is assumed to be still valid. New particularities that cannot be ignored are adapted or reduced within that framework, which has become a tableau. Neoconservatism presents the inverse error. The new particularities are treated as the necessary basis for a politics that will recreate the tried-and-true structures of receptivity.

5. Two extraordinary studies suggest the sweep of the problem. Kantorowicz's *The King's Two Bodies* (Princeton: Princeton University Press, 1957) articulates the medieval Christian background of the development of the notion of sovereignty toward its modern form. The dense scholarship presented in lucid prose follows conceptual and political perigrinations that make the modernist wonder how contemporary his modernity truly is. J. G. A. Pocock's *The Machiavellian Moment* (Princeton: Princeton University Press, 1975) is of comparable sweep, if less brilliant in prose. The evolution of Florentine *virtù* through Venetien faith in stable institutions toward the volatile English synthesis of the two moments which crosses the Atlantic to found the republic based on particular virtue is a fascinating prehistory of that political logic that creates the modern state on the basis of the separation of public and private affairs. A critique using both notions will be found in my *Lè penseé politique de la Révolution amèricaine* (Paris: Ramsey, 1986).

6. Habermas's criticism of Marx's tendency toward a "positivism" that generalizes technical rationality at the expense of communication and emancipation should be recalled here. The general critique of "reification" from Lukács through Horkheimer and Adorno's "Dialectics of Enlightenment" to Habermas's recent theses concerning the "colonization of the *Lebenswelt*" belong in this context of the philosophical reflection on politics. The limit of these approaches is their neglect of the political moment.

7. The theoretical issue has contemporary parallels. The domination of the capitalist economy confronts external and internal limits which are its own product. This too is a modern structure. The moral and material difficulties cannot be blamed on outside agitators or external scarcity. The loss of social sense is captured in Habermas's phrase, the "colonization of the life-world (*Lebenswelt*)." The material difficulties are compounded by the surfeit of goods that neither subjective nor objective built-in obsolescence can eliminate. The contemporary response is dual. The philosophical moment of sociality is articulated by new forms of "movement" and communal experience that attempt to reopen a public space of receptivity. The political aspect appears in attempts to expand the objects of public and social concern. These efforts are not always successful. The movement experiences run the risk of creating the kind of "democratic" social conformism feared by thinkers like Tocqueville and Mill. The extension of politics runs the complementary risk that the

private sphere is extended so far into the public that the public space itself is privatized. The great victory that inaugurated the modern age by securing the right of privacy against royal intervention is forgotten. These risks should not hide the benefits, at least in the Western democracies. The sphere of material equality has widened; the objects with which politics can legitimately concern itself have increased. The sphere of rights has been expanded. The condition of the possibility of these developments, and the real grounds of their realization, can be found in the structures implicit in the Kantian argument. The ground of some of the errors can be found in the neglect or misunderstanding of the international dimension. "Third Worldism," the condemnation of "Western imperialism," and the (naïve) neglect of the Soviet variety, as well as variety of psychologically or sociologically explicable blind spots, explain the difficulties of the Left. I am unable to explain the errors of the Right aside from its rhetorical anticommunism, naïve nationalism, or short-sighted self-interest, thus finding myself in the interesting company of Daniel Bell's criticism of his erstwhile neo-conservative friends. (See his contribution to the special 50th Anniversary issue of *Partasen Review*, "Our Country—1984.")

8. Two objections should be answered at this point. The first calls on other political texts, especially the "Critique of the Gotha Program," as instances of a "better" Marxian politics. Marx's biting refutations of the German Socialists' misunderstanding of the difference between socialist and reformist demands justify the attribution to him of a more developed sense of the political. The difficulty lies elsewhere. Marx's "Critique" was a program that was to function on the soil of capitalism. It was to articulate transitional demands similar to those appended to the *Manifesto*. This context rules out more detailed discussion of them here. The question of transitional demands is a tactical issue, whose political justification has to be articulated in the methodological moment of the system. Transitional demands do not replace the revolution Marx sought to found philosophically.

   It might also be objected that, especially in *Capital*, Marx distinguishes between the systematic anarchy of capitalist production which pits individual capitalists against one another, and the planned structure adopted for each individual capitalist factory. Even in this case, Marx is aware of the ideological structures that mystify necessarily the individual capitalist. *Capital* reconstructs a system of social relations that works by preserving its asymmetrical premises. What is good for the individual capitalist may not be good for the system, and vice versa.

   Capital itself is inconsistent frequently for the same reasons that Marx's politics are inconsistent. For example, volume 1 offers two quite different explanations of the introduction of "labor-saving" (i.e., labor-intensifying) machinery. The first suggestion is that new inventions are introduced when the class struggle makes them necessary in order to discipline the working class. The second argument is a purely economic demonstration of the kind of calculation the capitalist makes before deciding to invest. The former argument corresponds to the phenomenological aspect of the method, presenting the theory of class struggle. The latter articulates the logical demonstration of the crisis-prone structure that proves a theory for revolutionary practice.

9. Cornelius Castoriadis has denounced this stance for treating the proletariat as "the constitutional monarch of history." It is given the credit when it is correct; error is attributed to its ministers. (See Castoriadis' preface to the collection of his political essays, "La question de l'historie du mouvement ouvrier," in *L'experience du mouvement ouvrier* (Paris: UGE, 1974). English translation in *Telos*, 30 (Winter, 1976).

10. Marx uses the term *accomodation* only once in his lengthy polemic. The specific use refers to a moment where Hegel is inconsistent even with his own "mystifying" method (cf., Cotta edition, p. 383). The tenor of Marx's "invertive critique" accents the "real" civil society that Hegel's "idealism" hides.

11. Such a syncretism is presented by a variety of authors, of whom I shall mention here only my own earlier attempt, "Kant's Political Theory: The Virtue of His Vices," *Review of Metaphysics*, vol. 34, no. 2, December 1980, pp. 325-350. *Caveat emptor!* I will be citing here, without pagination, for the translation by L. W. Beck in *On History* (Indianapolis: Bobbs-Merill, 1963).

12. The basis of the argument is moral, but it becomes central to the late political theory. In the remarks introducing the Definitive Articles, Kant asserts that "All men who can reciprocally influence each other must stand under some civil constitution." The justification for this duty, which itself is the precondition for any and all other duties, needs to be demonstrated.

13. This is clearly at Frederick the Great, to whom Kant later makes an apparently fawning reference. Meinecke's *Die Idee der Staatsräson* (München: R. Oldenburg, 1976) gives a lengthy list of such arguments in the chapter devoted to Frederick. The Political Testament of 1752 explicitly breaks with the moralism of the young prince's "Anti-Machiavelli." Sixteen years later, at the end of the Seven Years War, Frederick writes: "Let it be deelpy impressed in your mind that there are no great Princes who do not have the idea in their head of expanding their kingdom [*Herrschaft*]" (pp. 357-358). Kant expected his reader to be able to read.

14. Albert Hirschmann's *The Passions and the Interests* (Princeton: Princeton University Press, 1977) develops the logic of the "race of devils" toward an understanding of the gradual victory of *homo economicus* over his competitors. Kant was surely aware of the pattern traced by Hirschmann, which was reaching its climax when he was writing. This reinforces the suggestion that Kant's politics differs from those of Hegel and Marx due to the difference in their conceptions of civil society.

15. This "should" is based on systematic considerations. That the Secret Article was added to the second edition and that Kant may have wanted to keep a symmetry in his text could explain its place. I cannot give any better explanation, any more than I can explain the difference Kant

intended by the distinction between the supplements (*Zusätze*) and the appendixes (*Anhänge*). Hence, I refer to both as "supplementary materials.

16. This point is presented in luxurious detail in Hans Saner's well-documented but theoretically uninteresting *Kants Weg vom Krieg zum Frieden* (Munchen: R. Piper Verlag, 1967).
17. In the discussion of the Definitive Articles, the difficulties of this domain will appear to be much greater than Kant pretends here. If my argument were only philological, the contradiction of this sentence to the interpretation I will give of international law would be a problem.
18. The nineteenth-century French republican translator of Kant, J. Barni, notes that this should have led Kant to oppose a hereditary monarchy ("Kant et la révolution française," *Revue de Paris*, 15 mars 1856, pp. 481-508).
19. My article, "Rousseau and the Origin of Revolution" (*Philosophy and Social Criticism*, vol. 6, vo. 4, pp. 349-370), does not deal with the difficulty that guides the following presentation of Kant. The reasons for Rousseau's inability to articulate a theory of representation would need to be integrated into the interpretation offered there. Rousseau's notion of political economy could be reinterpreted from this point of view.
20. One must pay homage to Kant's historical sense. He does not discuss the question of empire in this article, where he limits himself to more polemical remarks, comparing savages to the European states (where the difference is that they eat their victims while the Europeans use them to increase the numbers of their subjects and the quantity of their instruments, in preparation for the new wars). He returns briefly to the issue in the First supplement, where he notes that such an empire would quickly become a "soulless despotism," its laws would lose their vigor, anarchy would emerge gradually.

    The justification of Kant's theoretical-historical argumentation was presented more than a century after he wrote. The historian Otto Hintze posed the question of the origins of the representative constitution in an essay by that title. Hintze's comparativist history demonstrates that western Europe was the only place where such a political form developed precisely because of the rise and role of international diplomacy which meant that a de facto federation of independent states existed and would persist in spite of any attempt to subsume them under an empire. This is, unfortunately, not the place for a lengthy excursus; fortunately, Hintze's essay has been translated into English in Felix Gilbert, ed., *The Historical Essays of Otto Hintze* (New York: Oxford University Press, 1975). Practical and contemporary implications are drawn in my essay, "La République et l'ordre international," *Intervention* (Paris), no. 3, March 1983, pp. 91-99.
21. Andrè Glucksmann's polemic against contemporary "pacifism," *La Force du vertige* (Paris: Grasset, 1983) does not follow up the interesting suggestion of its penultimate chapter, that the logic of nuclear deterrence returns us to the age of Pufendorf and Grotius. The task of

elaborating a "law of war" would again be incumbant upon us moderns. Kant's proposal in "Perpetual Peace" can be given contemporary significance in this context.

22. Kant never demonstrates the impossibility of a modern world empire. The distinction between the philosophical-logical moment and its political-phenomenological correlate suggests the kind of argument that could serve as proof. The desire for empire is present constantly. It is constitutive of the politics of the sovereign state. This phenomenological desire cannot be grounded. The logical conditions of receptivity that would make necessary this political possibility are not demonstrable. The public debate, the judgmental learning to think in the place of the other, the refusal to close off further enlightenment: these fundamental Kantian demonstrations of the conditions of receptivity to political action depend on the coexistence of a plurality of independent beings. World empire would be a politics that eliminates the political. It would be identical to its apparent opposite, the politics of autarchy.

23. I am drawing conclusions about the relation of national and international politics that are only implicit in Kant. There are some historical interpretations that justify this reading, especially for the events that Kant's political theory attempted to explain. Jacques Godechot's *La grande nation* (Paris: Aubier Montaigne, 1983) and Robert Palmer's *The Age of Democratic Revolution* (Princeton: Princeton University Press, 1959 and 1964) suggest this type of interpretation. Although Godechot notes that these arguments were viciously attacked by the Left at the time (9), similar ideas are presented for example in Theda Skocopol's *States and Social Revolutions: A Comparative Analysis of France, Russia, and China* (Cambridge: Cambridge University Press, 1979). From the point of view of contemporary international politics, cf. Stanley Hoffmann, *Une morale pour les monstres froids* (Paris: Editions du Seuil, 1982) and my review in *Intervention* (March, 1983), as well as my suggestion about the "peace movement's" failure in "D'une nouvelle gauche á une autre," *Esprit*, July 1983.